Luke-Acts

Luke-Acts

Foundations for Christian Worship

JOHN PAUL HEIL

CASCADE *Books* • Eugene, Oregon

LUKE-ACTS
Foundations for Christian Worship

Copyright © 2018 John Paul Heil. All rights reserved. Except for brief quotations in critical publications or reviews, no part of this book may be reproduced in any manner without prior written permission from the publisher. Write: Permissions, Wipf and Stock Publishers, 199 W. 8th Ave., Suite 3, Eugene, OR 97401.

Cascade Books
An Imprint of Wipf and Stock Publishers
199 W. 8th Ave., Suite 3
Eugene, OR 97401

www.wipfandstock.com

PAPERBACK ISBN: 978-1-5326-3580-9
HARDCOVER ISBN: 978-1-5326-3582-3
EBOOK ISBN: 978-1-5326-3581-6

Cataloguing-in-Publication data:

Names: Heil, John Paul

Title: Luke-Acts : foundations for Christian worship / by John Paul Heil.

Description: Eugene, OR: Cascade Books, 2018 | Includes bibliographical references and indexes.

Identifiers: ISBN 978-1-5326-3580-9 (paperback) | ISBN 978-1-5326-3582-3 (hardcover) | ISBN 978-1-5326-3581-6 (ebook)

Subjects: LCSH: Bible. Luke—Criticism, interpretation, etc. | Bible. Acts—Criticism, interpretation, etc. | Worship in the Bible.

Classification: BS2589 H3 2018 (paperback) | BS2589 (ebook)

Manufactured in the U.S.A.   04/06/18

Contents

Abbreviations | vii

1. Introduction: Worship in Luke-Acts | 1
2. Locations, Leadership, and Times for Worship | 8
3. True and False Worship | 31
4. Supplicatory Worship | 39
5. Laudatory Worship | 63
6. Baptismal Worship | 92
7. Meals and Eucharistic Worship | 106
8. Conclusion | 141

Bibliography | 153
Index | 161

Abbreviations

AB	Anchor Bible
AnBib	Analecta Biblica
ANTC	Abingdon New Testament Commentaries
AUSTR	American University Studies, Series 7: Theology and Religion
BBR	*Bulletin for Biblical Research*
BBRSup	*Bulletin for Biblical Research, Supplements*
BDAG	Danker, Frederick W., Walter Bauer, William F. Arndt, and F. Wilbur Gingrich. *Greek-English Lexicon of the New Testament and Other Early Christian Literature.* 3rd ed. Chicago: University of Chicago Press, 2000
BECNT	Baker Exegetical Commentary on the New Testament
Bib	*Biblica*
BibInt	*Biblical Interpretation*
BZNW	Beihefte zur Zeitschrift für die neutestamentliche Wissenshaft
CBQ	*Catholic Biblical Quarterly*
CTQ	*Concordia Theological Quarterly*
CurTM	*Currents in Theology and Mission*
EDB	*Eerdmans Dictionary of the Bible.* Edited by David Noel Freedman. Grand Rapids: Eerdmans, 2000.
EDNT	*Exegetical Dictionary of the New Testament.* Edited by Horst Balz and Gerhard Schneider. ET. 3 vols. Grand Rapids: Eerdmans, 1990–1993
EstBib	*Estudios biblicos*
ETL	*Ephemerides Theologicae Lovanienses*

ExpTim	*Expository Times*
FF	Foundations and Facets
JBL	*Journal of Biblical Literature*
JSNT	*Journal for the Study of the New Testament*
JSNTSup	Journal for the Study of the New Testament Supplement Series
JTS	*Journal of Theological Studies*
LNTS	The Library of New Testament Studies
NICNT	New International Commentary on the New Testament
NIDB	*New Interpreter's Dictionary of the Bible.* Edited by Katharine Doob Sakenfeld. 5 vols. Nashville: Abingdon, 2006–2009
NTL	New Testament Library
NTS	*New Testament Studies*
PRSt	Perspectives in Religious Studies
RB	*Revue biblique*
RivB	*Rivista biblica italiana*
RTP	Revue de théologie et de philosophie
SBLMS	Society of Biblical Literature Monograph Series
SBLStBL	Society of Biblical Literature Studies in Biblical Literature
ScEs	*Science et esprit*
SNTSMS	Society for New Testament Studies Monograph Series
SP	Sacra Pagina
TynBul	*Tyndale Bulletin*
WBC	Word Biblical Commentary
WUNT	Wissenschaftliche Untersuchungen zum Neuen Testament
ZNW	*Zeitschrift für die neutestamentliche Wissenschaft und die Kunde der älteren Kirche*

1

Introduction
Worship in Luke-Acts

There have been scholarly treatments of various aspects of the theme of worship in Luke-Acts. For example, several scholars have addressed the role of the Jerusalem temple with regard to worship in Luke-Acts.[1] The role of praise responses for laudatory worship has been examined.[2] The Lukan emphasis upon prayer has long been noted and variously presented.[3] The significance of the many Lukan meal scenes for eucharistic worship has been discussed.[4] The theme of worship in general for both Luke and Acts has been briefly treated.[5] But, to my knowledge, there has not been a more comprehensive presentation that considers all of the various dimensions and different types of worship in Luke-Acts.

With this book I aim to offer a more comprehensive investigation of the various aspects regarding the theme of worship that is so prevalent throughout Luke-Acts. Accordingly, there will be chapters on the following topics: the locations, leadership, and times for worship (ch. 2); true and false worship (ch. 3); laudatory worship (ch. 4); supplicatory worship (ch.

---

1. Peterson, *Engaging with God*, 136–65; Holmås, "My House," 393–416; Head, "Temple in Luke's Gospel," 101–19; Walton, "Tale of Two Perspectives," 135–49; Perrin, *Jesus the Temple*, 61–65; Thompson, *Acts*, 145–73.

2. De Long, *Surprised by God*.

3. Feldkämper, *Der betende Jesus*; Plymale, *Prayer Texts*; Crump, *Jesus the Intercessor*; Holmås, *Prayer*; Millar, *Calling on the Name*, 167–200.

4. Heil, *Meal Scenes*; Koenig, *Feast*, 181–93; Esposito, *Jesus' Meals*.

5. Borchert, *Worship*, 32–42, 61–82.

5); baptismal worship (ch. 6); and meals and eucharistic worship (ch. 7). I thereby hope to demonstrate that Luke-Acts provides its audience with a foundation for, as well as key insights into, all of the various dimensions of Christian worship.

As a brief anticipation and overview of the results of my presentation, the person of Jesus Christ provides the key for each of the above topics regarding worship. With the arrival of Jesus, and especially his being raised from the dead by God, the preeminent locations, leadership, and times for worship move beyond the Jerusalem temple, Jewish synagogues, Sabbath, and the Jewish feasts of Passover and Pentecost to worship in and by the Christian community. As Son of God and Lord, Jesus becomes an object of true worship along with God the Father. Jesus not only exemplifies but serves as a subject for laudatory worship. Jesus teaches about prayer, engages in it, and serves as an object for supplicatory worship. Jesus not only took part in the ritual worship of being baptized by John but as the risen and exalted Lord baptizes believers with the Holy Spirit in the sacrament of baptism. And the many meal scenes throughout Luke-Acts provide numerous insights foundational for proper celebrations of the Eucharist.

Methodological Presuppositions

I consider the Gospel of Luke and the Acts of the Apostles to be two volumes of a unified narrative (hence the term "Luke-Acts"; cf. Luke 1:1–4; Acts 1:1–2), written by the Luke associated with Paul.[6] I will treat the various aspects and dimensions of the theme of worship in Luke-Acts by means of a narrative-critical, audience-oriented exegetical methodology. The focus will be on the responses expected by the implied or ideal audience members, the audience presupposed by the text, as they hear the narrative unfold and develop.[7] With regard to the theme of worship, Luke-Acts presupposes an audience with knowledge of the OT scriptures and of such Jewish religious institutions as the synagogue, Sabbath observance, Jerusalem temple, ritual

---

6. Tannehill, *Narrative Unity* (2 vols.). "These works have long been ascribed to Luke, assumed to be Paul's loyal co-worker (Col 4:14; 2 Tim 4:11; Phlm 24)" (Garland, *Luke*, 21). See also Padilla, *Acts*, 22–31; Green, *Gospel of Luke*, 20–21.

7. Resseguie, *Narrative Criticism*; Maxwell, *Hearing Between the Lines*; Dinkler, *Silent Statements*. Luke-Acts, like all of the other NT writings, was intended to be performed publicly in a communal liturgical setting rather than read privately by individuals. Although the conventional term "the reader" can be and often is employed to designate the recipients of these writings, the term "the audience" is technically more appropriate. Actually, "the reader" would be the one who reads the material publicly for the benefit of a communal gathering of hearers.

cleansings, meal fellowship, Jewish feasts such as Passover and Pentecost, prayer, fasting, almsgiving, etc.[8] I understand Luke-Acts to have been written in the latter half of the first century for a specific community or communities of Christians located in the Mediterranean regions of the Roman empire, but with a general relevance for all Christian believers.[9]

I agree with the view that Luke-Acts has "formative and normative functions" for Christian believers. Luke-Acts presents "Jesus and the Apostles as paradigms of Christian life and thought; when Luke wrote, Christianity needed definition, identity and legitimation, and Luke-Acts provided all three."[10] It is most plausible and very likely that much of the material in Luke-Acts, as well as in the other Synoptic Gospels, had its origin in liturgical celebrations of the Eucharist.[11] That a considerable amount of the teaching in Luke-Acts occurs in its many meal scenes suggests that portions or all of one or both volumes of Luke-Acts were publicly performed in the meal setting of a eucharistic celebration.[12] At any rate, as I hope to show, Luke-Acts was written to be heard primarily by the church as a liturgical community and provides its audience of Christian believers with a rich array of models and teaching foundational for all facets of their life of worship.[13]

---

8. Hays, *Echoes of Scripture*, 191–280.

9. For detailed discussions regarding such introductory issues as authorship, dating, location, etc. for Luke-Acts, see Just, *Luke 1:1—9:50*, 1–32; Green, *Gospel of Luke*, 1–25; Garland, *Luke*, 21–38; Carroll, *Luke*, 1–16; Edwards, *Gospel According to Luke*, 1–21; Wolter, *Gospel According to Luke*, 1–39; Gaventa, *Acts*, 21–59; Spencer, *Journeying through Acts*, 13–31; Pervo, *Acts*, 1–26; Peterson, *Acts*, 1–52; Kurz, *Acts*, 13–20; Schnabel, *Acts*, 21–43; Padilla, *Acts*, 13–122; Holladay, *Acts*, 1–70.

10. Eve, *Writing the Gospels*, 37.

11. According to Farkasfalvy ("Eucharistic Provenance," 35–36), "the basic understanding of Jesus' mission and ministry as presented by the Synoptics is best understood in this eucharistic context of early Christian worship and it was in this context that not only the individual episodic pieces were formulated, rehearsed, and fixed but the literary genre of the gospels—the model for assembling, linking, and organizing these units into a composition—took its origin. . . . The way Jesus is portrayed . . . is the result of the eucharistic setting in which the Jesus tradition was formed, chiseled into oral patterns, and finally turned into literary compositions which the early church canonized." See also Esposito, *Jesus' Meals*, 355–64.

12. Downing, "Theophilus's First Reading," 91–95.

13. The statement by Just ("Luke's Canonical Criterion," 256n26) regarding Luke can be applied also to Acts: "Luke's Gospel is a book of the church, written for the church, to be used by the church in its proclamation of the Gospel to the unbaptized and the baptized. The community that receives Luke's Gospel is a catechetical and eucharistic body. His Gospel prepares the baptized for the Eucharist and catechizes the unbaptized."

The Lukan Prefaces (Luke 1:1–4; Acts 1:1–2)

Both volumes of Luke-Acts are addressed to an individual named "Theophilus" (Luke 1:3; Acts 1:1), who represents and characterizes Luke's broader communal audience of Christian believers, those who, like Theophilus (Luke 1:3–4), already have some knowledge of the Jesus tradition.[14] In the past many had set their hand to compile a narrative concerning the deeds or events that have been fulfilled among "us" (1:1), that is, Luke, Theophilus, and all the members of Luke's audience. As a "divine passive," the perfect passive participle, "have been fulfilled" (πεπληροφορημένων), refers not only to God's past fulfillment of prophetic promises in accord with his providential plan, but to their ongoing significance.[15] The events that have been fulfilled among us in accord with the promised fulfillment of God's scriptural plan center around Jesus (Luke 4:21), his ministry, and especially his suffering, death, and resurrection (24:44–46). As will be indicated in Acts, the Lord Jesus, raised from the dead by God in the past, continues to be active and effective among us.[16]

The events that God has brought to fulfillment among us were handed down to us by "those who from the beginning were eyewitnesses and became ministers of the word" (1:2). The term "eyewitnesses" refers to those who had a firsthand, personal experience of the events.[17] The terms "eye-

---

14. The name "Theophilus" connotes "beloved of God" and/or "lover of God." His name provides the only explicit reference to God in the preface to Luke, although God's activity is implicit throughout. "Theophilus is best regarded not as an interested non-Christian, but as a catechumen or a neophyte. Because Luke dedicates the two volumes to Theophilus, it means that his opus is not a private writing; Theophilus stands for the Christian readers of Luke's own day and thereafter" (Fitzmyer, *Gospel According to Luke I–IX*, 300).

15. "Because of the framework within which these events are 'fulfilled'—that is, the divine framework of God's purpose—those among whom these events are complete (the 'among us' of v. 1) cannot be restricted to the first generation of men and women who participated in Jesus' ministry and to whom he appeared after his resurrection. Luke's inclusion of himself in this 'us' guarantees this, but even more significant is the tense of the verb, 'have been fulfilled'—perfect, denoting the continuance of completed action. Luke has in mind the Christian community, with its organic unity across generations" (Green, *Gospel of Luke*, 39–40). See also Butticaz, "Le récit," 607–25; Papademetriou, "Illustrating the Meaning," 365–87.

16. "The effect of Jesus' life, death, and resurrection lives on. Luke will chronicle one of the immediate effects, the rise of the church, in his second volume. In Acts, Luke makes the point that Jesus continues to work in the world as the exalted Lord (Acts 1:1–5)" (Bock, *Luke 1:1—9:50*, 57). See also Thompson, *Acts*.

17. "We should note that the Greek word used in v. 2 for 'eyewitnesses' (αὐτόπται) does not have a forensic meaning, and in that sense the English word 'eyewitnesses,' with its suggestion of a metaphor from the law courts, is a little misleading. The αὐτόπται are

witnesses" and "ministers of the word" (ὑπηρέται τοῦ λόγου) refer to the same group, more or less synonymous with what Luke later calls "witnesses" (μάρτυρες), those who not only experienced the risen Lord but bear witness about him to others.[18] Noteworthy in this regard, the risen Lord appointed Paul as a "minister and witness" (ὑπηρέτην καὶ μάρτυρα) of the things he has seen regarding the risen Jesus and of the things in which the risen Jesus will appear to him (Acts 26:16). The "word" (λόγου) of which they are ministers or witnesses (Luke 1:2) is the word about the events God has fulfilled among us (1:1), central to which is the climactic resurrection and exaltation of Jesus. Luke later refers to it as the "word [λόγον] of the gospel" (Acts 15:7), the "gospel of the grace of God" (20:24).

Although not an eyewitness "from the beginning" (Luke 1:2), Luke was an eyewitness of some of the later events, as indicated by the inclusion of himself in the "we" sections in Acts 16:10–17; 20:5–15; 21:1–18; and 27:1—28:16.[19] And, with the writing of his Gospel, Luke himself became a "minister of the word [λόγου]" (Luke 1:2), as indicated by the preface to his second volume, which refers to his Gospel as the first "word": "I produced the first word [λόγον] about all, O Theophilus, of the things Jesus began to do and to teach" (Acts 1:1). That the Gospel concerned all that Jesus *began* to do and to teach implies that Acts will include what Jesus, as the risen and exalted Lord, continued to do and to teach.

After Luke had investigated anew everything accurately (Luke 1:3a), that is, all of the events fulfilled among us (1:1), and that were handed down to us (1:2), he decided to put in writing an orderly account of them for Theophilus (1:3b). Theophilus may then realize or recognize the certainty or assurance "concerning" (περί) the "words" of which he was instructed orally (1:4), the words "concerning" (περί) the events fulfilled among us

---

simply firsthand observers of the events" (Bauckham, *Jesus and the Eyewitnesses*, 117). By "eyewitnesses" Luke "has in mind 'witnesses' as that term is developed later—that is, people empowered by the Spirit who '. . . cannot keep from speaking about what [they] have seen and heard' (Acts 4:20). And for Luke, 'seeing' is insufficient unless one's eyes are opened, as the Emmaus-story demonstrates (Luke 24:13–35)" (Green, *Gospel of Luke*, 41).

18. The noun for "witness" occurs in Luke 24:48; Acts 1:8, 22; 2:32; 3:15; 5:32; 10:39, 41; 13:31; 22:15, 20; 26:16; and the verb used for "witness" (διαμαρτύρομαι) to the word of the gospel occurs in Acts 2:40; 8:25; 10:42; 18:5; 20:21, 24; 23:11; 28:23. Note also the reference to a similar expression, the "service of the word" (διακονίᾳ τοῦ λόγου), to which the twelve apostles devoted themselves (Acts 6:4).

19. "The first-person singular and plural passages in the Acts narrative defend and project the narrator's personal knowledge as eyewitness or researcher and, therefore, his credentials for telling the story accurately so that, as Luke 1:4 claims, Theophilus and by extension all readers can be assured of the truth of the information" (Campbell, *"We" Passages*, 90). See also Thompson, "Paul," 429.

(1:1), and summed up as "the word" (1:2). Later in Acts, Apollos, who was "instructed" (κατηχημένος) in the way of the Lord, but knew only the baptism of John (Acts 18:25), had the way explained to him "more accurately [ἀκριβέστερον]" by Priscilla and Aquila (18:26). Similarly, Theophilus, who was orally "instructed" (κατηχήθης), may have more certainty or assurance from Luke's orderly writing, based on Luke having investigated everything "accurately" (ἀκριβῶς).

Near the conclusion of Luke's Gospel the risen Jesus explained to the two disciples who had left Jerusalem for Emmaus (24:13) the prophetic scriptural words regarding the divine necessity for him as the Christ to suffer before entering into the glory of his resurrection (24:25–27). But it was not until he celebrated a eucharistic meal with them that their eyes were opened and they "recognized" (ἐπέγνωσαν) him as the risen Lord (24:31, 35), and thus recognized the certainty not only that Jesus was raised but they he was still with them. Similarly, Luke wrote the "words" of Luke-Acts (Acts 1:1) so that "you"—Theophilus and the audience—"may recognize" (ἐπιγνῷς) the "certainty" (ἀσφάλειαν) concerning the "words" (Luke 1:4) about the events fulfilled among us (1:1), the certainty that Jesus was raised and is still active among them.[20] Peter expressed the knowledge of this certainty regarding the risen Lord explicitly and emphatically: "With certainty [ἀσφαλῶς] therefore let all the house of Israel know [γινωσκέτω] that God has made him both Lord and Christ, this Jesus whom you crucified!" (Acts 2:36).[21]

In the writing of the "words" of Luke-Acts for Theophilus (Acts 1:1), Luke himself, as noted, has become a "minister of the word" (Luke 1:2). But Luke-Acts provides Theophilus, already instructed of the "words" (1:4) concerning the events fulfilled by God among us (1:1), with an orderly sequence of accurately investigated "words" (1:3), which enable him and the audience of believers he represents to likewise become "ministers of the word." Luke-Acts not only makes the resurrection faith of the members of the audience more certain (1:4), but enables them, as "ministers of the word," to share their faith with others. It enables them to bring to faith and baptism those

---

20. Notably, Luke 1:4 and 24:31 contain the first and last occurrences of the verb ἐπιγινώσκω in the Gospel, thus serving as a kind of literary inclusion.

21. Just, "Luke's Canonical Criterion," 256–60. "Luke-Acts . . . glories in the deaths of Jesus, Stephen, Paul (proleptically) and others, and projects them as exemplary: precisely, examples that may have to be followed. But it repeatedly insists on the 'proven' Christian reward of ultimate resurrection. . . . In the last analysis, Christian ἀσφάλεια is underwritten by ἀνάστασις: the resurrection both of Jesus and of humankind" (Moles, "Luke's Preface," 480). Note that ἀσφάλεια ("certainty") is the final, emphatic word that concludes the periodic sentence of the preface to the Gospel (Luke 1:1–4), suggesting that it serves as a one-word summary of the purpose of Luke-Acts.

who are receptive but also to explain the faith to those who are not. Most of all, Luke-Acts enables believers, as "ministers of the word," to celebrate and practice their faith in accord with the different dimensions enriching the life of Christian worship that Luke-Acts presents to its audience. The "certainty" (1:4) regarding the risen and exalted Lord Jesus that Luke-Acts provides for believers is the foundational key for their life of Christian worship.[22]

---

22. "As a liturgical document, it [Luke, but also Acts] cannot be understood outside the church's worship life. Because it is liturgical, it is also catechetical in that it prepares unbaptized hearers of the Word for Baptism and nurtures the baptized" (Just, *Luke 1:1—9:50*, 19).

2

Locations, Leadership, and Times for Worship

Luke-Acts provides its audience with a foundation for the movement from the preeminent locations for worship in the Jerusalem temple and Jewish synagogues to worship in Christian communities and houses. Christians become the new leaders of true worship in contrast to the leadership associated with the temple and synagogues (chief priests, elders, synagogue officials, etc.). A foundation is laid for a transition from worship in Jewish synagogues on the seventh day of the week, the Jewish Sabbath, to worship in houses of Christians on the first day of the week, the Christian Sunday. The annual celebration of the Jewish Passover meal provides a basis for the celebration of Christian eucharistic meals. And the exuberant outpouring of the Holy Spirit on believers during the Jewish feast of Pentecost in Jerusalem provides a basis for the Christian celebration of Pentecost.

From Jerusalem Temple to Christian Community

The Temple Sanctuary in Luke

The narrative of Luke's Gospel begins and ends in the Jerusalem temple (1:9; 24:53), forming a literary inclusion that indicates this Gospel's concern for worship. The opening scene of the infancy narrative (chs. 1–2) takes place in the "sanctuary" or "holy place" (ναός; 1:9, 21, 22) within the larger complex of the "temple" (ἱερόν).[1] The priest Zechariah was divinely chosen by lot for

---

1. Although Luke sometimes uses terms such as "house" or "holy place" for the

the once in a lifetime privilege of entering the sanctuary of the Lord to make the sacrificial incense offering at the afternoon Tamid service (1:9).[2] But before Zechariah can complete the cultic ritual, the angel of the Lord appeared to him, standing at the right of the altar of incense (1:11). The angel informed Zechariah that his prayer, implicitly for a child (1:5–7), who will have significance for the whole people (1:10, 17), has been heard.[3] Notably, the detailed ritual of the incense offering is not narrated. It seems to be ignored—interrupted and overshadowed by the divine intervention of the angelic appearance, already preparing the audience for a loss of importance regarding temple ritual worship in favor of a new divine initiative.[4]

The next and final occurrence of the term "sanctuary" in the Gospel further indicates how the temple is losing its importance as a preeminent place for worship. Immediately before the death of Jesus "the veil of the sanctuary [ναοῦ] was torn down the middle" (23:45) by God (divine passive). Whichever of the two possible veils or curtains is meant—the inner one separating the holy of holies from the holy place or the outer one separating the holy place from the temple proper—this is a divine indication that the temple is losing its importance as a preeminent place for worship.[5] This is confirmed in the next verse as the dying Jesus performs an act of worship, quoting from one of the psalms associated with temple worship not in the temple but from the cross: "Father, into your hands I entrust my spirit" (23:46; cf. LXX Ps 30:6). Jesus has thus provided the members of the audience with a model prayer not only for their lives but for the moment of their own deaths. Jesus, as a result of his death (and resurrection), rather than the Jerusalem sanctuary/temple has become the preeminent focus for the worship of God.[6]

---

temple complex in general, he most often uses the term ἱερόν for it, "but in the Gospel ναός is used consistently with reference to the 'sanctuary' as distinct from the larger temple precinct (1:9, 21, 22; 23:45; cf. 'shrine' in Acts 17:24; 19:24)" (Green, *Gospel of Luke*, 70n30).

2. Hamm, "Tamid Service," 221.

3. "The object of Zechariah's prayer is not specified, but the immediate context and the following words of the angel would imply that he had been praying not only for the good of Israel but also for a child (vv. 6–7). The angel's words imply too that the child to be born to him will also help Israel" (Fitzmyer, *Gospel According to Luke I-IX*, 325).

4. "The cultic action is never narrated, since, as the narrator has it, it is not through the Temple cult that God visits his people" (Coleridge, *Birth*, 33). "The normal routines of temple worship are underway when heaven intervenes" (Carroll, *Luke*, 28).

5. "The tearing of either curtain would make the point that God is at work" (Bock, *Luke 9:51—24:53*, 1860).

6. "Luke portrays the rending of the temple veil as a symbol of the destruction of the symbolic world surrounding and emanating from the temple, neutralizing the

The Temple Sanctuary in Acts

The term "sanctuary" occurs in Paul's speech to the Athenians at the Areopagus, when he declares that God "does not dwell in handmade sanctuaries [οὐκ ἐν χειροποιήτοις ναοῖς κατοικεῖ]" (Acts 17:24). This reminds the audience of Stephen's speech in Jerusalem in which he similarly declared that "the Most High does not dwell in [houses] handmade [οὐχ ὁ ὕψιστος ἐν χειροποιήτοις κατοικεῖ]" (7:48). That God does not dwell in, and thus is not confined to be worshiped in, houses made by humans includes the "house" that Solomon built for God (7:47; cf. 7:49), the Jerusalem temple. The focal point for true worship is neither pagan sanctuaries nor the Jerusalem sanctuary but the risen Jesus. When Paul observed the objects of worship in Athens, he found an altar on which was inscribed, "To an Unknown God." What they unknowingly worship, Paul proclaimed to them (17:23), namely the risen Jesus. Indeed, Paul's Areopagus speech is framed by references to the risen Jesus (17:18, 32), which prompted some to say ironically that Paul seems to be a proclaimer of "strange deities" (17:18).[7]

The term "sanctuary" occurs for a final time in Acts with the introduction of the silversmith Demetrius in Ephesus who made silver "sanctuaries" or "shrines" (ναούς) of the goddess Artemis (Acts 19:24).[8] He declared that Paul has persuaded and misled a large crowd by saying that gods made through "hands" (χειρῶν) are not gods at all (19:26). This adds an implicit idolatrous character to the Jerusalem sanctuary and temple, which Stephen included in the "handmade" (χειροποιήτοις) houses in which the Most High does not dwell (7:48). The danger that the "temple" (ἱερόν) of the great

---

centrality of the temple in preparation for the centrifugal mission of Jesus' followers—not *to* Jerusalem, but *from* it, and to the 'end of the earth' (Acts 1:8)" (Green, *Gospel of Luke*, 826; emphases original). "Jesus' death suggests that it is no longer necessary to worship God in the temple" (Bock, *Luke 9:51—24:53*, 1861). See also Sylva, "Temple Curtain," 239–50.

7. "To be sure, there are examples of the apostles praying and preaching in the temple. Yet, in light of the speeches of Stephen and Paul at the Areopagus, the reader understands that the temple is no locus to meet with God. Second, by using the same intertexts, terminology and theological logic for *both* the Jerusalem temple and pagan temples, Luke has relativized the importance of the former. He wants his readers to move forward with worship that is centered on Christ" (Padilla, *Acts*, 187; emphasis original). See also Rowe, *World Upside Down*, 27–41; Jipp, "Paul's Areopagus Speech," 579–81; Pervo, *Acts*, 433.

8. "Demetrius is presented as an idol-maker and one who worshipped the very idols he made. . . . He is depicted as hypocritical, claiming to be distressed by the possible downfall of the Artemis cult when in reality the omniscient narrator has already informed his audience that material possession was what drove Demetrius' indignation" (Padilla, *Speeches*, 171).

goddess Artemis will be regarded as nothing and that she whom the whole province of Asia and the world worship will have her greatness taken away (19:27) implicitly applies to the magnificent Jerusalem temple (Luke 21:5) as well. As indicated in Ephesus where the name of the Lord Jesus "was magnified [ἐμεγαλύνετο]" (Acts 19:17), implying that he was worshiped, like the Lord God (Luke 1:46; Acts 10:46), the new focus of true worship is the risen Jesus rather than handmade sanctuaries/temples/idols.

The Temple in Luke

The term "temple" occurs for the first time in Luke when Simeon came into "the temple" (τὸ ἱερόν) when the parents brought in the child Jesus (2:27). Simeon, divinely informed that he would not see death before he had seen the Christ of the Lord (2:26), blessed God (2:28), and declared that "my eyes have seen your salvation [τὸ σωτήριόν]" (2:30), implicitly personified in "the child [τὸ παιδίον] Jesus" (2:27) whom Simeon had taken into his arms (2:28).[9] Simeon added that this salvation God has prepared before all peoples (2:31), as "a light for revelation to the gentiles, and for glory to your people Israel" (2:32).[10] The focus of worship regarding the salvation that includes all peoples, even the gentiles, is not the temple, the preeminent place for Jewish worship, but the person of Jesus. This is confirmed by the elderly Jewish prophetess Anna (2:36), who never left "the temple," worshiping with prayer and fasting night and day (2:37). She praised God and spoke to all those awaiting the redemption of Jerusalem about the child Jesus (2:38), who represents the implicit answer to her prayers in the temple.

When his parents found the twelve-year-old Jesus "in the temple" (2:46), he said to them, "Did you not know that it is necessary for me to be in the things of my Father?" (2:49).[11] That it is necessary for Jesus to be "in the things" (ἐν τοῖς) of his Father while "in the temple" (ἐν τῷ ἱερῷ) implies his concern for the true worship of God.[12] In the temple he was sitting amid the teachers and asking questions of them (2:46). All who heard him were astounded at his "answers [ἀποκρίσεσιν]" (2:47). This prepares the audience for when the chief priests and scribes (20:19) asked Jesus (20:21) while he

---

9. The movement from the focus on "the temple" to "the child" Jesus as the personification of "the salvation" of God is enhanced grammatically by the fact that all three terms are accusative neuter singular nouns.

10. In Acts 26:23 Paul declared that the Christ, as the first of the resurrection of the dead, would proclaim "light to the people as well as to the gentiles."

11. On the significance of Jesus' relation to God in Luke's infancy narrative, see Harris, *Davidic Shepherd King*, 46–48.

12. Sylva, "Cryptic Clause," 132–40.

was teaching "in the temple [ἐν τῷ ἱερῷ]" (20:1) if they should pay tax to Caesar or not (20:22). They were amazed at his "answer [ἀποκρίσει]" (20:26) to pay to Caesar what belongs to Caesar, i.e., the denarius in Caesar's "image [εἰκόνα]" (20:24), but to God what belongs to God (20:25), i.e., the entire human person created in the "image" (εἰκόνα) of God (LXX Gen 1:26). In the temple Jesus taught the temple leaders that true worship of God involves giving over to God one's entire being.[13]

For his third temptation of Jesus, the devil made him stand on the pinnacle of "the temple" and told him that if he is the Son of God to throw himself down (Luke 4:9). The devil then quoted from one of the psalms (LXX Ps 90:11–12) used in temple worship to suggest that God will protect his Son at this highest point in the temple, a traditional place of divine refuge (4:10–11).[14] Jesus countered with his own quotation from scripture: "You shall not test the Lord your God" (Deut 6:16 in Luke 4:12). In the context this includes not testing the Lord God to perform a salvific act related to worship in the temple. Rather, as Jesus emphatically proclaimed in overcoming the temptation to worship the devil, "The Lord [κύριον] your God shall you worship [προσκυνήσεις]" (Deut 6:13 in Luke 4:8), without regard to a specific place of worship. Since Jesus is also "Lord [κύριος]" (1:43; 2:11; 3:4), he is ironically indicating to the audience that he also is to be worshiped, as happened when the disciples "worshiped" (προσκυνήσαντες) the risen "Lord [κύριος]" (24:34) outside of the temple (24:52; cf. 24:53).[15]

The temple location does not assure proper worship. In a parable that Jesus addressed to those confident of themselves that they are righteous while despising others (18:9), two men went up into "the temple" to pray,

---

13. Although the twelve-year-old Jesus asked questions of the teachers in the temple, all who heard him were astounded at the answers not of the teachers but of Jesus, which foreshadows the amazement at the answer of the adult Jesus teaching in the temple implicitly about the proper worship of God. That these are the only two occurrences of the term "answer" (ἀπόκρισις) in Luke (2:47; 20:26) enhances this connection.

14. "The devil shifts the temptation to the temple because it is the place where God's protection is particularly effective" (Garland, *Luke*, 183). "If the location of the test—the temple's pinnacle or 'wing' (πτερύγιον)—suggests divine protection on which human faith may rely, there is an ironic twist. Refuge comes from God, not from the temple" (Carroll, *Luke*, 104).

15. "Even within the single word κύριος Luke is careful to preserve a distinction between the κύριος χριστός and the κύριος πατήρ or ὁ θεός. On the other hand, in light of 1:43 there is a unity between the heavenly and the earthly κύριος such that they are both κύριος with respect to their basic identity" (Rowe, *Early Narrative*, 55). "Luke demonstrates that Jesus fully shares YHWH's divine identity when he characterizes Jesus as the one who is capable of carrying out YHWH's responsibilities and functions and, therefore, worthy to receive the recognition associated with the superior position he shares with his Father YHWH" (Henrichs-Tarasenkova, *Luke's Christology*, 171).

one a Pharisee, the other a tax collector (18:10). Although addressed to God, the Pharisee's prayer is about himself, arrogantly thankful that he is not sinful like the rest of humanity, or even like this tax collector (18:11). His pseudo prayer includes a reference to what he has done by fasting and tithing, not what God may do for him (18:12). The tax collector prayed for God himself, rather than for the temple sacrifices, "to make atonement" (ἱλάσθητί) for him as a sinner (18:13).[16] This man went down to his home justified by God rather than the Pharisee in the temple, since everyone who exalts himself will be humbled, but the one who humbles himself, like the tax collector, will be exalted by God (18:14). Jesus thus taught that divine mercy and forgiveness come not from being in the temple or from temple sacrifices, but from authentically praying to God.[17]

At the conclusion of his final and fateful journey to Jerusalem (9:51), Jesus entered "the temple" and began to drive out those selling things (19:45). He quoted from scripture that "my house [God's temple] shall be a house of prayer, but you have made it a den of robbers!" (Isa 56:7 and Jer 7:11 in Luke 19:46). While he was teaching every day in "the temple," implicitly about true worship, the chief priests, scribes, and those prominent among the people, that is, the leadership ultimately responsible for making the temple a den of robbers rather than a house of true worship, were seeking to destroy him (19:47). One day as he was teaching the people in "the temple" (20:1), he told them a parable (20:9) which portrayed him as the beloved son (20:13) killed by tenant farmers representing the Jewish leaders (20:14–15). He then quoted scripture that "the stone" (the son) that "the builders" (the Jewish leaders, 20:19) rejected has become (by his resurrection) "the cornerstone" (LXX Ps 117:22 in Luke 20:17) of a new "temple" or household of true worship, namely the Christian community.[18]

---

16. "The prayer should not be translated 'be merciful to me' because the verb ἐλέεω (see 18:38) is not used. Rather, the verb ἱλάσκομαι is used, which occurs in Heb 2:17 to mean 'make an expiation.' Related noun forms occur in Rom 3:25; Heb 9:5; 1 John 2:2; 4:10 to refer to an atonement sacrifice; and this seems best to fit the setting if it occurs during the daily sacrifice for the people" (Garland, *Luke*, 719). See also Hamm, "Tamid Service," 224.

17. "The tax collector experiences the anguish of the temple's promise of atonement from the daily sacrifice and the reality of his own sinful life. The forgiveness offered in the temple sacrifice confirmed by the priestly benediction does not apply to the likes of him. In his brokenness, he cries out, 'God, make atonement for me!' . . . From Luke's perspective, God is preparing an atonement sacrifice that will expiate this man's sin apart from the temple sacrifices" (Garland, *Luke*, 719–20).

18. "The transformation of the rejected stone into the cornerstone corresponds to Jesus' vindication after his rejection (i.e., his resurrection). This vindication-resurrection of Jesus will thus establish him as the centre-piece of a restored 'temple'" (Head, "Temple," 116). "The citation from the psalm (cited again in Acts 4:11) implies that a

While some were speaking about "the temple," admiring its beauty (21:5), Jesus predicted its eventual destruction (21:6). Although during the day Jesus was teaching in "the temple," at night he went out and stayed on the Mount of Olives (21:37). All of the people, however, would get up early in the morning to listen to him in "the temple [τῷ ἱερῷ]" (21:38).[19] To the chief priests, the guards of "the temple," and the elders who had come to arrest him, Jesus said, "Have you come out as against a robber [λῃστήν], with swords and clubs?" (22:52). This ironically recalls that they, the temple leadership, are the ones who have made the temple a den of "robbers" (λῃστῶν) rather than a house of true worship (19:46). When he was with them daily in "the temple," implicitly teaching about true worship, they did not stretch out their hands against him, because they feared the people (20:19). But now is their "hour and the authority of the darkness" (22:53), the time for them to reject him, so that he might become the cornerstone of a new edifice for worship, the Christian community.[20]

After the disciples worshiped the risen Jesus as he was taken up into heaven, they returned to Jerusalem with great joy (24:51–52). And they were continually in "the temple" (τῷ ἱερῷ) blessing God (24:53). Although Luke's Gospel ends with the disciples worshiping in the temple, that worship has been radically transformed. Their "blessing" (εὐλογοῦντες) God in the temple includes a reciprocal blessing of the heavenly Jesus for his twice, and thus emphatically, mentioned blessing of them: "He blessed [εὐλόγησεν] them" (24:50), "and as he was blessing [εὐλογεῖν] them, he parted from them and was taken up into heaven [by God, divine passive]" (24:51).[21] In blessing God in the temple, then, the disciples are continuing their "worshiping" (προσκυνήσαντες) of the risen "Lord" (κύριος) Jesus (24:34) in accord with Jesus' previous proclamation: "The Lord [κύριον] your God shall you worship [προσκυνήσεις]" (4:8).[22] The disciples' worship of the heavenly Lord

---

new structure is to be built, but Luke's second volume will make clear that it is not to be a literal building made of stone (see Acts 7:44–53)" (Garland, *Luke*, 795).

19. "These verses [21:37–38] form an *inclusion* with 20:1, marking the narrative closure not only of Jesus' eschatological discourse but also of Luke's narration of the teaching of Jesus in the temple. They underscore the temple context in which Jesus' teaching has taken place, as well as the overwhelmingly positive response of 'the people' ('all'!) to Jesus" (Green, *Gospel of Luke*, 743).

20. "Jesus' rebuke specifically links the temple officialdom with Satan's dominion and its moral darkness. They will have their hour, but it is an hour that will only last until the resurrection" (Garland, *Luke*, 886).

21. Mekkattukunnel, *Priestly Blessing*.

22. That the only occurrences in Luke's Gospel of the verb προσκυνέω are in 4:7–8 and 24:52 enhances this connection. "Luke is clear that worship of the God of Israel entails worship of the risen Jesus as Lord" (Hamm, "Tamid Service," 230). In Luke-Acts

Jesus in the temple prepares for the transition to worshiping the heavenly Lord Jesus apart from the temple (Acts 7:59–60).[23]

The Temple in Acts

The first occurrence of the term "temple" (ἱερόν) in Acts continues to indicate the transition for the location of worship from the Jerusalem temple to the houses of the Christian community with the notice that while the apostles continued to gather together in "the temple," they were breaking bread "from house to house [κατ' οἶκον]" (2:46) and "praising God" (2:47). And the transcendence of Jesus over the temple continues.[24] When Peter and John were going up into "the temple" (3:1), a crippled man, who was placed at the gate of "the temple" called "Beautiful Gate" every day to beg for alms from those entering "the temple" (3:2), asked them for alms as they were about to enter "the temple" (3:3). Instead, in the name of Jesus Christ he was enabled to rise and walk (3:6). He entered "the temple" with them, "praising God" (3:8). Jesus Christ, rather than the temple, enabled the man who used to sit at the Beautiful Gate of "the temple" (3:10) to join in the worship of "praising God" that takes place not only in the temple (3:8–9) but in the houses of the apostles (2:47).[25]

"worship is denied images, the devil, and mere mortals, and allowed only in the case of God. Their worship of Jesus signifies that the disciples have, at last, recognized Jesus for who he is" (Green, *Gospel of Luke*, 862).

23. "After Jesus' ascension, the temple serves as God's house for Jesus' joyfully worshiping disciples, but the situation is temporary. Soon the promised Spirit will come upon them when they are gathered—not in the temple, but *in a house* (οἶκος [Acts 2:2]). The worship of the emerging Christian community will center in house churches. Filled with the Spirit, the church will no longer be bound to any single location" (Just, *Luke 9:51—24:53*, 1057; emphasis original).

24. Luke "views the role of the Jerusalem temple as having come to an end and its ultimate purpose is now found in the risen Lord Jesus, who not only replaces the temple but provides more for God's people than even the temple was able to provide" (Thompson, *Acts*, 147).

25. There is an emphatic focus on the temple here, and implicitly its inadequacy, as the term occurs seven times in Acts 2:46—3:10. "Ultimately the story appears more radical than conventional, focusing more on the beggar's miraculous leap over strict temple boundaries than the apostles' and other worshippers' customary visit to the sanctuary at the appointed hour of prayer" (Spencer, *Journeying through Acts*, 55). "The healing allows the man to walk into the temple proper for the first time (Lev 21:17–20; 2 Sam 5:8 prohibited his entry as a lame man)" (Bock, *Acts*, 162). "[I]t is the inadequacy of the temple system together with the overcoming of that old-system inadequacy through Jesus that is being highlighted here" (Thompson, *Acts*, 154).

All the people astounded ran together toward Peter, John, and the healed man in Solomon's portico within the Jerusalem temple (3:11). Peter and John were confronted by the temple leadership—the priests, the commander of "the temple," and the Sadducees (4:1), who put them in custody (4:3). The next day the Jewish leadership (4:5) together with temple leaders—Annas the high priest and all of the high priestly class (4:6)—inquired by what power or name the man was healed (4:7). Peter replied that it was in the name of Jesus Christ the Nazorean whom they crucified, but whom God raised from the dead, that this man stands before them healed (4:10).[26] Recalling and reinforcing for the audience Jesus' previous pronouncement to the Jewish leaders (Luke 20:17), Peter declared that the "stone"/Jesus rejected by them, the temple leaders, as the "builders," has ironically become the "cornerstone" (Acts 4:11; cf. LXX Ps 117:22) of a new edifice for true worship with new leadership, the Christian community. There is salvation in no one other than Jesus, the new "cornerstone" (4:12).[27]

The apostles continued to gather together in Solomon's portico within the temple (5:12). The high priest and the Sadducees eventually had them put in prison (5:17–18). But the angel of the Lord freed them from prison (5:19) and told them to go and stand in "the temple" and "tell the people all the words of this life" (5:20). So they entered "the temple" and were teaching the people (5:21). When the commander of "the temple" and the chief priests heard of it, they were greatly perplexed (5:24). Then it was reported to them that the men they had put in prison are in "the temple" and are teaching the people (5:25). Even after they had been beaten by the temple leaders (5:40), the apostles every day both in "the temple" and "from house to house [κατ' οἶκον]" (cf. 2:46) did not stop teaching and proclaiming the good news that Jesus was the Christ (5:42). This continues the transition from worship in the temple to worship in houses and from the temple leadership to the apostles' leadership, teaching the people that Jesus, not the Jerusalem temple, is the new focus for true worship.[28]

---

26. "The power of the divine name to deliver and protect God's people is a prominent theme in Israelite worship, linked to the localization of this name in the Solomonic temple. In Solomon's Portico, Peter now makes clear that the name of Jesus represents God's glory and strength revealed within, but not restricted to, the temple arena" (Spencer, *Journeying through Acts*, 57).

27. "In this context, therefore, the inadequacy of the temple system is now contrasted with Peter's message about the all sufficiency of Jesus" (Thompson, *Acts*, 156).

28. "As Jesus' authorized delegates, the apostles are the new leaders over the true people of God (4:23—5:42). More specifically, the apostolic teaching that Jesus has fulfilled all of God's saving promises, including all that the temple pointed to, should be followed rather than the teaching of the temple leadership" (Thompson, *Acts*, 164).

Locations, Leadership, and Times for Worship

Eventually even a large group of temple priests became obedient to the faith (6:7). But false witnesses testified against Stephen, a prominent Christian leader (6:8), that he never stops speaking words against this "holy place," the temple (6:13). Although Jesus did predict that the temple "will be destroyed" (Luke 21:6), they falsely claim to have heard Stephen say that Jesus himself "will destroy" this "place," the temple (Acts 6:14). Stephen went on to point out that the Jerusalem temple was not always the exclusive place for worship, as God said that the people will come out of slavery in Egypt and "they will worship me in this place" (7:7), Mount Horeb/Sinai (Exod 3:1, 12). And God told Moses that the "place" where he is standing is "holy" ground (Acts 7:33). Although Solomon built a "house," the temple, for God (7:47), the Most High does not dwell in handmade things (7:48). Indeed, as the Lord God asks, what kind of "house" can be built for him, or what is to be a "place" for his resting (Isa 66:1 in Acts 7:49). True worship cannot and never has been limited to the Jerusalem temple.[29]

To show that he is not against the Jewish law and its cultic customs (21:21), Paul purified himself together with four men who had taken a vow (21:23) and entered "the temple" (21:26). But Jews from Asia who had seen Paul in "the temple" (21:27) accused him of teaching against this "place" and of bringing Greeks into "the temple," thus defiling this "holy place" (21:28). They had previously seen Trophimus the Ephesian in the city with Paul and erroneously supposed that Paul had brought him into "the temple" (21:29). As a result, the whole city was stirred up and there was a running together of the people; they seized Paul and dragged him out of "the temple," and "immediately the doors were shut" (21:30). On the literal level the doors of the temple were shut by the temple officials, but on the symbolic level they were shut by God (divine passive), in correspondence to the Jewish rejection of Paul and the movement away from the Jerusalem temple as the preeminent location for worship to worship focused on the risen Lord Jesus in the Christian community.[30]

---

29. "Stephen consistently highlights the dynamic presence of God with his people outside the holy place (temple), city (Jerusalem) and land (Israel) and ultimately casts the temple as a 'hand-made' human creation (on a par with the golden calf!) where the Most High God most certainly 'does not dwell'" (Spencer, *Journeying through Acts*, 91). "Although it is unlikely that Stephen is criticizing the actual building of the temple, he has relativized the temple as the location for God's presence as well as declared that God is greater than the temple. However, Stephen also points beyond the temple to Jesus [Acts 7:55–60]" (Thompson, *Acts*, 169–70).

30. "The action makes good sense on the literal level: the keepers of the Temple close the gates once the polluter has been expelled from it in order to keep the riot outside the sacred precincts. But does Luke also intend a symbolic 'shutting the gates' that marks Paul as an outsider to the cultic life of Judaism, and at the same time the final

In his defense to the people of Jerusalem (22:1), Paul recounted that while he was praying in "the temple," he fell into a trance (22:17) and heard the Lord telling him to leave Jerusalem at once, because they will not accept Paul's testimony about Jesus (22:18). Rather, Paul is to go far away to the gentiles (22:21). The high priest Ananias and Jewish leaders falsely charged Paul (24:1) before Felix (24:3) of trying to desecrate "the temple" (24:6). Paul replied that he went up to Jerusalem to worship (24:11), and did not stir up a crowd or cause a disturbance in "the temple" (24:12, 18). To Festus, Paul declared that he committed no crime against "the temple" (25:8). To King Agrippa, Paul explained that the Jews seized him in "the temple" and tried to kill him (26:21). But Paul had simply announced what the prophets and Moses foretold (26:22), that the Christ was to suffer and be the first of the resurrection of the dead, to proclaim light to the Jewish people and to the gentiles (26:23). The focus of true worship for all peoples thus moves from the Jerusalem temple and its leaders to the risen Lord Jesus and the Christian community.[31]

From Jewish Synagogues and Sabbath to Christian Community and Sunday

Jewish Synagogues and Sabbath in Luke

Jesus taught in Jewish synagogues, glorified by all (Luke 4:15), implicitly on the Sabbath.[32] This is confirmed with the notice that when Jesus came to his home town of Nazareth, he entered, according to his custom, on the day of the Sabbath into the synagogue (4:16). He read a passage taken from Isaiah (61:1–2; 58:6): "The Spirit of the Lord is upon me, because he has anointed me to bring good news to the poor; he has sent me to proclaim freedom to captives and recovery of sight to the blind, to send away the oppressed in freedom, to proclaim the year of the Lord's favor" (Luke 4:18–19).[33] As

---

response of the non-Christian Jerusalem Jews to the apostle?" (Johnson, *Acts*, 382). "This scene involves the final shutting out of Paul and his message from the temple precincts—the temple doors are closed against him" (Witherington, *Acts*, 652).

31. "[T]he broader work of God which Luke narrates deconstructs any notion of sacred space that is narrower than the world, for that world is the arena of God's saving activity" (Walton, "Tale of Two Perspectives," 148).

32. "The synagogue was the religious, social, and educational nucleus of a Jewish community.... Jewish synagogues... were 'assembly halls' or auditoriums, which functioned primarily as worship centers where Torah was read and expounded" (Edwards, *Gospel According to Luke*, 135).

33. The phrase "year of the Lord's favor" (ἐνιαυτὸν κυρίου δεκτόν) "takes on a

the eyes of all in the synagogue were looking intently at him (4:20), Jesus declared to them that "today this scripture has been fulfilled in your ears" (4:21). Jesus has come to bring the salvation that Jewish leaders, including those of the synagogue, have not provided. "Today," the day of the Sabbath, marks the arrival of "the year/time of the Lord's favor," an allusion to the year of Jubilee (Lev 25:10), a metaphor for the time of salvation that fulfills yet transcends the eschatological rest foreshadowed by Sabbath time.[34]

Although all in the synagogue spoke well of him, they questioned his ordinary human origin as one who is merely the son of Joseph (4:22), but, as ironically known by the audience, he is also the Son of God (1:35; 3:22; 4:3, 9), and thus worthy of being "glorified by all" (4:15) as an object of divine worship. After pointing out that no prophet is accepted in his native place (4:24), Jesus implicitly compared himself to the prophets Elijah and Elisha, who extended their prophetic ministries beyond non-receptive Israelites to gentiles (4:25–27). With the implication that they are similarly non-receptive of the divine salvation now being brought by Jesus on the "today" of this special Sabbath, all in the synagogue were filled with rage (4:28). They tried to throw him off the cliff on which their town was built, but Jesus escaped (4:29–30). This rejection of Jesus by those in the synagogue in his native town on the day of the Sabbath begins to indicate and prepare for the transition from worship in Jewish synagogues on the Sabbath to worship in Christian communities and houses on Sunday.[35]

Jesus then went down to Capernaum and was teaching them on the Sabbath (4:31). They were astonished at his teaching for his "word" was with authority (4:32), recalling the "words" of grace, words of the "year of the

---

double meaning. In the first and most obvious sense, κύριος refers to God, and the year of God's favor is proclaimed by Jesus as having arrived. In the second and more subtle sense, κύριος refers also to Jesus, and ἐνιαυτὸν κυρίου δεκτόν expresses the nature of his ministry as κύριος in the succeeding story—the year of the Lord's favor is in fact the ministry of the Lord" (Rowe, *Early Narrative*, 81).

34. "The Sabbath is the basis, both calendrically and theologically, for the whole system of Israelite feasts and festivals. . . . This year [of Jubilee] ultimately finds its source in the Sabbath" (Burer, *Divine Sabbath*, 38, 117n43). "Since Jesus quotes from Isaiah, not Leviticus, it is more likely that he is drawing on Jubilee *imagery* to refer to the day of salvation" (Garland, *Luke*, 200; emphasis original). "Thus the true Sabbath, which has come with Christ, is not a literal, physical rest but is seen as consisting in the salvation that God has provided. . . . It includes the good news of deliverance, liberation and forgiveness brought by the mighty works and preaching of Jesus (Luke 4)" (Lincoln, "From Sabbath," 215).

35. "It is hard to overstress the importance of this scene in Luke's Gospel [4:14–30]. In modern political terms this is where Jesus launches his campaign, announces his manifesto. The way he inaugurates his mission here in Nazareth and the response he receives set a pattern that will run throughout the Gospel" (Byrne, *Hospitality*, 45).

Lord's favor" (4:21), that were coming from his mouth on the Sabbath in the Nazareth synagogue (4:22).[36] In the Capernaum synagogue there was a man having a spirit of an unclean demon (4:33), who, in ironic contrast to those in the Nazareth synagogue, knows the divine identity of Jesus as the Holy One of God (4:34; cf. 1:35). After Jesus expelled the demon from the man (4:35), amazement came over all and they asked one another about this "word," for with authority and power Jesus commands the unclean spirits and they come out (4:36). In implicit contrast to the mere human authority and inability of the usual synagogue teachers, with divine authority and power the word of Jesus has brought salvation to this man in the synagogue. He did this appropriately on the Sabbath, actualizing the "year/time of the Lord's favor" (4:19) whose fulfillment he announced on a previous Sabbath (4:21).[37]

Foreshadowing the transition from worship in synagogues to worship in houses, Jesus, arising from the Capernaum synagogue on the Sabbath, entered the house of Simon (4:38a).[38] Simon's mother-in-law was afflicted with a severe fever, so that those in the house, performing an act of supplicatory worship, asked Jesus about her (4:38b). Just as Jesus had "rebuked" the demon that he had expelled in the synagogue, so he "rebuked" the demonic fever, and it "left" (ἀφῆκεν) her (4:39a), so that Jesus has freed her from this demonic power. In answer to the supplicatory prayer of those in the house, Jesus has actualized for this woman the salvation previously described as "freedom" (ἄφεσιν) to captives and sending away the oppressed in "freedom [ἀφέσει]" (4:18). As a result of Jesus "arising" (ἀναστάς) from the synagogue and entering the house (4:38), this woman "arose" (ἀναστᾶσα) and, in restoration to her role in meal hospitality, was "serving" those at table in the house (4:39b). This story thus presents the audience with a paradigm for their supplicatory worship of Jesus in Christian houses.[39]

---

36. "Frequent references to Jesus teaching and even healing on the Sabbath and in synagogues reinforces Luke's salvation-history motif that the gospel arises from the heart of Israel and its worship" (Edwards, *Gospel According to Luke*, 144).

37. "The crowd's amazement underscores that this event was not a normal occurrence every Sabbath in the synagogue" (Garland, *Luke*, 216). "The amazement reflects the occurrence of a work of divine power" (Bock, *Luke 1:1—9:50*, 435).

38. "The move from synagogue to household may seem unwarranted, given the apparent success of Jesus' ministry in the synagogue. In fact, this change of venue is proleptic, establishing a pattern of things to come" (Green, *Gospel of Luke*, 224).

39. "As her 'serving' at a meal can also have the meaning of 'serving' in a more comprehensive sense, this healed woman acts as a model for the audience to likewise 'serve' Jesus and the community in gratitude for their own personal experiences of the salvation Jesus brings them. Serving at a meal is thus a Lukan paradigm for Christian service in general" (Heil, *Meal Scenes*, 19).

On a Sabbath Jesus was going through grain fields, and his disciples were picking and eating the heads of grain, rubbing them in their hands (6:1), which accentuates their doing work in violation of the Sabbath rest. Jesus countered the Pharisees' objection to this (6:2) with a reference to what David did when he and "those who were with him" were hungry (6:3). He went into the house of God, and, taking the bread of the Presence (Lev 24:5-9), ate and gave to "those with him"—bread that it is not permitted anyone to eat but the priests (Luke 6:4; cf. 1 Sam 21:1-6). As the messianic Son of David (Luke 1:27, 32, 69; 2:4, 11; 3:31), Jesus has similarly allowed his disciples, as those with him, to do what was otherwise not permitted on the Sabbath. Then Jesus announced, "Lord [κύριός] of the Sabbath is the Son of Man" (6:5).[40] This recalls that on a Sabbath (4:16) Jesus declared the fulfillment of the scripture that indicates that "the year/time of the Lord's [κυρίου] favor" (4:19), the era of divine salvation that brings the eschatological rest anticipated by the Sabbath, has arrived with him as the Son of Man.[41]

On another Sabbath Jesus entered the synagogue and was teaching, and a man was there whose "right" (δεξιά) hand, the one key to his livelihood, was withered (6:6).[42] The scribes and Pharisees closely watched Jesus to see if he would heal on the Sabbath, so that they might find a reason to accuse him (6:7). Jesus knew their thoughts (cf. 2:35; 5:22), and told the man to stand amid them (6:8). Jesus then asked them if it is permitted on the Sabbath "to do good or to do evil, to save life or destroy it" (6:9). Looking around at them all, he told the man to stretch out his withered hand; the

---

40. "Luke's Jesus makes a startling claim and equates his authority with God's precisely in his identity as κύριος.... Through the use of the word κύριος, Luke does, then, actually provide a justification for the Son of Man's authority over the Sabbath rather than simply asserting that he has this authority. As has been developed in the Gospel narrative to this point, there exists a continuity in identity between the God of Israel and Jesus" (Rowe, *Early Narrative*, 109-10). "God instituted the Sabbath (Gen 2:2-3), and Jesus expressly claims God's prerogatives, presuming preeminence over Sabbath! The purpose of the Sabbath, as originally intended by God, cannot be understood by Moses, and especially not by the rabbinic tradition subsequent to Moses, but only by Jesus, who is Lord of the Sabbath" (Edwards, *Gospel According to Luke*, 180).

41. "The Lukan hearer would know that the movement in the Christian church from worship on the Sabbath to worship on the first day of the week is one of the major results of Jesus' fulfillment of the Sabbath. This Sabbath controversy points to Jesus as Lord of the Sabbath, King of the new era of Salvation" (Just, *Luke 1:1—9:50*, 254). "Jesus, in declaring the onset of the eschatological Jubilee, has made this day ('today,' 4:21) the day for providing for humans. Jesus is less concerned with abrogating Sabbath law, and more concerned with bringing the grace of God to concrete expression in his own ministry, not least on the Sabbath; what is more, according to Luke, as lord of the Sabbath he has the authority to do just that!" (Green, *Gospel of Luke*, 252-53).

42. "The healing of the right hand is urgent because it executes the main work" (Von der Osten-Sacken, "δεξιός," 1.286).

man did so and his hand was restored (6:10). Jesus thus further illustrated that he is the divine Lord of the Sabbath (6:5). On this day of the Sabbath in the synagogue Jesus has appropriately saved and thus brought divine salvation (1:69, 71, 77; 2:30; 3:6) to this man with the withered right hand. He has thus actualized and made personal for this man the "year/time of the Lord's favor" (4:19), the new era of divine salvation, which not only accords with but supersedes the significance of Sabbath time.[43]

The Lukan theme of the transition from a focus on synagogues to houses continues. At Capernaum (7:1) Jesus healed the slave of a Roman centurion not in the synagogue that this gentile had built for the Jews (7:5) but in his house (7:10). When Jesus was not far from his house, the centurion sent friends to tell Jesus that he need not come to his house (7:6); the mere authoritative word of Jesus from afar will effect the healing (7:7). Jesus declared that not even in Israel, including implicitly in the synagogues, has he found such faith (7:9). The faith of this gentile resulted in Jesus' healing of his slave in his house (7:10). Similarly, Jairus, although a ruler of the synagogue, begged Jesus to enter not into the synagogue but into his house (8:41), because his daughter was dying (8:42). After someone from the synagogue ruler's house announced that the daughter had already died (8:49), Jesus, calling for him not to be afraid but only to have faith and she will be saved (8:50), entered the house (8:51) and there, as a result of faith, raised the daughter of the synagogue ruler to life (8:54–55).

The negativity toward Jewish leadership regarding synagogues continues. Jesus warned against the behavior of the Jewish leaders—Pharisees and scribes—who love the seats of honor in synagogues (11:43; 20:46), demonstrating their false leadership and inability to lead people in true worship. Ironically, they desire for themselves the honor that should be given to God in synagogues as places of worship. And Jesus warned his disciples that Jewish synagogues will be places where they will be persecuted by Jewish leaders because of his name (12:11; 21:12), rather than places where they can participate in true worship.

---

43. "The miracle demonstrates conclusively that Jesus is Lord of the Sabbath and that the new era of his salvation has arrived. As Jesus said in his Nazareth sermon (4:16–30), he must fulfill the messianic ministry he was anointed to do. Healing the man's withered hand is an act of goodness and an act of salvation, one absolutely permitted, suitable, *required* on the Sabbath" (Just, *Luke 1:1—9:50*, 258; emphasis original). "Against these Pharisees and scribes, Jesus refuses to represent Sabbath observance as a litmus test for faithfulness to God. More fundamental for him is God's design to save—a purpose that is not incompatible with Sabbath observance but, in fact, is embodied in God's purpose for the Sabbath. . . . For Jesus, 'today,' including the Sabbath day, is the day when divine salvation is available to those who need it (see 4:21)" (Green, *Gospel of Luke*, 256).

When Jesus was teaching in one of the synagogues on the Sabbath (13:10), he told a crippled woman (13:11) that she has been "set free" (ἀπολέλυσαι) from her infirmity (13:12). She then "glorified God," performing an act of true worship, disclosing that she recognizes God's power at work in what Jesus had done for her on the day of the Sabbath (13:13). The ruler of the synagogue, indignant that Jesus had healed on the Sabbath, objected that there are six days when "it is necessary" (δεῖ) to work, so come on those days to be healed but not on the day of the Sabbath (13:14). Speaking as the "Lord," recalling that he is the divine "Lord" of the Sabbath (6:5), Jesus then pointed out that each of them, on the Sabbath, does work as he "loosens" (λύει) his ox or donkey and leads it to water (13:15).[44] Directly countering the ruler of the synagogue, Jesus asserted that "it was necessary" (ἔδει) that this "daughter of Abraham" whom Satan had bound for eighteen years be "loosened" (λυθῆναι) by God (divine passive) from this bondage appropriately in a synagogue on the day of the Sabbath (13:16).[45]

Indeed, this healing was divinely necessary because on the day of the Sabbath in the Nazareth synagogue Jesus announced the arrival of the time of divine freedom for captives and the oppressed (4:18). The "year/time of the Lord's favor" (4:19), the new era of divine salvation, has "today," the day of the Sabbath, arrived with him and his ministry (4:21). As the divinely authoritative "Lord" of the Sabbath (6:5), Jesus provides the healing and freedom that the ruler of the synagogue would deny this oppressed woman on the Sabbath. It is the time that not only accords with but supersedes the significance of the Sabbath as a time of restorative and salvific rest for human beings in honor of God.[46]

The movement from synagogues to houses continues, as on a Sabbath Jesus went not into a synagogue but into the house of one of the leaders of the Pharisees, and they were closely watching him (14:1; cf. 6:7). In front

---

44. "Jesus speaks directly to the ruler in v. 15, and he speaks as 'the Lord.' This is a strategic title, for Luke has already emphasized the Jesus is '*Lord* of the Sabbath' (6:5). In rebutting the ruler's Sabbath pronouncement, Jesus offers not simply an alternative rabbinic opinion; he speaks with the authority of the very God who established Sabbath (Gen 2:2–3)" (Edwards, *Gospel According to Luke*, 396; emphasis original).

45. "The synagogue leader's view led him to function as a barrier to the healing of this woman, and, thus to represent the synagogue and Sabbath as entities segregating this needy woman from divine help. Jesus' view led him to regard today, this day, even a Sabbath day, as the right time for the redemptive purpose of God to be realized" (Green, *Gospel of Luke*, 524–25).

46. "Jesus does not revoke the law of Moses but interprets it differently according to his messianic mission to set free the oppressed. He is under a 'must' from God, and this Sabbath day belongs to the 'today' of divine liberation that Jesus announced in 4:18–21" (Garland, *Luke*, 549).

of Jesus was a man suffering from dropsy or edema (14:2), a swelling of the body due to the retention of fluid. Jesus asked the scholars of the law and the Pharisees whether it is permitted on the Sabbath to heal or not (14:3; cf. 6:9). They remained silent, so Jesus, taking hold of the man, healed him and "set him free [ἀπέλυσεν]" (14:4; cf. 13:12). He then said to them, "Which of you, if a son or an ox falls into a well, will not immediately pull him out on the day of the Sabbath?" (14:5; cf. 13:15). Once again Jesus demonstrated that he is the divine Lord of the Sabbath (6:5). He has actualized and made personal for this man the freedom he proclaimed (4:18) in the "year/time of the Lord's favor" (4:19), the new era of divine salvation, that has arrived on the "today" that includes and accords with the Sabbath (4:21). And this time he did so not in a synagogue but in a house.[47]

The details regarding the burial preparations for Jesus during the time surrounding the Sabbath and his resurrection on the next day, the first day of the week, begin to indicate the transition from the Sabbath to Sunday as the day appropriate for Christian worship. It was the day of preparation (Friday) and the Sabbath (Saturday) was beginning (23:54) when the women who had followed Jesus from Galilee (23:55) prepared spices and perfumed oils to anoint the body of Jesus, and then on the Sabbath day itself they rested according to the commandment (23:56). It was on the next day, the first day of the week, Sunday, that they went to the tomb, taking the spices they had prepared (24:1). It was on this day, not the Sabbath, that they received the divine revelation of Jesus' resurrection (24:2-8). This begins to provide a foundation for the transition from the Sabbath, the last day of the week, to Sunday, the first day of the week, as the weekly day most appropriate for Christian worship.[48]

---

47. "A distinguishing feature of Lk 14:1-6, besides the dropsical man himself, is the fact that the healing takes place in the house of a Pharisee on the Sabbath and not in a synagogue" (Esposito, *Jesus' Meals*, 298). "Jesus' point is that scribal specifications have missed the salvific purpose of God resident in the Sabbath; Jesus, in declaring the onset of the eschatological Jubilee, has made this day, even the Sabbath day ('today,' 4:21), the day of divine benefaction for the needy" (Green, *Gospel of Luke*, 548). "Sabbath healings have produced no change in the leadership. Where is God working? Where is the evidence of his authority? Where is his power and presence displayed? It resides in Jesus, not in the leadership" (Bock, *Luke 9:51—24:53*, 1259).

48. "The first day of the week is the only day, apart from the Sabbath, to receive explicit attention in the New Testament. It figures prominently, of course, in the Resurrection narratives of all four Gospels" (Lincoln, "From Sabbath," 382). See also McGowan, *Ancient Christian Worship*, 218-23.

Jewish Synagogues and Sabbath in Acts

The negativity toward members of Jewish synagogues and their leaders despite the gospel being preached to them in synagogues continues in Acts. Members of the so-called Synagogue of Freedmen were among those who debated against and eventually killed a Christian leader, Stephen (Acts 6:9). Saul, one of the consenting witnesses to the murder of Stephen (7:58; 8:1), went to the high priest (9:1) and requested letters from him to the synagogues in Damascus to authorize Saul to arrest Christians there (9:2), presumably in their houses as part of his attempt to destroy the church (8:3). After he became a believer in Damascus (9:3–19), Saul immediately was preaching in the synagogues there that Jesus is the Son of God (9:20). But after he confounded, presumably in their synagogues, the Jews who lived in Damascus (9:22), they eventually conspired to kill him (9:23), but he escaped and returned to Jerusalem (9:24–26).

When Barnabas and Saul arrived in Salamis on the island of Cyprus, they proclaimed the word of God in the synagogues of the Jews (13:5). Although they had traveled through the whole island as far as Paphos (13:6), it was the Roman proconsul Sergius Paulus, an intelligent gentile and not a Jew from the synagogue, who summoned Barnabas and Saul to hear the word of God (13:7). When the proconsul saw Saul/Paul (13:9) cause Elymas the magician, who wanted to turn the proconsul away from the faith, to become blind (13:8–11), he became a believer (13:12). But evidently no one from the synagogues of the Jews on Cyprus became a believer.

In Pisidian Antioch Paul and Barnabas entered the synagogue on the day of the Sabbath (13:14) and Paul preached at length (13:15–41). As they were leaving, those in the synagogue invited them to speak about these things on the next Sabbath (13:42). When the meeting of the synagogue had broken up, many of the Jews and God-fearing proselytes followed Paul and Barnabas, who, speaking with them, persuaded them to remain in the grace of God (13:43). On the following Sabbath almost the whole city gathered to hear the word of the Lord (13:44). But when the Jews saw the crowds, they were filled with jealousy and contradicted what was said by Paul, reviling him (13:45). Both Paul and Barnabas spoke boldly and said, "It was necessary that the word of God be spoken to you first, but since you reject it and condemn yourselves as unworthy of eternal life, now we are turning to the gentiles" (13:46). Hearing this, the gentiles rejoiced and glorified the word of the Lord and believed (13:48). But the Jews stirred up persecution against Paul and Barnabas and expelled them from their region (13:50).

In Iconium Paul and Barnabas entered the synagogue of the Jews and spoke in such a way that a large multitude of both Jews and Greeks believed

(14:1). But the disbelieving Jews stirred up and poisoned the minds of the gentiles against the "brothers," that is, believers (14:2). Eventually there was an attempt by both the gentiles and the Jews, together with their leaders, to mistreat and stone Paul and Barnabas (14:5). They became aware of it and fled to the Lycaonian cities of Lystra and Derbe and the surrounding region (14:6). There they continued to proclaim the good news (14:7). Once again members and leaders of the Jewish synagogue rejected the gospel and instigated a persecution, but with the favorable result that it caused the word of the Lord to spread elsewhere.

In Philippi (16:12), on the day of the Sabbath, Paul and those with him went outside the city gate along the river where they thought there would be a Jewish place of prayer, and, sitting down, they spoke with the women who had come together there (16:13). This "place of prayer" (προσευχή) was the equivalent to a synagogue, and occurs here probably because there were not the ten Jewish men needed for an official synagogue.[49] One of the women, named Lydia, a gentile worshiper of God, listened, and the Lord opened her heart to heed what was spoken by Paul (16:14). After she and her household were baptized, she urged Paul and those with him that if they consider her to be a believer in the Lord to enter and stay at her house, and she persuaded them (16:15). This begins the movement in Acts from the synagogues of the Jews to the houses of gentiles as places for Christian fellowship and worship.

In Thessalonica there was a synagogue of the Jews (17:1), and according to the custom of Paul, he went in to them, and on three Sabbaths conversed with them from the scriptures (17:2). He explained and demonstrated that it was necessary for the Christ to suffer and rise from the dead, and that the Jesus whom Paul was proclaiming to them is the Christ (17:3). Some, including Jews, Greeks, and prominent women, were convinced and joined Paul and Silas (17:4). But eventually the Jews stirred up the crowd and the city officials (17:8), so that Paul and Silas were sent by their fellow believers to Beroea, where they went into the synagogue of the Jews (17:10). The Jews there were more receptive (17:11), so that many of them believed, as did quite a few reputable Greek women and men (17:12). But the Jews from Thessalonica came to Beroea, inciting and stirring up the crowds (17:13). Consequently, Paul was sent away by his fellow believers (17:14) to Athens (17:15–16) where he conversed in the synagogue with the Jews and the gentile worshipers, but with no mention of success in the synagogue there (17:17).

---

49. The word προσευχή "is nearly always equivalent to συναγωγή [synagogue] in the sense of a cultic place. But many consider that the προσευχή in Ac 16:13, 16 was not a regular synagogue because it was attended only by women" (BDAG, 878–79).

Locations, Leadership, and Times for Worship

In Corinth (18:1) Paul conversed in the synagogue every Sabbath, attempting to convince both Jews and Greeks (18:4). He testified to the Jews that Jesus is the Christ (18:5). But when they opposed and reviled him, he announced that from now on he will go to the gentiles (18:6). Leaving there, he entered the house of a man by the name of Titius Justus, a gentile worshiper of God, whose house was next to the synagogue (18:7). It was only after leaving the Jewish synagogue for a gentile house that Crispus, the ruler of the synagogue, believed in the Lord together with his whole household, and many of the Corinthians who heard, after Paul left the synagogue for the house, believed and were baptized (18:8).[50] This continues the movement in Acts from the synagogues of the Jews to the houses of gentiles as places for Christian fellowship and worship.[51]

In Ephesus, Paul entered the synagogue and conversed with the Jews (18:19). He eventually left them, with no mention of anyone in the synagogue becoming a believer (18:20-21). Later, a Jew named Apollos arrived in Ephesus (18:24). He had been instructed in the way of the Lord, and spoke and taught accurately about Jesus, although he knew only the baptism of John (18:25). He began to speak boldly in the synagogue, but when Priscilla and Aquila, associates of Paul (18:2-3), heard him, they took him aside and explained the way of God to him more accurately (18:26), but there is no mention that he had any success in bringing people to faith in the synagogue in Ephesus. He eventually traveled to Achaia (18:27), and, demonstrating through the scriptures that Jesus is the Christ, he vigorously refuted the Jews, notably "in public" rather than in their synagogues (18:28).

When Paul returned to Ephesus, he entered the synagogue and spoke boldly for three months, conversing and convincing about the kingdom of God (19:8). But when some became hardened and disbelieved, reviling the Way before the multitude, Paul withdrew from them and took the disciples with him, every day conversing in the lecture hall of Tyrannus (19:9). This continued for two years, so that all in the province of Asia heard the word of the Lord, both Jews and Greeks (19:10) in the lecture hall of Tyrannus, a gentile location, rather than in the synagogue of the Jews.

---

50. "It is possible that Crispus had also been converted during Paul's synagogue ministry, though the narrative sequence implies that it was after Paul moved to the house of Titius Justus" (Peterson, *Acts*, 512). "With the possible exception of Gamaliel (5:34-39), temple and synagogue leaders throughout Acts have doggedly opposed the gospel, yet Crispus becomes a believer" (Gaventa, *Acts*, 257-58).

51. "The opposition in the synagogue forces Paul to transfer his teaching activity from there to the house of a certain Titius Justus, a God-fearer who had heard Paul preach and teach in the synagogue, had evidently come to faith in Jesus, and made his house available as a new center of preaching and teaching" (Schnabel, *Acts*, 759).

The theme of the transition from Jewish synagogues to Christian houses as the location for worship and from the Sabbath to Sunday as the day for Christian worship reaches its climax in Acts when Paul and those with him arrived in Troas (20:6). On "the first day of the week" (τῇ μιᾷ τῶν σαββάτων) they gathered to break bread (20:7), which Christians did regularly in their houses as part of their worship (2:46). This recalls and resonates with "the first day of the week" (τῇ μιᾷ τῶν σαββάτων) as the day for the revelation of Jesus' resurrection (Luke 24:1), Sunday as the day that became most appropriate for weekly Christian worship.[52] In contrast to the Jewish "synagogue" (συναγωγή) gathering for worship, Paul and those with him "gathered" (συνηγμένων) to break bread (Acts 20:7) in the upstairs room of the house where they "gathered" (συνηγμένοι) for worship (20:8), further indicating the transition from Jewish synagogues to houses for Christian worship.[53]

In his defense before the Jews in Jerusalem, Paul recounted how he used to beat and imprison believers in the various synagogues (22:19). In his defense before Felix, Paul pointed out that he was not found conversing with anyone or stirring up a crowd in the temple or in the synagogues or throughout the city (24:12). On the contrary, Paul worships the God of the Jewish ancestors, believing everything that is according to the law and that is written in the prophets (24:14), which were read aloud every Sabbath in the synagogues (15:21). And in his defense before King Agrippa, Paul repeated how he used to punish and force believers to blaspheme many times in all of the synagogues (26:11). In Acts, then, synagogues became places where believers were persecuted, and where the gospel, whose scriptural origins accord with synagogue worship, was preached but rejected by Jews, so that gentile houses rather than Jewish synagogues became the places for Christian fellowship, teaching, and worship.

Passover and Pentecost

Luke places great emphasis on the Jewish Passover context of Jesus' institution of the Eucharist, mentioning the term "Passover" (πάσχα) six times in the narrative leading to it (22:1–15). After the notice that the Feast of Unleavened Bread, which is called the Passover, was coming near (22:1), when the day for sacrificing the Passover lamb arrived (22:7), Jesus gave Peter and

---

52. That these are the only two occurrences in Luke-Acts of the phrase "first day of the week" enhances this connection.

53. The term "synagogue" (συναγωγή) means "gathering together" and is used to refer to a "gathering place" or "place of assembly" (BDAG, 963).

Locations, Leadership, and Times for Worship

John instructions to prepare for them to eat the Passover (22:8).[54] They were to ask the master of a certain house for the location of a room where Jesus may eat the Passover with his disciples (22:11). After they had prepared the Passover (22:13), Jesus announced to the apostles (22:14) that he has eagerly desired to eat this Passover with them before he suffers (22:15). He then instituted the Eucharist (22:17–20), which included his reinterpretation of the bread as his body, suggesting that he is the new sacrificial Passover lamb, and they are to do this in "remembrance" (ἀνάμνησιν) of him (22:19), replacing the remembrance of the Passover (Exod 12:14).[55] The Christian eucharistic meal is thus based upon but supersedes the Jewish Passover meal.[56]

The Jewish feast of Pentecost originally celebrated the spring harvest (Lev 23:9–21; Deut 16:9–11). Later, this pilgrimage festival, observed fifty days after Passover, became associated with the giving of the Mosaic law and the making of the Sinai covenant, key elements of the origins of the Jewish community.[57] When the day of Pentecost had arrived, the disciples in Jerusalem were all together in one place (Acts 2:1). The risen Jesus had told the disciples previously that he would send the promise of his Father, that is, the gift of the Holy Spirit, upon them and that they were to stay in Jerusalem until they are "clothed with power from on high" (Luke 24:49). This promise

54. Passover was an annual pilgrimage festival celebrated in Jerusalem that included a "ritual observance of Israel that celebrates Yahweh's deliverance of the community from Egypt. The observance took place on the 14th day of Nisan and included the slaughter of a lamb and its consumption in a meal shared by the whole family. Passover eventually became associated with the seven-day Festival of Unleavened Bread that began on the 15th of Nisan" (Gorman, "Passover," 1013).

55. "As Jesus has substituted himself for the Passover lamb, so the memento of him is to replace the ἀνάμνησις of the Passover meal" (Fitzmyer, *Gospel According to Luke X–XXIV*, 1401).

56. "The disciples prepared for this meal with expectations of celebrating another Jewish Passover with its fixed ritual of remembering God's gracious deliverance out of Egypt. But what the disciples experienced on this night in which Jesus was betrayed was not another Jewish Passover, but *Jesus' Passover*, in which he took the fixed ritual of the Passover Seder and gave everything in this meal new meaning. He gave it *Christological* meaning, as he interpreted the food at the meal, the story of the exodus, the broken bread and the cup of blessing *in terms of himself*. He took the old Passover meal and he made it his meal by instituting a new meal that supersedes all previous meals of God's table fellowship" (Just, *Luke 9:51—24:53*, 817–18; emphases original).

57. "[T]he evidence from sectarian Judaism and from the Targums suggests associations between Pentecost and the giving of the Torah were very much 'in the air' in the period covered by Acts" (Turner, *Power*, 281–82). See also Fitzmyer, *Acts*, 233–37. "Jesus reinterprets the Passover to signify the inauguration of a new covenant in his blood, and the promised renewal of God's relationship with Israel is experienced fifty days later through the gift of his Spirit, as a direct result of Jesus' redemptive death and resurrection. Some reflection of the pattern of salvation and covenant renewal in Exodus is thus reflected in Luke-Acts" (Peterson, *Acts*, 131–32).

was fulfilled on the day of Pentecost as the apostles were all filled with the Holy Spirit and began to speak in different tongues as the Spirit enabled them to proclaim (Acts 2:4) the gospel to the many and various pilgrims from around the world who had come to Jerusalem for Pentecost (2:5–11). This marks the transition from the Jewish to the Christian feast of Pentecost, which celebrates the sacred origin of the church.[58]

Summary

Throughout Luke-Acts the focus of true worship for all peoples moves away from the Jerusalem temple and its Jewish leaders to the risen Lord Jesus and the leaders of the Christian community. Luke-Acts presents its audience with a concerted theme of the transition from inadequate worship, disbelief, and rejection of the gospel in Jewish synagogues, often on the Sabbath, to true worship, belief, and fellowship in Christian communities and houses, especially on the first day of the week, Sunday, the day of the revelation of the resurrection of the Lord Jesus (Luke 24:1; Acts 20:7). The Christian eucharistic meal is based upon but supersedes the Jewish Passover meal (Luke 22:15–20). And the exuberant outpouring of the Holy Spirit upon the believers in Jerusalem (Acts 2:1–11) marks the transition from the Jewish to the Christian feast of Pentecost, which celebrates the origin of the church's empowerment for its missionary activity.

---

58. "Although the text of Acts fails to make any specific reference to Sinai or the Sinai covenant, it is probable that the writer of Acts understood the descent of the Spirit to mark the sacred beginning of the Christian community in a way that paralleled the sacred origin of the Israelite community at Sinai. As such, Pentecost functions as a celebration of the founding of the Christian community and the beginning of its evangelistic mission" (Gorman, "Pentecost," 1027).

3

True and False Worship

Luke-Acts provides its audience with a foundation for recognizing and avoiding false worship in order to appreciate and practice true worship. True worship of the Lord God includes worship of the Lord Jesus. False worship involves attempts to worship earthly status, wealth, pagan idols, the devil, or human beings rather than God. Jesus and the Christian leaders not only warn against engaging in false and idolatrous worship, but teach matters that are foundational for true and authentic worship.

The Lord Jesus as Object of True Worship in Luke

For the second of his three temptations of Jesus (Luke 4:1–13), the devil took him up and showed him all the kingdoms of the world in a moment of time (4:5). The devil told him that he would give him "all this authority and their glory," for it has been given to the devil who may give it to whomever he wishes (4:6). All of it will be given to Jesus if he worships the devil (4:7). This rings ironic for the audience, having heard that Jesus has already been given the Holy Spirit of God (3:22) and that he is the Son of God who will give him the throne of David his father (1:32), and he will reign over the house of Jacob forever, and of his kingdom there will be no end (1:33).[1] The implication is that the pursuit of earthly authority and the earthly glory based on wealth amounts to worshiping the devil. Jesus overcame the devil's

---

1. "Whatever rule the devil exercises is that allowed him by God; he can only delegate to Jesus what has already been delegated to him. What Jesus is offered, then, is a shabby substitute for the divine sonship that is his by birth" (Green, *Gospel of Luke*, 195).

temptation to false worship with a quotation of the scriptural word of God: "The Lord [κύριον] your God shall you worship and him alone shall you serve [Deut 6:13]" (Luke 4:8). But true worship includes the worship of Jesus, who shares with God a divine identity as "Lord [κύριος]" (1:43; 2:11).[2]

Simon Peter addressed Jesus as "master" (ἐπιστάτα), when he told him that although they had labored all night and caught no fish, at the word of Jesus he will lower the nets (5:5). When Peter saw the great number of fish that filled both boats (5:6–7) as a result of the divine authority manifested by Jesus, he fell down at the knees of Jesus in a gesture of supplicatory worship, confessing his sinfulness and now addressing Jesus as divine Lord:[3] "Depart from me, for I am a sinful man, Lord [κύριε]" (5:8). Jesus answered his prayer by telling him not to fear, implicitly forgiving his sinfulness, and, with divine empowerment, transforming him from one who catches fish to one who catches people for the kingdom of God (5:10; cf. 4:43).[4] Similarly, when a leper saw Jesus, he "fell on his face," a gesture of worshipful devotion, and beseeched him with an act of supplicatory worship, addressing him as divine Lord: "Lord [κύριε], if you wish, you can make me clean" (5:12).[5] Jesus answered his prayer, cleansing him by means of his divine authority (5:13; cf. 2 Kgs 5:7).[6]

The Lord Jesus as Object of True Worship in Acts

In replacing Judas (Acts 1:15–20), Peter told his fellow believers that it was necessary that one of the men who accompanied them the whole time the "Lord" Jesus associated with them (1:21) must become with them a witness of his resurrection (1:22). They proposed two men (1:23), and praying,

---

2. Rowe, *Early Narrative*, 55; Henrichs-Tarasenkova, *Luke's Christology*, 171.

3. On "fell down [προσέπεσεν] at the knees" (5:8) as a worshipful "gesture of a suppliant," see BDAG, 884.

4. "Luke surely intends readers to hear 'Lord' as a divine title, confessing both Peter's sin and his faith" (Edwards, *Gospel According to Luke*, 155–56). "Jesus' response, 'Do not fear,' is his word of absolution to Peter. The miracle of bringing fish into the boat is the miracle of making the unworthy sinner fit to stay in the presence of the holy God. It is the miracle of the forgiveness of sins" (Just, *Luke 1:1—9:50*, 209). See also Rowe, *Early Narrative*, 82–89.

5. On "falling [πεσών] on the face" (5:12) as a sign of devotion before divine beings, see BDAG, 815.

6. "The reference to Jesus as 'Lord' . . . is accompanied by language and posture appropriate to worship, and it echoes Peter's address to Jesus immediately before in 5:8" (Edwards, *Gospel According to Luke*, 160). "He [the leper] attributes to Jesus the power and grace of God to do as he wills (Wis 12:18), to forgive his sins and to cleanse him" (Garland, *Luke*, 240). See also Rowe, *Early Narrative*, 89–92.

they addressed the risen, heavenly Jesus as divine Lord: "You, Lord, who know the hearts of all, show which of these two you have chosen [ἐξελέξω]" (1:24). This recalls and resonates with the fact that it was Jesus who originally "chose" (ἐξελέξατο) the apostles (1:2), "having chosen" (ἐκλεξάμενος) twelve apostles from his disciples (Luke 6:13). The prayer to the divine Lord Jesus was answered through the casting of lots, which indicated that Matthias was to be numbered with the eleven apostles (Acts 1:26).[7] And when Stephen was being stoned to death, he prayed to the heavenly Lord Jesus (7:55–56), calling out, "Lord Jesus, receive my spirit!" (7:59; cf. Luke 23:46). Then he fell to his knees, a gesture of supplicatory worship, and cried out in a loud voice, "Lord, do not hold this sin against them!" (7:60; cf. Luke 23:34).

When Simon, the magician (8:9), offered money to the apostles to buy the power to bestow the Holy Spirit (8:18–19), Peter told him to repent of his wickedness and pray to the "Lord," the heavenly Lord Jesus (cf. 8:16), for forgiveness (8:22). Simon then asked Peter to pray for him to the "Lord" (8:24). The members of the church at Antioch (13:1) were worshiping the "Lord," the heavenly Lord Jesus (cf. 12:17, 23), and fasting (13:2a). Their prayer to the Lord Jesus was answered when the Holy Spirit told them to "set apart for me Barnabas and Saul for the work to which I have called them" (13:2b). And in Ephesus the name of the heavenly "Lord" Jesus "was magnified [ἐμεγαλύνετο]" (19:17), that is, praised or glorified as an act of doxological worship (cf. Luke 1:46; Acts 10:46).

True and False Worship in Luke

When Jesus entered the Jerusalem temple, he began to expel "those selling" (Luke 19:45), that is, those engaged in selling the things necessary to carry out the sacrificial system of worship in the temple. In expelling them, Jesus confronted these sellers with a composite scriptural quotation in which God himself is the speaker: "My house will be a house of prayer [Isa 56:7], but you have made it a den of robbers [Jer 7:11]" (Luke 19:46). This implies that the sellers in the temple have robbed the people by taking their money and thus enabling them to engage in what amounts to false worship. They thereby fail to make the temple, God's house, a place for the authentic worship of God. It

---

7. "The opening and closing 'frame' in Acts 1 regarding the apostles 'chosen' by Jesus, and the 'frame' regarding 'the day he was taken up', together with the immediately preceding reference to 'the Lord' Jesus in this context (1:21) all indicate that 'the Lord' who is being prayed to in 1:24 is Jesus. Luke shows then that Jesus not only has such authority that he may be prayed to, but Jesus is also continuing to direct affairs from 'heaven'" (Thompson, *Acts*, 50).

recalls and resonates with Jesus' previous pronouncement that "you cannot serve God and money [literally, "mammon"])" (16:13).[8] But by his continual teaching of the people in the temple (19:47; 20:1; 21:37), Jesus will indicate to the audience what makes for the authentic worship of God.[9]

While teaching in the temple, Jesus told the people a parable (20:9–19) in which a man, representative of God, planted a vineyard, representative of Israel/the temple, and leased it to tenants, representative of the Jewish leaders in charge of temple worship. After the tenants killed the man's son, representative of Jesus (20:15), Jesus told the people that the man will come and put the tenants to death and give the vineyard to others (20:16). He then quoted a scripture passage (LXX Ps 117:22) according to which "the stone," that is the son, Jesus, "the builders," that is, the tenants as builders/leaders of the temple, "rejected" by killing him "has become," by being raised from the dead by God, "the cornerstone" of a new edifice (20:17). The implication is that the risen Lord Jesus will be the foundation for a new edifice, a new communal "house," the Christian community, which will replace the temple whose leaders failed to make it God's house of true worship (19:46).

As he continued to teach in the temple, Jesus indicated the characteristics of the true worship to be practiced by his followers. Rather than offering God sacrificial animals in the temple, and analogous to the coin for the tax, made in the "image" of Caesar (20:24), they are to "give to God what belongs to God" (20:25), that is, the human person made in the "image" and likeness of God (Gen 1:26). Rather than giving to God dead animals in sacrificial worship, they are to give themselves as living human beings to God, since "he is not the God of the dead, but of the living, for all live to him" (Luke 20:38). As indicated by David, who, as the speaker of Ps 110:1, calls both God and the Christ "Lord," Jesus is worthy of being an object of true worship (20:41–44; cf. 4:8).[10] And in the temple Jesus pointed to

---

8. "Mammon" (μαμωνᾶς) appears in Luke 16:13 and Matt 6:24 "personified as a power that comes into competition with God's claim on humankind.... Jesus rejects securing one's life through possessions and property, inasmuch as it would be an attempt to secure one's life by submitting to a false lord" (Balz, "μαμωνᾶς," 2.383).

9. "The volume of trade in the Court of the gentiles was conducted on a scale commensurate with the grandeur of Herod's temple itself; it was crucial for the maintenance of proper worship and for the financial gain of the Sadducees and Sanhedrin" (Edwards, *Gospel According to Luke*, 555). "Far from being a place for authentic worship, the temple, in the hands of its powerful custodians, has become a refuge for those who engage in unjust, exploitative economic practices" (Carroll, *Luke*, 389). "Those in charge were taking advantage of the worshipers. In the very presence of God, as it prepares to worship, the nation dishonors God. Something about the current practice is too commercial" (Bock, *Luke 9:51—24:53*, 1579).

10. On the indications of the Lord Jesus Christ sharing a divine identity with the Lord God in Luke 20:41–44, see Rowe, *Early Narrative*, 170–77.

a poor widow who put into the temple treasury her whole livelihood as a sacrificial offering (21:1–4). This characterizes how Jesus will offer his own life as an act of sacrificial worship and serves as a paradigm for the true, self-sacrificial worship to be practiced in the Christian community that is to replace the temple.[11]

True and False Worship in Acts

In his speech during his defense before the high-priest and the Sanhedrin (Acts 6:12, 15; 7:1) Stephen pointed out to the Jewish leaders that their ancestors had engaged in false worship when they asked Aaron to make gods for them who will go before them (7:40). Then "they made an idol in the form of a calf" (ἐμοσχοποίησαν) and engaged in idolatrous worship as they rejoiced in the "works of their hands" (7:41). God then turned and gave them over "to serve/worship" (λατρεύειν) the host of heaven (7:42), the idolatrous images "you made to worship [προσκυνεῖν]" (7:43). Solomon later built a house for God (7:47), the forerunner of the Jerusalem temple in Stephen's day, but the Most High does not dwell in things "handmade [χειροποιήτοις]" (7:48). This insinuates that the worship conducted by the Jewish leaders in the handmade Jerusalem temple amounts to idolatrous worship, just as the Jewish ancestors worshiped the images "you made [ἐποιήσατε]" (7:43) and rejoiced in the "works of their hands [χειρῶν]" (7:41).[12]

In Caesarea there was a Roman centurion named Cornelius (10:1). He was a devout and God-fearing man along with his whole household, who prayed regularly to God (10:2), and thus engaged in acts of authentic worship, as an angel of God who appeared to him (10:3) indicated (10:4). But when Peter entered his house, Cornelius, "falling at his feet" in a dramatic act of devotional obeisance toward Peter, performed an act of false worship as he "worshiped" (προσεκύνησεν) him (10:25). Peter, however, raised him up, saying, "Arise, I myself am also a human being" (10:26). This reminds the audience that true worship must be directed toward the Lord God: "the Lord your God shall you worship [προσκυνήσεις]" (Luke 4:8),

---

11. "Her sacrificial giving demonstrates selfless devotion to God (like Anna's, 2:36–38) and models what it means to give back to God what is God's (20:25). She gives her whole self" (Garland, *Luke*, 818). "She is exactly what Jesus called his disciples to be: completely devoted to the work of the Lord" (Just, *Luke 9:51—24:53*, 781).

12. "The fact that every occurrence of the term χειροποίητος (handmade) in the LXX refers to idols especially strengthens the idea that Stephen is charging his audience with idolatry here. Thus Stephen indicates that the idolatry characteristic of Israel's history of rejecting God is still present in the generation of those who have rejected the Lord Jesus" (Thompson, *Acts*, 169).

which, however, includes worship of the risen Lord Jesus, as indicated by the disciples who were "worshiping" (προσκυνήσαντες) him at the conclusion of the Gospel (24:52). Furthermore, "falling at the feet" is a gesture of worship appropriate not for the merely human Peter but for the divine Lord Jesus (8:41; 17:16).[13]

King Herod Agrippa I, the grandson of King Herod the Great, had James, the brother of John, killed (Acts 12:1-2) and imprisoned Peter (12:3-4). But, in answer to the prayer of the church for Peter (12:5), the Lord sent his angel and rescued Peter from the hand of Herod (12:11). After Herod then went to Caesarea (12:19), on an appointed day, clothed in royal robes and sitting on the judgment seat, he addressed the assembled crowd (12:21), who cried out, "The voice of a god, and not of a man!" (12:22). Immediately an angel of the Lord struck Herod down because he did not "give the glory to God," and he was eaten by worms and died (12:23). Herod thus was arrogantly about to allow himself to be worshiped as a false god, rather than, in contrast to Peter (10:25-26), preventing it and leading the crowd to the proper worship of giving glory to the true God, like the Samaritan who "gave glory to God" after being miraculously healed by the divine Lord Jesus (Luke 17:18).[14] This underscores for the audience how true worship must be directed to the Lord God/Jesus rather than to human beings.[15]

After Paul healed a lame man at Lystra (Acts 14:8-10), the crowds cried out, "The gods resembling human beings have come down to us!" (14:11). Calling Barnabas "Zeus" and Paul "Hermes" (14:12), the priest of Zeus together with the crowds intended to offer them sacrificial worship (14:13). But the apostles Barnabas and Paul dramatically tore their garments (14:14) and declared that they are of the same nature as the crowds, human beings, who are proclaiming to them the good news that they should turn from the false worship of dead idols to the true worship of the "living God" (14:15).[16] This reinforces for the audience that true worship consists

---

13. "From the standpoint of Luke's literary purposes, Cornelius 'worshiped' Peter so that Peter could reject this inappropriate response, just as Paul rejects such a response in [Acts] 14:15 (cf. 28:6). By contrast, those who 'fell at the feet' of Jesus (Luke 8:41; 17:16) or 'worshiped' him (24:52) were not reproved because such veneration was appropriate for him" (Keener, *Acts*, 2.1781).

14. "According to v. 23, the punishment was for failure to honor God, whose angel acted before Herod had the opportunity to reject this adulation (as had Peter in 10:25-26) or (as in Josephus *Ant.* 19.246) to tolerate it" (Pervo, *Acts*, 314).

15. "Agrippa kept divine honor for himself instead of glorifying the true source of his honor (cf. Rom 1:21). By contrast, the ministry of the apostle he had sought to kill, Peter, led to people glorifying God (Acts 4:21; 11:18), as would the ministry of Paul (13:48; 21:20)" (Keener, *Acts*, 2.1965).

16. "The 'living' God stands in contrast to and implies 'dead' idols" (Bock, *Acts*,

in worshiping not human beings (10:25-26; 12:22-23), but the "living" (ζῶντα) God, including the "living" (ζῶντα) divine Lord Jesus, risen from the dead (Luke 24:5; Acts 1:3). It reminds the audience to practice the true worship of giving themselves as living human beings to the living God to whom they belong as the God who gave them life (Luke 20:25), the God who is not the God of the dead but of the "living" (ζώντων), for all "live" (ζῶσιν) to him (20:38).

While Paul was in Athens, "his spirit was aroused within him, seeing that the city was full of idols" (Acts 17:16), and thus heavily involved in false worship.[17] Some of those with whom he conversed declared that he seems to be a proclaimer of foreign deities, because he was proclaiming the good news about "Jesus" and the "Resurrection" (17:18). Ironically, for the audience, they were indirectly attesting to the divine status of the risen Lord Jesus. Paul went on to explain that the "Unknown God" inscribed on one of their altars, whom "you worship" (εὐσεβεῖτε) without knowing it is what Paul is proclaiming to them (17:23). This "Unknown God" includes not only the Creator God, who now commands all people everywhere to repent (17:24-30), but the man he appointed to judge the world in righteousness by raising him from the dead (17:31). Hearing about "resurrection" from the dead, some scoffed and others were dismissive (17:32), so that he left (17:33). The implication for the audience is that true worship includes worship not only of the Creator God but of the Jesus whom he raised from the dead.[18]

Demetrius, a silversmith, addressed those who were engaged with him in the business of making silver shrines to the goddess Artemis in Ephesus (19:24-25). He warned them that Paul misled a large crowd by saying that gods made by hands are not gods at all (19:26).[19] There is a danger that the

478).

17. "As Luke tells it, Paul does not think the Athenians are particularly pious but exceptionally superstitious—or in Jewish theological language, idolatrous" (Rowe, "Grammar of Life," 39).

18. "Thus, at the end of his address before the Areopagus Council, Paul expresses his conviction that people who approach the one true God should also approach Jesus.... It is ultimately impossible to distinguish between God's action and the action of Jesus.... As Paul provides an exposition of the God whom he proclaims—the God acknowledged in Athens as an 'unknown god'—he speaks of the one true God and he speaks of Jesus" (Schnabel, *Acts*, 742). "Luke has bracketed the speech (17:18, 32) and ended Paul's discourse with references to the resurrection in order to foreground the challenge that the risen Jesus presents to pagan religion" (Jipp, "Paul's Areopagus Speech," 587). See also O'Toole, "Paul at Athens," 185-97; Rowe, *World Upside Down*, 39-41.

19. "Paul's point would be not only that idols are empty of any power but also that the one true God must be worshiped" (Bock, *Acts*, 608-9).

temple of the "magnificent" (μεγάλης) goddess Artemis will be regarded as nothing, and she whom the whole world "worships" (σέβεται) will have her "magnificence" (μεγαλειότητος) taken away (19:27).[20] Ironically for the audience, this has already happened. After the attempt of some itinerant Jewish exorcists to invoke the name of the Lord Jesus over those with evil spirits (19:13) was thwarted (19:14–16), fear fell upon all the Jews and Greeks in Ephesus, and the name of the Lord Jesus "was magnified [ἐμεγαλύνετο]" (19:17). This resonates with the worship of those in the household of Cornelius who "were magnifying" (μεγαλυνόντων) God (10:46), and of Mary who said, "My soul magnifies [μεγαλύνει] the Lord" (Luke 1:46). The true worship of God and the divine Lord Jesus has thus replaced false, idolatrous worship.

Summary

Luke-Acts provides its audience with a foundation for practicing the true worship of the Lord God and the divine Lord Jesus rather than the false worship of earthly status, wealth, idols (Acts 7:40–48; 17:16–33; 19:14–27), the devil (Luke 4:5–8), or human beings (Acts 10:25–26; 12:22–23; 14:11–15). With the risen Lord Jesus as its foundational "cornerstone" (Luke 20:17), the Christian community is to become a new household of true worship to replace the Jerusalem temple whose leaders failed to make it God's "house of prayer" (19:46), a communal place for true worship. True worshipers are to "give to God what belongs to God" (20:25), that is, the total human person made in the "image" and likeness of God (Gen 1:26). Rather than giving to God dead animals in sacrificial worship in the temple, they are to give themselves as living human beings to God, since "he is not the God of the dead, but of the living, for all live to him" (Luke 20:38). In imitation of the poor widow (21:1–4), who prefigures the Lord Jesus himself, true worshipers are to give their whole lives to God in acts of self-sacrificial worship.

---

20. "Through the mouth of Demetrius, Luke thus juxtaposes starkly the competing perspectives that form the clash of the gods: to understand rightly the Christian mission is to perceive the 'danger' posed to Artemis of the Ephesians. It is, consequently, to witness to the prospective disintegration of religiously dependent economics" (Rowe, *World Upside Down*, 46).

4

Supplicatory Worship

Supplicatory worship refers to prayers of petition or supplication. In Luke-Acts people pray to both the Lord God and the divine Lord Jesus. Jesus not only teaches about how to pray to God, but he himself prays to God frequently and at important and critical moments in his ministry, providing the foundational paradigm and empowerment for Christian prayer.[1]

Praying to God in Luke

Praying to God occurs in the very first scene of the Lukan narrative, as the multitude of the people "was praying" (προσευχόμενον) in the Jerusalem temple outside of the sanctuary at the hour of the incense offering (Luke 1:10). Their communal praying, implicitly for the benefit of the people of Israel, complements that of the elderly priest Zechariah, implicitly for a child (1:5–13).[2] The angel of the Lord told Zechariah that his supplicatory

---

1. Prayer has been aptly described as a "primary means of communication that binds together God and humankind in intimate and reciprocal relationship. Its foundational assumption is the belief that the Creator of the world is both available for human address and committed to a divine-human partnership that sustains, and when necessary restores, the world in accordance with God's creational design.... The ultimate goal of this partnership, as articulated in Jesus' model prayer, is that God's will be done 'on earth as in heaven'" (Balentine, "Prayer," 1077, 1079).

2. "If analogy with other prayers at the time of sacrifice in the LXX are any indication, then we may assume that these prayers are on behalf of the nation of Israel. This assumption gains strength from the descriptions and words of the pious Jews throughout the birth narrative, concerned as they are with divine intervention on behalf of Israel" (Green, *Gospel of Luke*, 71).

"prayer" (δέησίς) to God has been answered; his wife Elizabeth will bear him a son, John (1:13), which is also the implicit answer to the prayer of the people, as John will "prepare a people fit for the Lord" (1:17), not only for the Lord God but the Lord Jesus (1:43; 2:11). This is confirmed by the praying of the elderly prophetess, Anna (2:36), who never left the temple, worshiping with supplicatory fasting and "prayers" (δεήσεσιν) night and day (2:37).[3] The birth of the Lord Jesus is the implicit answer to her prayers for the Jewish people, as she gave thanks to God and spoke about the child Jesus, personified salvation (2:30), to all who were awaiting the redemption of Jerusalem (2:38).

The Pharisees and scribes (5:30) told Jesus that the disciples of John and of the Pharisees fast often and offer "prayers" (δεήσεις), whereas his disciples continue to eat and drink (5:33). Referring to his disciples as the "wedding guests" of the messianic nuptial banquet that has now arrived with him, Jesus explained that it is not appropriate for his disciples to fast while he, the "bridegroom," is with them (5:34). But the time will come when he is taken away from them, and then his followers will appropriately engage in the supplicatory worship of fasting (5:35). This indicates the value of fasting together with praying as part of Christian supplicatory worship in the future.[4] Indeed, in the midst of their worshiping of the Lord and fasting, the members of the church in Antioch (Acts 13:1) were told by the Holy Spirit to set apart Saul and Barnabas for the work to which they have been called by the Lord (13:2). Then fasting and "praying" (προσευξάμενοι), they laid their hands on them and sent them off (13:3).

Jesus exhorted the disciples he sent out to work among the people to be "harvested" for the kingdom of God (Luke 10:1–9) to "pray" (δεήθητε) to the Lord of the harvest to send out workers into his harvest, since "the harvest is abundant but the workers are few" (10:2). Later, after Jesus had finished "praying" (προσευχόμενον), one of his disciples asked him to teach them "to pray" (προσεύχεσθαι), just as John taught his disciples (11:1). Jesus told them that whenever "you pray" (προσεύχησθε), say: "Father, may your name be held holy, may your kingdom come. Give us each day our daily bread, and forgive us our sins, for we ourselves forgive everyone who sins against us, and do not lead us into temptation" (11:2–4). Jesus thus provides his disciples and the audience with a model prayer for their communal supplicatory worship. They are to submit to God by praying first for the

---

3. Fasting was a "deliberate and often prolonged abstinence from food and sometimes drink.... Fasting seems to lend an air of extra dedication to religious acts such as prayer" (Smith-Christopher, "Fasting," 456).

4. "Thus, Luke anchors the custom of early Christian fasting in a saying of Jesus" (Fitzmyer, *Gospel According to Luke I-IX*, 599).

advancement of God's salvific plan (kingdom) for the world, before presenting God with petitions for their daily needs, forgiveness of their sins, and divine assistance in avoiding and overcoming temptations.[5]

Jesus then told a parable about how God will certainly answer prayers of supplication, as he implicitly contrasts divine with human behavior. Among human beings, if a friend goes to a friend at midnight requesting three loaves of bread (11:5), because he has nothing to give a traveling friend who has visited him (11:6), the friend being asked may be reluctant to respond because he and his family are in bed (11:7). Nevertheless, if he does not get up and give to the petitioner because of friendship, because of the rude "shamelessness" (ἀναίδειαν) of the petitioner he will get up and give him whatever he needs (11:8).[6] The implicit point is not to hesitate to pray to God, even with shameless audacity, because God will certainly give to one who prays to him whatever that person needs. This point is then emphasized as Jesus encourages the audience to practice supplicatory worship, because those who ask from God will certainly receive, those who seek from God will certainly find, and for those who, by praying, metaphorically "knock" God will open (11:9–10).[7]

In continuing to teach about supplicatory worship, Jesus again compared human with divine behavior. He asked the rhetorical questions, "What father among you whose son asks for a fish, will give him a snake instead of a fish? Or if he asks for an egg, will give him a scorpion?" (11:11–12). If even evil human beings know how to give good things to their children, how much more will the Father from heaven give the Holy Spirit to those asking him (11:13). Although those engaged in supplicatory worship may not receive precisely what they pray for, God will never give them anything

---

5. The fact that Jesus himself taught this thoroughly Jewish prayer "transforms it into a quintessential Christian prayer" (Edwards, *Gospel According to Luke*, 336). "To pray not to be led into temptation is to pray not to succumb to that temptation. . . . Taken together, the petitions for bread, for forgiveness, and for keeping them from succumbing to temptation are petitions to help the disciples be kept in the one, true saving faith" (Just, *Luke 9:51—24:53*, 470).

6. "In Luke 11:8 ἀναίδεια refers to the insensitivity, the rudeness, of the man who comes asking in the middle of the night. . . . It is how the petitioned man evaluates the conduct of the petitioner" (Snodgrass, *Stories with Intent*, 443–44). "One point that can be stated categorically is that the traditional translation of ἀναίδεια as 'persistence' is incorrect" (Crump, *Knocking on Heaven's Door*, 67).

7. "The parable says in effect: 'If a human will obviously get up in the middle of the night to grant the request even of a rude friend, will not God much more answer your requests? . . . Nothing in the parable of the Friend at Midnight teaches persistence in prayer. Rather the parable teaches the certainty of a God who hears prayer and responds" (Snodgrass, *Stories with Intent*, 447, 448). See also Crump, *Knocking on Heaven's Door*, 60–76.

detrimental but only what he knows is beneficial for them. Even if petitioners do not explicitly ask for the gift of the Holy Spirit, but only for what they think they need, God will give those asking/praying to him the Holy Spirit, as the greatest good which everyone needs. Just as the Holy Spirit enabled the praying Jesus not to succumb to temptation but to submit to God (3:21–22; 4:1–13, 14, 18; 10:21), so the Holy Spirit will enable those who pray not to succumb to temptation (11:4) but submit their wills to the will of God.[8]

Jesus then told them another parable, again contrasting human with divine behavior, about the necessity for them "to pray" (προσεύχεσθαι) always without losing heart (18:1). A widow used to come to a judge, who neither feared God nor respected people (18:2), seeking justice against her adversary (18:3). Although for a long time the judge was unwilling (18:4), he decided to give her justice, lest she eventually harm him (18:5). If this is how an unrighteous human judge behaves (18:6), then surely God will give justice to his chosen ones who call out to him day and night, as God, unlike the judge, will be patient toward them (18:7). God will surely give them justice quickly; but when Jesus, as the Son of Man, comes to finalize the kingdom of God (17:20–37), will he find faith on earth? (18:8). The point is for the audience to pray continually without losing heart, confident that God will surely answer in a timely manner. Such praying will assure that one is found faithful when Jesus comes again to bring to completion the kingdom of God at the end of the age.[9]

To some who were convinced that they were righteous and despised everyone else, Jesus told a parable about authentic prayer (18:9). Two men went up to the temple "to pray" (προσεύξασθαι), one a Pharisee and one a tax collector (18:10). The Pharisee "prayed" (προσηύχετο) to and/or about himself, thus not an authentic prayer to God, as he thanked God that he is not like the rest of sinful humanity, or even like this tax collector (18:11). He presented God with his own accomplishments (18:12), rather than with

---

8. "Luke does not say that the Father gives the Holy Spirit to 'those who ask for it.' He says that he gives the Spirit to those who pray" (Crump, *Jesus the Intercessor*, 133). "In 11:1–13, Jesus commends and models prayer, then reveals its basis: trust in God's gracious provision, experienced most deeply as guidance and empowerment by God's own Spirit" (Carroll, *Luke*, 253).

9. "Communicating the parable should concentrate on two primary areas: the character of God, who is *not* like the uncaring, unrighteous judge, but is merciful, patient, and eager to assist his people, and the necessity of staying alert and ready for God's vindication and judgment. . . . A primary path to alertness and faithfulness is prayer, constant involvement with God as we interpret and deal with the world in which we live" (Snodgrass, *Stories with Intent*, 461–62; emphasis original). See also Crump, *Knocking on Heaven's Door*, 77–89.

a genuine petition. But the tax collector prayed for God to be merciful to him as a sinner (18:13). The tax collector, implicitly forgiven, went home "made righteous" (δεδικαιωμένος) by God (18:14a), whereas the Pharisee, convinced he was one of the "righteous" (δίκαιοι) but despised others (18:9), did not. For everyone who, like the Pharisee, exalts himself will be humbled by God, but the one who, like the tax collector, humbles himself will be exalted by God (18:14b). Authentic prayer is praying with a humble acknowledgment of one's sinfulness to a God who is merciful and forgiving.[10]

Jesus warned his disciples to beware of the scribes who like to go around in long robes, love greetings in the marketplaces, seats of honor in synagogues, and places of honor at banquets (20:46). They devour the property of widows, and as a pretext they "pray" (προσεύχονται) at length. Rather than an answer to such insincere praying, they will receive a severe condemnation (20:47). They thus present the audience with an example of inauthentic prayer. In contrast, Jesus had already exhorted his disciples and thus the audience to "pray" (προσεύχεσθε) for those who mistreat them (6:28). Finally, Jesus exhorted the disciples and thus the audience to be alert at all times, "praying" (δεόμενοι) to escape all of the coming tribulations and to stand before Jesus as the Son of Man (21:36). This reinforces Jesus' previous parable about praying constantly and not losing heart (18:1), in order to be found faithful when he comes again as the Son of Man (18:8).

Praying of Jesus to God in Luke

When all the people were baptized by John, Jesus also was baptized and, while he was "praying" (προσευχομένου), "heaven was opened [by God, divine passive]" (3:21). Then in response to his praying, which placed him in a supplicatory stance of submission to God, the Holy Spirit descended upon him and God declared him to be his beloved Son with whom he is well pleased (3:22).[11] Filled with the Holy Spirit, Jesus was led by that Spirit into the wilderness (4:1) to be tempted by the devil (4:2-13). The Holy

---

10. "The Pharisee stands before God in self-congratulation, the tax collector stands before God in prayer" (Edwards, *Gospel According to Luke*, 506). "God is not a God impressed with pious acts and feelings of superiority. He is, rather, a God of mercy who responds to the needs and honest prayers of people" (Snodgrass, *Stories with Intent*, 474).

11. "Prayer itself, irrespective of what is actually said, is communication with the divine realm. As such it places one in the ideal position to receive whatever God may have to give.... Luke does not say that Jesus prayed specifically for the Spirit.... The Spirit descends in Lk. 3:21f because filling Jesus with the Spirit was the Father's particular will for him at that particular time" (Crump, *Jesus the Intercessor*, 115).

Spirit enabled Jesus to overcome the temptations of the devil, including the temptation to worship the devil rather than God (4:5–8). Jesus returned to Galilee "in the power of the Spirit" (4:14). And in the synagogue at Nazareth Jesus declared that, in fulfillment of scripture (4:21), the Spirit of the Lord, which he received as a result of praying to God, has anointed him to bring good news to the poor, to proclaim freedom for the oppressed (4:18), and "the year of the Lord's favor" (4:19), that is, the new era of messianic salvation, the time of the kingdom of God.

The word about Jesus spread all the more and many crowds were coming together to hear and be cured of their illnesses (5:15). But Jesus was withdrawing to deserted places and "praying" (5:16). One day as Jesus was teaching, Pharisees and teachers of the law were sitting there who had come from every village of Galilee and Judea and Jerusalem, and the power of the Lord was with him to heal (5:17), implicitly as a result of his praying. The "power" (δύναμις) of the Lord is synonymous with the Holy Spirit, as was indicated when the angel Gabriel told Mary that the Holy Spirit will come upon her and the "power" (δύναμις) of the Most High will overshadow her (1:35). The power of the Lord that was with Jesus to heal, the Jesus who returned to Galilee in the "power" (δυνάμει) of the Spirit (4:14), is thus the power of the Holy Spirit Jesus received while praying after his baptism (3:21–22).[12]

At another key moment in his ministry Jesus went out to a mountain "to pray," and he spent the night in "prayer" to God (6:12). As a result of his praying, which again placed him in a supplicatory stance of submission to God, he not only chose his twelve apostles on the next day (6:13–16), but "power" (δύναμις) was coming out from him and he healed all (6:19) those who came to him (6:17–18). This was the "power of the Spirit" (4:14) he received as a result of praying (3:21–22; 5:16; 6:12).[13] It was as a result of his "praying" (9:18) that Jesus evoked from his disciples their first confession of his identity as the Christ of God (9:20). And after Jesus went up a mountain "to pray" (9:28), it was while he was "praying," and implicitly as a result of it, that he was temporarily transformed into a heavenly figure (9:29). This indicates to the audience that it is God's will for Jesus ultimately to enter into

---

12. "His regular, intensive prayer life explains how the power to heal was with Jesus (5:17). He spent hours with God in prayer. Luke notes Jesus as praying at key moments, and this prayer occurs before his first conflict with the Pharisees" (Garland, *Luke*, 241).

13. "Jesus' communication with God *on the mountain at night* (6.12) is counterpointed with his election of the Twelve *on the next day* (6.13–16) as well as with his acts of power in response to the seeking crowds *at the foot of the mountain* (6.17–19), implying some kind of causal relationship between Jesus' prayer and these events" (Holmås, *Prayer*, 91; emphases original).

heavenly glory after his death (9:26), but only—in contrast to Moses and Elijah, prophetic leaders who attained heavenly glory (9:30–31) without being put to death—after he is put to death by his people (9:22, 35).[14]

After his last supper with his apostles (22:14–20) Jesus told Simon Peter that "Satan has demanded to sift all of you like wheat" (22:31; cf. 22:3). But then Jesus declared that "I have prayed" (ἐδεήθην) concerning Simon that his faith may not fail, and that when he has turned back after denying Jesus (22:34), Peter is to strengthen his "brothers" (22:32), that is, his fellow believers. The effectiveness of Jesus' intercessory prayer for Peter becomes evident later when Peter stood up in the midst of the "brothers" (Acts 1:15), and, addressing them as "brothers" (1:16), strengthened them as he authoritatively instructed them on the necessity of replacing Judas as one of the twelve apostles (1:16–22). They then proposed two candidates (1:23) and, "praying" (προσευξάμενοι), they beseeched the risen Lord Jesus to show which of the two he has chosen (1:24; cf. Luke 6:13; Acts 1:2) to take the place of Judas (1:25). In answer to their prayer, which came about as a result of Jesus praying for Peter, it was indicated that Matthias would replace Judas (1:26), thus restoring the number of apostles to the original twelve.[15]

When Jesus went out to the Mount of Olives and his disciples followed him (Luke 22:39), he exhorted them to "pray not to enter into temptation" (22:40), the Satanic temptation to reject God's will (4:13; 8:13; 11:4). Jesus then knelt down and "prayed" (22:41) for his Father to take this "cup," his suffering and death, away from him, but submitting his will to the will of his Father (22:42). In answer to his prayer, there appeared to him an angel from heaven, strengthening him (22:43). Being in agony, he "prayed" more earnestly, and that "his sweat became like drops of blood falling to the ground" (22:44) indicated the external manifestation of his inner struggle (sweat) to accept the necessary death (blood; cf. 22:20) God has willed for him.[16] When he rose from "prayer" and found his disciples sleeping from

---

14. Heil, *Transfiguration*, 257–79. "The revelatory event in the setting of prayer is a proleptic experience of Jesus' future glory (cf. 9:26–27) providing a sanction of his suffering as the very pathway to that glory" (Holmås, *Prayer*, 97).

15. "Thus *the perseverance of the disciples' faith, the survival of Satanic trials, is shown to be founded on the intercession of the earthly Jesus*. . . . Luke has grounded not only this ongoing perseverance, but also the initial perception and confession of Jesus as the Christ, in the power of Jesus' prayers" (Crump, *Jesus the Intercessor*, 157; emphasis original). "Luke has provided the reader with important clues to Peter's upcoming transformation from one who denies in the moment of crisis (Lk. 22.54–62) to becoming a self-conscious leader of the restored community (Acts 1–15): the sustenance of Peter's faith and his revitalization as a leader is firmly rooted in divine providence and assistance catalysed by Jesus' intercession" (Holmås, *Prayer*, 105).

16. After presenting the text-critical evidence, Crump (*Jesus the Intercessor*, 117–21)

grief (22:45), unable to pray, he exhorted them anew to rise and "pray so that you do not enter into temptation" (22:46). This dramatic and decisive prayer of Jesus thus provides his disciples and the audience not only the model but the empowerment to be strengthened to submit to God's will through prayer.[17]

Jesus prayed for those who crucified him (23:33), when he said, "Father, forgive them, for they do not know what they are doing" (23:34).[18] He thus provides a model for the audience to be generous in forgiving those who sin against them in accord with how he taught his disciples to pray, when he told them to address God as "Father" (11:2) and pray for him to "forgive us our sins, for we ourselves forgive everyone who sins against us" (11:4). Jesus thus exemplified his exhortation for his followers to "pray" for those who mistreat them (6:28), and he went beyond his teaching that if someone repents, forgive him (17:3), as he prayed for the forgiveness of those who killed him without any indication of their repentance.[19] That "they do not know what they are doing" foreshadows Peter's address to the Jewish people (Acts 3:12) responsible for putting Jesus to death (3:15), when he said, "And now, brothers, I know that you acted in ignorance, just as your leaders did" (3:17; cf. 13:27). He then called them to repentance, so that their sins may be wiped out (3:19).[20]

Immediately before Jesus breathed his last, he prayed, quoting from a psalm of the suffering righteous one (cf. LXX Ps 30:6), "Father, into your

---

concludes that "it is possible to be fairly confident in asserting that the weight of the internal evidence more than answers the objections made against these verses and tips the scales very strongly in favour of the authenticity of Lk. 22:43-44" (p. 121). See also Pope, "Downward Motion," 261-81.

17. A subtle difference in wording between Jesus' initial command, "Pray not to enter [μὴ εἰσελθεῖν] into temptation" (22:40), and the renewed, concluding command, "Pray so that you do not enter [ἵνα μὴ εἰσέλθητε] into temptation" (22:46), accords with the changed situation. Now that, and only because, Jesus was able to pray and be strengthened in praying, can the disciples and the audience fulfill his command to pray not to enter into temptation (cf. 11:4), confident of likewise being strengthened by praying to submit themselves to God's will. See Heil, *Transfiguration*, 297-300.

18. Regarding the questionable authenticity of Jesus' prayer here, Crump (*Jesus the Intercessor*, 84) states, "The external evidence regarding Lk. 23:34a is far from clear, but the greater weight of evidence lies in favour of the text's authenticity. The combination of this external evidence with the very weighty internal arguments decisively tips the balance in favour of this prayer being an original part of Luke's gospel."

19. "The prayer, however, is characteristic of Jesus' entire ministry in Luke. He forgives those who show no demonstrable sign of having repented, and it lays the foundation for the apostles' ministry (24:47)" (Garland, *Luke*, 923).

20. "That for which Jesus prayed on the cross, Peter proclaims in Acts. In point of fact, Jesus' prayer for forgiveness of the ignorant Jews at his crucifixion opens the way for their conversion, as described in Acts" (Holmås, *Prayer*, 110-11).

hands I entrust my spirit" (Luke 23:46). This prayer of the dying Jesus complements and climaxes his previous prayer of total submission to the will of God: "Father, if you are willing, take this cup away from me; yet not my will but yours be done" (22:42). It inspired the centurion who saw what had happened to perform an act of doxological worship, as he "glorified" God and declared, "Certainly this man was righteous/innocent [δίκαιος]" (23:47).[21] This confession of the dying Jesus as righteous foreshadows the later references to Jesus as God's "Righteous One [δίκαιον]" (Acts 3:14; 22:14). The praying of Jesus has thus provided both the model and the empowerment for the audience to submit themselves completely to the will of God and become "right" with God by praying, not only throughout life but at the time of death with confidence of ultimately being raised by God like Jesus to heavenly life.[22]

Praying to the Divine Lord Jesus in Luke

Jesus left the synagogue in Capernaum where with his divine authority he had expelled the demon of an unclean spirit from a man (Luke 4:31–37). He then entered the house of Simon whose mother-in-law was afflicted by a severe demonic fever, and those in the house interceded on her behalf as "they asked him about her" (4:38). They thus performed an act of supplicatory worship, implicitly asking Jesus to exercise his divine power and heal her. Jesus then answered their implicit intercessory prayer to him. Just as he had previously "rebuked" (ἐπετίμησεν) the demon in the synagogue (4:35), he stood over the mother-in-law and "rebuked" (ἐπετίμησεν) the demonic fever and it left her, so that she was able to arise and serve them (4:39). This healing of the mother-in-law provides a model and incentive for the audience to offer prayers of intercession to Jesus on behalf of the sick.

Overcome with astonishment (5:9) after witnessing a miraculous catch of abundant fish (5:1–7), Simon Peter "fell down at the knees of Jesus" in a gesture of supplicatory worship, confessing his sinfulness: "Depart from me, for I am a sinful man, Lord" (5:8). Jesus answered his prayer not by departing but instead by telling him not to fear, implicitly forgiving his

---

21. "Luke's description of the confession as 'glory to God' has already indicated that more than mere innocence is intended. Jesus is proclaimed a Just Man, who is right with God" (Crump. *Jesus the Intercessor*, 93).

22. "Jesus' dying prayer awaits his vindication in the resurrection, prayer articulating hope and faith in God to save him. . . . The sequential unfolding of Jesus' dedication to prayer in the framework of his mission to Israel presents him as one who is confidently and persistently committed to God in prayer, steadfastly anticipating his vindication in difficulties and trials" (Holmås, *Prayer*, 114).

sinfulness, and, with divine empowerment, transforming him from a sinful man who catches fish to one who catches people for the kingdom of God (5:10; cf. 4:43).[23] Similarly, when a leper saw Jesus, he "fell on his face," a gesture of worshipful devotion, and "beseeched" (ἐδεήθη) him with an act of supplicatory worship: "Lord, if you wish, you can make me clean" (5:12).[24] Jesus answered his prayer, immediately cleansing him by means of his divine authority (5:13; cf. 2 Kgs 5:7). These prayers provide the audience with models encouraging them to direct their own prayers for forgiveness and healing to Jesus.

At Capernaum there was a centurion who had a slave who was about to die (7:1-2). He sent elders of the Jews to intercede with Jesus on his behalf to come and save the life of his slave (7:3). They presented Jesus with an intercessory prayer of supplication as they repeatedly "implored" (παρεκάλουν) him earnestly on behalf of this deserving centurion (7:4), who had built the synagogue for them (7:5).[25] The centurion reinforced the intercessory prayer of the Jews with an expression of his faith in the divine power of Jesus' authoritative word, as he sent friends to address Jesus as "Lord [κύριε]" (7:6) and tell him only to pronounce the word of his divine power and his servant must be healed (7:7). Jesus praised his exemplary faith, as he told the crowd, "Not even in Israel have I found such faith" (7:9). In accord with his strong faith in the divine power of the Lord Jesus, the centurion received the answer to his intercessory prayer, as his slave was found in good health at his house (7:10). This healing serves as a model for the audience to pray on behalf of the sick with faith in the divine power of the Lord Jesus.[26]

When a woman who was a sinner learned that Jesus was at table in the house of a Pharisee, she brought in an alabaster jar of perfumed ointment (7:36-37). Her gestures of hospitality humbly directed toward the feet of Jesus served as an act of supplicatory worship, indicative of her repentance, love for Jesus, and faith in his divine power to forgive her sins. She stood

---

23. "Within the flow of Luke's narrative thus far, Simon thus serves a paradigmatic role in demonstrating the character of appropriate response to Jesus's mission" (Green, *Conversion*, 89).

24. "Ἐδεήθη describes the tone of his request. Δέομαι is often used of prayer and suggests an urgent request" (Bock, *Luke 1:1—9:50*, 473).

25. Luke "has the intensity of their effort come to expression in the fact that he describes it with recourse to the durative imperfect παρεκάλουν" (Wolter, *Gospel According to Luke*, 294).

26. "The address κύριε from a gentile centurion serves to foreshadow or prefigure the success of the gentile mission in Acts, wherein it is the gentiles who predominantly come to believe in Jesus as κύριος (e.g., Acts 13:47-49). The centurion represents those who will respond in faith to Jesus and acknowledge him as κύριος (e.g., Acts 10:36)" (Rowe, *Early Narrative*, 117).

Supplicatory Worship

behind Jesus at his feet, weeping in sorrow for her sins, bathed his feet with her tears, wiped them with her hair, kissed his feet, and anointed them with the perfumed ointment (7:38).[27] Jesus answered her implicit supplication for forgiveness, as he first told the Pharisee, who failed to extend gestures of hospitality toward Jesus (7:44-46), that "her sins, which were many, have been forgiven, for she has loved greatly" (7:47). Then he said to her, "Your sins are forgiven" (7:48), and dismissed her with the words, "Your faith has saved you; go in peace" (7:50). This sinful woman serves as a model for the audience to repent of their sins, no matter how numerous or great, to receive divine forgiveness through their supplicatory worship of Jesus.[28]

When a man possessed by demons (8:27) saw Jesus, he cried out and "fell down" before him in a gesture of supplicatory worship (cf. 5:8), but the unclean spirit/demon possessing him (8:29) shouted an inappropriate prayer of supplication: "I beseech [δέομαί] you, do not torment me!" (8:28; cf. 5:12). The many demons who had entered the man (8:30) continued the inappropriate supplication as they "implored" (παρεκάλουν) him not to order them to depart into the abyss (8:31; cf. 7:4), but "implored" (παρεκάλεσαν) him instead to let them enter a herd of swine, and Jesus let them (8:32). But then the demons and swine departed into the abyss, as they drowned in the lake (8:33). In contrast, the man from whom the demons had gone out performed a seemingly appropriate act of supplicatory worship, as he "beseeched" (ἐδεῖτο) to remain with Jesus (8:38). But Jesus gave him a more appropriate answer to his prayer, as he sent him home to proclaim what God had done for him, and he proclaimed what Jesus had done for him (8:39).[29] Thus, Jesus answers prayers in the way that he deems most appropriate.

Jairus, a ruler of the synagogue, "fell at the feet" of Jesus (cf. 5:8, 12) in a gesture of supplicatory worship and offered an intercessory prayer, as he "implored [παρεκάλει]" (cf. 7:4; 8:31, 32) Jesus to enter his house

---

27. Since the verb "weep" (κλαιω) has occurred previously in the narrative with the meaning of being sad and sorrowful, lamenting and mourning (6:21, 25; 7:13, 32), the woman's weeping is an expression of repentant sorrow for her sinfulness rather than a weeping for joy. See BDAG, 545. "Unbound hair on a weeping woman is naturally associated with grief, supplication, and gratitude" (Cosgrove, "Woman's Unbound Hair," 689). "The triple reference to the situation of the woman beside Jesus' 'feet' in v. 38 accentuates her humility" (Edwards, *Gospel According to Luke*, 228).

28. On Luke 7:36-50, see Heil, *Meal Scenes*, 43-53; Esposito, *Jesus' Meals*, 149-210.

29. "Jesus tells the healed man to narrate 'as many things as *God* has done for you' (8:39), and then the demoniac went to his town proclaiming 'as many things as *Jesus* had done for him' (8:39). What God does and what Jesus does are one and the same. God acts through Jesus; Jesus is the presence of God" (Just, *Luke 1:1—9:50*, 366-67; emphases original).

(8:41), for his only daughter was dying (8:42). On the way a hemorrhaging woman (8:43) touched the tassel of his cloak and immediately her bleeding stopped (8:44). Eventually she "fell down" before Jesus (cf. 5:8) in a gesture of worshipful humility, an implicit supplication for mercy, as she publicly confessed that she was the one who had touched his cloak and was healed (8:47).[30] Jesus said to her, "Daughter, your faith has saved you; go in peace" (8:48; cf. 7:50). Meanwhile, the daughter of Jairus died (8:49), but Jesus called for faith and she will be saved, just as faith saved the hemorrhaging woman. Jesus then answered the prayer of Jairus, as he raised the daughter to life from the "sleep" of death (8:51–55). This gives the audience a foundation for praying to Jesus on behalf of those who have fallen "asleep" in death, with faith that he can raise them to everlasting life in the kingdom of God.[31]

On the day after Jesus' transfiguration, which prefigures his future heavenly glory to be attained only after his "exodus" through suffering and death (9:28–37), a man performed an act of supplicatory worship. He interceded on behalf of his demon-possessed son (9:39), as he cried out to Jesus, "Teacher, I beseech [δέομαί] you to look at my son, for he is my only child!" (9:38; cf. 7:12; 8:42). The man went on to say, "I beseeched [ἐδεήθην] your disciples" to expel the demon but they could not (9:40).[32] Jesus then decried the faithlessness of this generation and asked, "How much longer will I be with you?" (9:41), with the implication that he will not be with them much longer, since he will soon undergo his "exodus" from this earth into heavenly glory (9:31). Jesus then answered the intercessory prayer of the father as "he rebuked the unclean spirit, healed the boy, and gave him back to his father" (9:42; cf. 7:15). The implication for the audience is that Jesus will continue to be able to answer their intercessory prayers of supplication even after his "exodus" into heavenly glory through his suffering, death, and resurrection.

A group of ten lepers (17:12) performed an act of supplicatory worship, as they prayed to Jesus implicitly for their healing, "Jesus, Master, have mercy on us!" (17:13). Jesus then answered their prayer. He told them to go and show themselves to the priests, and as they were going, they were cleansed (17:14). When one of them saw that he was healed, he returned,

---

30. "So, trembling, she falls before him . . . an act of respect and of begging for his mercy" (Bock, *Luke 1:1—9:50*, 797).

31. "Jesus' reference to the girl 'sleeping' may indicate to Jairus the way God would have believers regard all who die in faith" (Edwards, *Gospel According to Luke*, 258). "At this point, Jesus only forestalls death for this girl; his death and resurrection will release death's grasp on believers completely" (Garland, *Luke*, 370).

32. In Luke-Acts "the meaning of δέομαι/δέησις is restricted to spoken supplication, denoting 'to plead, to beg, to ask for with urgency (with the implication of a presumed need)'" (Holmås, *Prayer*, 24–25).

Supplicatory Worship

glorifying God with a loud voice (17:15). This one, a Samaritan, then "fell on his face" at the feet of Jesus, a gesture of worshipful devotion (cf. 5:12; 8:41), "thanking" him (17:16), thus paralleling his doxological worship of God (17:15) with an implication of Jesus' divine status and worthiness to likewise be an object of worship. Jesus confirmed this, as he declared that of the ten (17:17) only this foreigner has returned "to give glory" to God (17:18), implying that in thanking Jesus he was giving glory to God. Jesus then dismissed him, saying, "Your faith has saved you" (17:19; cf. 7:50; 8:48). The Samaritan leper serves as a model for the audience to pray with faith in Jesus and show gratitude toward God/Jesus when their prayers are answered.[33]

When Jesus approached Jericho, a blind man (18:35) performed an act of supplicatory worship, as he called out, "Jesus, Son of David, have mercy on me" (18:38; cf. 17:13), implicitly praying for Jesus to heal him. When he was rebuked by the crowd and told to be silent, he cried out all the more, intensifying his supplication, "Son of David, have mercy on me" (18:39). When Jesus asked him what he wanted, he made his prayer explicit: "Lord, let me see again" (18:41). Jesus answered his prayer as he told him, "Regain your sight; your faith has saved you" (18:42; cf. 7:50; 8:48; 17:19). Immediately the blind man not only regained his physical sight but received spiritual insight.[34] He became a disciple of Jesus, as he "followed" him (18:43; cf. 5:28) on his way to suffering, death, and resurrection in Jerusalem (18:31–33).[35] The blind man serves as a model for the audience to pray with faith to Jesus for the insight to deny themselves, take up their cross daily, and follow Jesus (9:23) in order to be saved, for "whoever wants to save his life will lose it, but whoever loses his life for my sake will save it" (9:24).

Two criminals were crucified with Jesus (23:33), representative of all sinners on behalf of whom Jesus was crucified, fulfilling the role of God's

---

33. "Luke's statement that the healed leper is 'giving thanks' to Jesus, εὐχαριστῶν αὐτῷ, suggests something more than the gratitude of one human being to another. In the four [sic] other occurrences of that verb in Luke-Acts, it always refers to thanksgiving to God in prayer: Luke 18:11; 22:17, 19; Acts 27:35; 28:15" (Hamm, "What the Samaritan Leper Sees," 284). "This is the only place in the entire NT where εὐχαριστέω refers to the giving of thanks *to Jesus!*" (Just, *Luke 9:51—24:53*, 655; emphasis original).

34. "'Your faith has saved you' emphasized that opened eyes enable both physical and *spiritual* sight. This man has received eternal salvation" (Just, *Luke 9:51—24:53*, 708; emphasis original).

35. "The blind man is transformed from being a beggar sitting along the way to a person who can see and follow Jesus on the way to Jerusalem. He now has both sight and insight. Jesus does not ask him to follow him, as he does the rich ruler (18:22), but his voluntarily following Jesus illustrates how those with nothing readily do so. He has no worldly attachments to encumber him and hold him back" (Garland, *Luke*, 742).

"suffering servant" (cf. LXX Isa 53:12). One of the criminals reviled him, failing to recognize that Jesus was being crucified as the Christ for the salvation of all people (23:39), while the other pointed out that they were justly condemned as criminals/sinners but that Jesus was innocent (23:41). He then performed an act of supplicatory worship, as he prayed, "Jesus, remember me when you come into your kingdom" (23:42).[36] This recalls Jesus' promise to his disciples that "I grant to you, just as my Father granted to me, a kingdom, that you may eat and drink at my table in my kingdom" (22:29–30). Jesus then answered his prayer, as he promised him that today, the day of his death with Jesus, he would be with Jesus in "paradise," the heavenly kingdom.[37] This criminal serves as a model for the audience to acknowledge their sinfulness and pray to join Jesus in the heavenly kingdom he has opened for them by his salvific death.[38]

Praying to God and/or the Risen Lord Jesus in Acts

The believers in Jerusalem devoted themselves with one accord to "prayer [προσευχῇ]" (Acts 1:14; 6:4) and to the "prayers [προσευχαῖς]" (2:42), presumably to God and/or Jesus (cf. 1:24). After Peter and John reported to their fellow believers that the chief priests and elders had told them not to speak or teach in the name of Jesus (4:18, 23), their fellow believers raised their voices with one accord to the sovereign Lord God, the Creator (4:24). They acknowledged to the Lord God that everything done to his holy servant Jesus accorded with what the hand and plan of God had predetermined to happen (4:25–28). They then performed an act of supplicatory worship, praying that the Lord God enable them to speak his word with all boldness (4:29), and stretch out his hand to heal through the name of his holy servant Jesus (4:30). As they "beseeched" (δεηθέντων), their prayer was answered; they were all filled with the Holy Spirit and spoke the word of God with

---

36. "Hearing Jesus' petition to the Father to forgive his executioners [23:34] gave this criminal the temerity to make a bold petition. He addresses Jesus as if he were God, who remembers people in his covenant mercy (Ps 106:4; Luke 1:54, 72; Acts 10:31)" (Garland, *Luke*, 926).

37. "'Paradise' refers to 'God's garden,' an eschatological image of new creation" (Green, *Gospel of Luke*, 823). "In Jewish literature, 'paradise' is a transcendent place of blessedness, a celestial Garden of Eden (Gen 2:8; 13:10; Josephus, *Ant.* 1.37), reserved for the righteous after death" (Edwards, *Gospel According to Luke*, 692).

38. "The petition of the penitent criminal is a witness that Jesus' death is not a defeat but a means of salvation. Luke's use of 'remember' is significant, for it recalls Mary's prayer in the Magnificat that God will 'help his servant Israel to remember mercy' (1:54). On the cross, his Suffering Servant Jesus fulfills that prayer" (Edwards, *Gospel According to Luke*, 692).

boldness (4:31). This encourages the audience to pray to God for courage and boldness to proclaim the word of the gospel despite opposition.[39]

"Praying" (προσευξάμενοι) implicitly for divine assistance, the apostles "laid hands on them" (6:6), that is, on the seven "filled with the Spirit and wisdom" (6:3), who were presented to them (6:5–6) to serve at table, so that the apostles may not neglect the service of the word of God (6:1–4).[40] Their prayer was answered, as indicated by the notice that the word of God continued to spread (6:7). This answered prayer encourages the audience to pray for divine assistance for those appointed to special tasks or offices within the church.

As Stephen was being stoned, in prayer he was "calling upon" (ἐπικαλούμενον) the risen Lord Jesus, whom he saw in heaven standing at the right hand of God (7:55–56): "Lord Jesus, receive my spirit" (7:59).[41] He thus imitated the dying Jesus' prayer of submission to God: "Father, into your hands I entrust my spirit" (Luke 23:46). Stephen then "fell to his knees" (Acts 7:60), imitating Jesus who likewise "fell to his knees" before he prayed (Luke 22:41), subjecting his own will to the will of his Father (22:42). The dying Stephen then cried out in a loud voice, as he prayed to Jesus, "Lord, do not hold this sin against them" (Acts 7:60). He thus imitated the dying Jesus' prayer of forgiveness: "Father, forgive them for they do not know what they are doing" (Luke 23:34). The prayers of the dying Stephen reinforce those of the dying Jesus as models for the audience to imitate. They are likewise to pray to God and/or the risen Lord Jesus to forgive those who harm them, and through prayer to entrust themselves to the divine will both during their life and at the time of their death.[42]

---

39. "[T]he praying church enjoys open access to none other than the 'Sovereign Lord (δεσπότης)' of all creation (4.24). The title δεσπότης applied to the God of Israel denoted his terrible, absolute authority over all earthly nations and rulers, indeed, over the entire universe" (Spencer, *Journeying through Acts*, 63–64). "Verse 31 dramatically depicts God's response to this prayer. The place itself is shaken, and those who are present experience the Holy Spirit again, as at Pentecost, and speak God's word with boldness" (Gaventa, *Acts*, 98). "In sum, this prayer is an expression of complete dependence on God, a recognition of his sovereignty, a call for God's justice and oversight in the midst of opposition, for an enablement for mission, and for the working of his power to show that God is behind the preaching of the name of Jesus in healing and signs" (Bock, *Acts*, 210). See also Hamm, "Acts 4:23–31," 225–37.

40. "By laying hands on the Seven, the disciples of the Jerusalem church pray that God would bless them in their new role" (Tipei, *Laying On of Hands*, 253).

41. "The account of Stephen's death provides a pointed narrative 'demonstration' of what Peter had declared in the words of LXX Joel 3.5: 'Everyone who calls on (πᾶς ὃς ἂν ἐπικαλέσηται) the name of the Lord shall be saved' (Acts 2.21)" (Holmås, *Prayer*, 190).

42. Kurz, "Narrative Models for Imitation," 171–89, esp. 187.

The apostles in Jerusalem sent Peter and John to the Samaritans who had accepted the word of God (8:14). When Peter and John went down to Samaria, they "prayed" (προσηύξαντο) that the Samaritans might receive the Holy Spirit (8:15), for the Spirit had not yet fallen upon any of them; they had only been baptized in the name of the Lord Jesus (8:16). Their prayer was answered as "they laid hands on them and they received the Holy Spirit" (8:17). This answered prayer encourages the audience to pray that new converts to the Christian faith receive the Holy Spirit, which enables them to become fully accepted by and united with all the other members of the church.[43]

In a house in Damascus, Saul/Paul "is praying [προσεύχεται]" (9:11), implicitly to regain the sight he lost after seeing the risen Lord and for divine guidance (9:3–9, 12).[44] Ananias, a disciple in Damascus (9:10), entered the house and, laying his hands on Saul, told him that the Jesus who had appeared to him sent Ananias so that he may regain his sight and be filled with the Holy Spirit (9:17). Saul's prayer was answered, as immediately something like scales fell from his eyes and he regained his sight (9:18). He was also presumably filled with the Holy Spirit to equip him for his mission to be the "chosen instrument" of the Lord Jesus "to carry my name before the gentiles and the kings and the sons of Israel" (9:15), and to suffer for the name of the Lord Jesus (9:16). This answered prayer of Saul/Paul serves as a model for the members of the audience to pray for the divine guidance and insight they need to play their respective roles in the evangelizing mission of the church.

In Joppa there was a disciple named Tabitha/Dorcas, who fell sick, died, and was placed in an upstairs room (9:36–37). After Peter was summoned from Lydda (9:38–39), he sent all out of the room, "fell to his knees," and "prayed [προσηύξατο]" (9:40a). Whereas Stephen similarly "fell to his knees" and cried out in prayer explicitly to the risen Lord Jesus (7:60), Peter prayed implicitly to Jesus for the power to heal and raise Tabitha (cf. 3:6, 16; 4:10; 9:34). When Jesus "fell to his knees and prayed [προσηύχετο]" (Luke

---

43. "As their prayer is favourably answered, it is affirmed that God now acts redemptively in a way that transcends conventional lines of ethnic and socioreligious distinction" (Holmås, *Prayer*, 194).

44. "As regards Saul, his prayers might have conveyed to God expressions of remorse for working against Jesus, whom he encountered in the light of divine glory; of repentance for fighting against God (cf. Gamaliel's warning in 5:39); and of regret for having been involved in the arrest, punishment, and execution of followers of Jesus. Saul also probably asks for guidance concerning his life, which the risen Lord had promised in the vision on the road to Damascus" (Garland, *Acts*, 447). "In praying continually (cf. the present tense), Saul conforms with characters attuned to God's purposes elsewhere in the Lukan story, suggesting his beginning renewal" (Holmås, *Prayer*, 204).

22:41), his prayer was answered as he was strengthened by an angel (22:43). Similarly, Peter's prayer was answered as he received the divine strength to heal and raise Tabitha, just as Jesus had raised the daughter of Jairus (8:51-55). Peter turned to her body and said, "Tabitha, rise up" (Acts 9:40b; cf. Luke 8:54). She opened her eyes, saw Peter, and sat up (Acts 9:40c). Peter then raised her up and presented her alive (9:41). This reinforces the foundation Luke-Acts provides for the audience to pray to the risen Lord Jesus not only for the sick but for the resurrection of those who have died.[45]

In Caesarea there was a Roman centurion named Cornelius (10:1) who was devout and God-fearing along with all his household. This gentile used to give many alms to the Jewish people and was "beseeching" (δεόμενος) God in prayer regularly (10:2). In response to his praying an angel of God appeared to him (10:3) and told him that his "prayers" (προσευχαί) and almsgiving have ascended as a memorial offering before God (10:4). Through his praying, which attuned him to God's will, he was chosen to play an important role in God's plan of including gentiles in the people of God, as the angel commanded him to send some men to Joppa and summon Peter to his household (10:5). After Peter arrived, Cornelius recounted how he was "praying" (προσευχόμενος) in his house when the angel appeared (10:30) and told him that his "prayer" (προσευχή) had been heard (cf. Luke 1:13) and his almsgiving remembered before God (Acts 10:31). That is why the prominent gentile Cornelius summoned the Jewish leader Peter from Joppa to his house in Caesarea (10:32).

While the men sent by Cornelius were approaching Joppa, Peter went up to the roof terrace "to pray" (προσεύξασθαι) about noon (10:9). In a hunger-induced trance (10:10) and in response to his praying, Peter saw heaven opened and a large sheet containing all the animals on earth (10:11-12). He was told to slaughter and eat, but replied that he had never eaten anything profane and unclean (10:13-14). He was then told that what God has made clean he is not to consider profane (10:15). He later applied what he saw as a consequence of his praying to the gentiles in the house of Cornelius, as he told them that although it is unlawful for a Jew to associate with a gentile, God has shown him that he should call no person profane or unclean (10:28). Eventually these gentiles received the Holy Spirit and were baptized (10:44-48). Peter recounted for the Jewish leaders that it was as a

---

45. "Luke underscores again the power of prayer as Peter intercedes for the woman. . . . Peter's prayer mediates life to Dorcas, as the Lord hears his appeal" (Bock, *Acts*, 378). "The accent on God's answering Peter's humble prayer by restoring Tabitha to life reactivates the Lukan notion of the resurrection hope being fulfilled in response to Israel's devoted prayers (cf. Acts 3.1 and especially 26.6-7) in a new salvation-historical situation" (Holmås, *Prayer*, 207).

consequence of his "praying" (προσευχόμενος) that all of this took place (11:5).⁴⁶ Cornelius and Peter model for the audience how praying can inform them of the role they are to play in God's salvific plan for all people.⁴⁷

After King Herod Agrippa I (12:1), the grandson of King Herod the Great, arrested Peter and imprisoned him (12:3-4), "prayer" (προσευχή) was earnestly being made by the church to God concerning him (12:5). In implicit response to the prayer an angel of the Lord appeared and rescued Peter from the prison (12:6-10). After being miraculously freed from the prison, Peter declared, "Now I truly know that the Lord sent his angel and rescued me from the hand of Herod and from all that the Jewish people were expecting" (12:11). That his rescue was in answer to the prayer of the church for him is confirmed as Peter went to the house of Mary, the mother of John who is called Mark, where there were many gathered together and they were "praying [προσευχόμενοι]" (12:12). When they ironically refused to believe Peter had been freed from prison in answer to their prayer (12:13-16), Peter reaffirmed how the Lord had led him out of the prison (12:17). This answered prayer of the church serves as a model encouraging the audience to have confidence in the power of their prayers on behalf of church leaders in need.⁴⁸

Among the prophets and teachers in the church at Antioch were Barnabas and Saul/Paul (13:1). While they were "worshiping" (λειτουργούντων) the Lord and fasting, the Holy Spirit said to set apart Barnabas and Saul for the missionary "work" (ἔργον) to which the Spirit has called them (13:2). Then fasting and "praying" (προσευξάμενοι) and laying hands on them, they sent them off (13:3). That it was by praying for them that Barnabas and Saul were able to fulfill their missionary work was confirmed when they returned to Antioch, where they had been handed over to the grace

---

46. "In 11:5, Peter begins by emphasizing that he was in prayer (10:9); Luke understands that this is a favorable time for revelations (10:30; 13:2; 22:17)" (Keener, *Acts*, 2.1823).

47. "The function of the element of prayer in the series of salvific events in Acts 11.5–18 is actually a miniature of the convincing quality of prayer in relation to the outworking of God's salvation in Luke's macro-narrative, in which . . . prayer serves as a catalyst for new departures in the story in order to establish divine causation and validation" (Holmås, *Prayer*, 211). See also Witherup, "Cornelius," 45–66; Shellberg, *Cleansed Lepers*, 197–218.

48. "Peter's deliverance is presented as an answer to this prayer, even though those who interceded for him were actually surprised by the outcome (vv. 15–17)" (Peterson, *Acts*, 362). "In Acts 12, the believers are cast as victims of the story's inherent irony: the wondrous divine intervention is catalysed by their prayer (v. 5), indeed, as the liberated apostle heads for the house of Mary, believers are still assembled there for prayer. Yet they are incognizant of the power of their prayers, weighed down by the hopelessness of the situation" (Holmås, *Prayer*, 215).

of God for the "work" (ἔργον) they had now fulfilled (14:26).⁴⁹ Similarly, "appointing" or "laying hands" (χειροτονήσαντες) on elders for each church and "praying" (προσευξάμενοι) with fasting, Paul and Barnabas entrusted them to the Lord in whom they had believed (14:23) to fulfill their role as church leaders.⁵⁰ These prayers provide a foundational model encouraging the audience to pray for church leaders, so that they may fulfill their roles in advancing the evangelizing and pastoral missions of the church.

In Philippi, after the Roman magistrates ordered the jailer to guard Paul and Silas securely, he put them in the inner cell and secured their feet (16:23–24). About midnight Paul and Silas, "praying" (προσευχόμενοι), were singing praise to God (16:25).⁵¹ In divine response to their praying, suddenly there was a great earthquake so that the foundations of the prison "were shaken" (16:26a) by God (divine passive), just as the place "was shaken" when those in Jerusalem were praying (4:31). All the doors of the prison "were opened," and the bonds of all "were loosened" (16:26b). After this dramatic divine response to their praying, the jailer fell down and asked the "sirs/lords" (κύριοι) what he must do to be saved (16:29–30). They told him to believe in the "Lord" (κύριον) Jesus and he and his household will be saved (16:31). Then the pagan Roman jailer and his household were baptized (16:33) and rejoiced at having come to faith in God (16:34).⁵² This

---

49. Paul and Barnabas were "the beneficiaries of the church's prayer for God's favour (or blessing) upon them. This was the only means by which they could have successfully accomplished their mission" (Tipei, *Laying On of Hands*, 256). "Acts 13.1–3 also provides yet another example in Luke-Acts of prayer accompanying selection and appointment to a new role (cf. Lk. 6.12–16; Acts 1.24–25; 6.6)" (Holmås, *Prayer*, 219).

50. "The original sense of the verb [χειροτονέω] is 'to stretch out the hand' . . . but in the first century CE the derivation was gradually forgotten, the meaning becoming simply 'to choose' or 'to appoint to office.' . . . [The laying on of hands] seems to be a sign of prayer" (Tipei, *Laying On of Hands*, 258, 261). "The ordaining of ministers with *prayer and fasting* recalls Paul and Barnabas' own commissioning by the church in Antioch (13.1–3). In this case, however, the ministers are appointed to stay and oversee local community affairs rather than sent out to spread the gospel further" (Spencer, *Journeying through Acts*, 162; emphasis original).

51. "The term προσεύχομαι can mean prayer that is spoken as well as prayer that is sung. Here the latter is specified (προσευχόμενοι ὕμνουν). . . . The singing might be accentuated to imply the joy and courage of the missionaries in the midst of dire straits" (Holmås, *Prayer*, 233). "Their *praying* may have included a cry for justice, release from prison, and freedom to continue their ministry in an unhindered way. At the same time, *singing hymns to God*, they acknowledged God's character and expressed their trust in him as their deliverer" (Peterson, *Acts*, 468; emphases original).

52. "Belief in the Lord Jesus Christ (v. 31) is equated with belief in the one true God (v. 34)" (Peterson, *Acts*, 470). "Thus far in the narrative, at least as far as conversions of individuals are concerned, only god-fearing gentiles have been recruited to the faith, but now we seem to have the first clear example of a pagan (i.e., a gentile with no

encourages the audience that their praying while being persecuted can not only free them from persecution but lead their persecutors to the true worship of God.

"Falling to his knees" to underscore the seriousness of the situation, Jesus "prayed" (Luke 22:41), submitting himself to God's will and receiving divine assistance to undergo his suffering and death (22:42–46). "Falling to his knees" at the time of his death, Stephen prayed for the Lord to forgive those who will kill him (Acts 7:60). "Falling to his knees," Peter "prayed" and received the divine power to raise Tabitha from the dead (9:40). "Falling to his knees" after his farewell address at Miletus to the elders of Ephesus (20:17–35), Paul "prayed," not alone but communally, together "with them all," implicitly for them and the divine strength to complete his fateful journey to Jerusalem (20:36).[53] "Falling on their knees" on the beach at Tyre, all of the disciples (21:3–4), Paul, and his companions were "praying" communally (21:5), reinforcing the supplication for divine guidance as Paul continues his fateful journey to Jerusalem (21:6; cf. 21:14).[54] These examples of praying while kneeling serve as models for the audience to likewise pray alone as well as with others at critical times of need for divine strength and guidance.

During his defense speech before the people of Jerusalem (21:39), Paul recounted that after he returned from Damascus to Jerusalem and was "praying" (προσευχομένου) in the temple, he fell "into a trance [ἐν ἐκστάσει]" (22:17). This recalls that when Peter went up to the roof terrace of a house in Joppa "to pray [προσεύξασθαι]" (10:9), a "trance" (ἔκστασις) came over him (10:10). He later recounted to the Jewish leaders in Jerusalem that while "praying" (προσευχόμενος) he saw "in a trance" (ἐν ἐκστάσει) a vision (11:5) of all the animals of the earth (11:6) that God had made clean (11:9), thus opening the way for gentiles to become Christians (11:15–18).

---

connection to the synagogue) turning to faith in Luke-Acts" (Holmås, *Prayer*, 233–34).

53. "Kneeling sometimes accompanied prayer in the OT, as here, although, for Jewish people standing was more common" (Keener, *Acts*, 3.3068). "Paul concludes and prays with them while kneeling, an indication of the solemn nature of the moment" (Bock, *Acts*, 632). "Kneeling is a gesture of humility before a superior, and at the same time a gesture of reverence before God. The prayer presumably contained intercession for the Ephesian elders in their tasks as leaders of the congregation, a blessing for the elders, and a petition for a safe journey for Paul" (Schnabel, *Acts*, 853).

54. "As in Miletus, Paul and the believers kneel down and pray, surely for a good outcome of the journey to Jerusalem, for strength in view of the trials that lie ahead, and for God's blessings for the Tyrian believers" (Schnabel, *Acts*, 855). "When they all fall on their knees together before they part, this signals a joint submission to God's will over the controversial trip. Luke . . . present[s] them as exemplars of prayerful surrender in the face of crisis" (Holmås, *Prayer*, 239–40).

Supplicatory Worship

While he was praying in the temple, Paul was told by the risen Lord Jesus to hurry and leave Jerusalem at once, because they will not accept his testimony about the Lord (22:18).[55] The Lord Jesus told him to go, because he will send Paul far away to the gentiles (22:21), thus to continue the mission begun by Peter. This reinforces for the audience how praying can indicate to them the role they are to play in God's salvific plan for all peoples (cf. 26:28–29).

Publius, the chief of the island of Malta (28:1), welcomed Paul and his companions and extended hospitality to them for three days (28:7). When the father of Publius became sick with a fever and dysentery, Paul went to him and, "praying" (προσευξάμενος), laid his hands on him and cured him (28:8; cf. 9:12; Luke 4:40; 13:13). Then the rest of the sick on the island came and were healed (Acts 28:9), implicitly by the divine power Paul received as a result of praying. Remarkably, none of those who were sick demonstrated the faith that elsewhere in Luke-Acts has led to healing (Luke 5:20; 7:9, 50; 8:48; 17:19; 18:42; Acts 14:9). Indeed, none of them have become Christian believers, and some on the island even idolatrously and ironically said that Paul was a god (28:6), after he was not harmed by a snake that fastened itself onto his hand (28:3–5). Paul's praying here serves as a model for the audience to likewise pray for the health and salvation even of nonbelievers.[56]

Summary

The births of John the Baptist and Jesus were answers to supplicatory prayers by venerable members of the Jewish people (Luke 1–2).

---

55. "Paul's vision implies that the risen Jesus is Lord of the temple, who reveals his will and commissions his servant in that context for his mission to the nations" (Peterson, *Acts*, 604–5). "Paradoxically, Jerusalem's recalcitrance resurfaces as the temple is used according to the purpose for which it was designed, i.e., to be a 'house of prayer' (Lk. 19.45–46)" (Holmås, *Prayer*, 246). "Paul undoubtedly shared Stephen's perspective on the temple's inadequacy, cf. 7:49; 17:24" (Keener, *Acts*, 3.3236).

56. "As far as the prayer theme is concerned, we thus see again, now for the last time in Luke-Acts, how God reaches out to new audiences and frontiers with the blessing of salvation in the context of prayer. The resurrection witness having successively reached Jews, Samaritans (Acts 8), god-fearing gentiles (Acts 10), and pagans (Acts 16), it is now extended even to barbarians [Acts 28:2, 4]" (Holmås, *Prayer*, 258). "The author suggests not only that the Christian movement has something to offer the general culture, an arrow for the apologetic quiver, but also that these gifts may also be shared with unbelievers. Here . . . is a proof text for the charitable missions conducted with no strings attached. Paul is an agent of *gratia universalis*" (Pervo, *Acts*, 676).

Jesus indicated the appropriateness of fasting together with praying after his death and resurrection as part of Christian supplicatory worship (5:30–35; Acts 13:2–3; 14:23).

Jesus taught his disciples to submit to God by praying for the advancement of God's salvific plan (kingdom) for the world, before presenting God with petitions for their daily needs, forgiveness of their sins, and divine assistance in avoiding and overcoming temptations (Luke 11:1–4). One should not hesitate to pray to God, even with shameless audacity, because God will certainly give to one who prays to him whatever that person needs (11:5–10). Although those engaged in supplicatory worship may not receive precisely what they pray for, God will never give them anything detrimental but only what is beneficial for them. Even if petitioners do not explicitly ask for the gift of the Holy Spirit, but only for what they think they need, God will give those praying to him the Holy Spirit, as the greatest good that everyone needs (11:11–13).

One should pray continually without losing heart, confident that God will answer in a timely manner. Such praying will assure that one is found faithful when Jesus comes again to bring to completion the kingdom of God at the end of the age (18:1–8). Authentic prayer is praying with a humble acknowledgment of one's sinfulness to a God who is merciful and forgiving (18:9–14).

As a result of the praying of Jesus all night (6:12), which placed him in a supplicatory stance of submission to God, he not only chose his twelve apostles on the next day (6:13–16), but power was coming out from him and he healed all (6:19) those who came to him (6:17–18). This was the power of the Spirit (4:14) he received as a result of praying (3:21–22; 5:16; 6:12). It was implicitly as a result of his praying (9:18) that Jesus evoked from his disciples their first confession of his identity as the Christ of God (9:20). And after Jesus went up a mountain to pray (9:28), it was while he was praying, and implicitly as a result of it, that he was temporarily transformed into a heavenly figure, which prefigured his future heavenly glory through his death and resurrection (9:29).

The dramatic and decisive prayer of Jesus on the Mount of Olives, through which he was divinely strengthened to undergo his suffering and death (22:39–46), provides the audience not only the model but the empowerment to be likewise strengthened to submit to God's will for them through prayer. In praying for the forgiveness of those who crucified him (23:33–34), Jesus provided a model for the audience to be generous in forgiving those who sin against them in accord with how he taught his disciples to pray (11:4; 6:28). The prayer of the dying Jesus, in which he entrusted his spirit into the hands of his Father (23:46), provides both the model and the

Supplicatory Worship

empowerment for the audience to submit themselves completely to the will of God by praying, not only throughout life but at the time of death with confidence of ultimately being raised by God like Jesus to heavenly life.

Jesus' healing of the mother-in-law of Simon Peter after a petition was made to him on her behalf (4:38–39), the petitionary prayer of Peter for forgiveness (5:8), the prayer of a leper for healing (5:12), and Jesus' healing of the slave of a gentile centurion after intercession was made for him (7:1–10) provide models for the audience to pray with faith in the divine power of the Lord Jesus to forgive them and to heal the sick. The forgiveness of a sinful woman by Jesus serves as a model for the audience to repent of their sins, no matter how numerous or great, to receive forgiveness by demonstrating their faith and love through their supplicatory worship of Jesus (7:36–50). The criminal who prayed to Jesus on the cross (23:42) serves as a model for the audience to acknowledge their sinfulness and pray to join Jesus in the heavenly kingdom he has opened for them by his salvific death. And Jesus' raising of the daughter of Jairus (8:41–55) gives the audience a foundation for praying to Jesus on behalf of those who have fallen "asleep" in death, with faith that he can raise them to everlasting life in the kingdom of God.

The miraculous healing of a Samaritan leper by Jesus in answer to prayer (17:12–19) provides a model for the audience to pray with faith in Jesus and show gratitude toward God/Jesus when their prayers are answered. Similarly, Jesus' healing of a blind man at Jericho (18:35–43) serves as a model for the audience to pray with faith to Jesus for the insight to deny themselves, take up their cross daily, and follow Jesus (9:23) in order to be saved, for "whoever wants to save his life will lose it, but whoever loses his life for my sake will save it" (9:24).

The answered prayers of the community of believers in Jerusalem (Acts 4:29–31; 6:6–7) encourage the audience to pray to God for boldness to proclaim the word of the gospel despite opposition and for divine assistance for those appointed to special tasks or offices within the church.

The prayers of the dying Stephen (7:59–60) reinforce those of the dying Jesus as models for the audience to imitate. The members of the audience are likewise to pray to God and/or the risen Lord Jesus to forgive those who harm them, and through prayer to entrust themselves to the divine will not only during their life but at the time of their death.

The answered prayer of Peter and John for the Samaritans to receive the Holy Spirit (8:15–17) encourages the audience to pray that new converts to the Christian faith likewise receive the Holy Spirit, which will enable them to become fully accepted by and united with all the other members of the church. The answered prayer of Saul/Paul (9:11–20) serves as a model for the audience to pray for the divine guidance and insight they need to play their respective roles in the evangelizing mission of the church. And the prayers of Cornelius and Peter model for the audience how praying can inform them of the role they are to play in God's salvific plan for all people (10:1—11:18).

Peter's raising of Tabitha/Dorcas after praying (9:36–41) reinforces the foundation Luke-Acts provides for the audience to pray to the risen Lord Jesus not only for the sick but for the resurrection of those who have died.

The answered prayer of the church for the freeing of the imprisoned Peter (12:1–17), the prayers of the church at Antioch for Barnabas and Paul (13:1–3), the prayers of Barnabas and Paul for the elders in local churches (14:23), and the praying by the imprisoned Paul and Silas (16:25–34) provide foundational models encouraging the audience to pray not only for themselves when in need but for the needs of church leaders, so that they may fulfill their roles in advancing the evangelizing and pastoral missions of the church.

The examples of Paul praying while kneeling, like Jesus (Luke 22:41), Stephen (Acts 7:60), and Peter (9:40), before his fateful journey to Jerusalem (20:36; 21:3–6) serve as models for the audience to pray alone as well as with others at critical times of need for divine strength and guidance. And Paul's praying before healing the pagan father of Publius, the chief of the island of Malta (28:8–9), provides a model for the audience to pray for the health and salvation even of nonbelievers.

5

Laudatory Worship

In the biblical tradition laudatory worship comprises not only praising, but thanking, glorifying, magnifying, and blessing God. All of creation can join human beings for laudatory worship.[1] One can offer laudatory worship indirectly or implicitly to God by invoking, acknowledging, or declaring God's blessing or glory on persons or things.[2] Laudatory worship often includes expressions of joy.[3] In Luke-Acts God's activity in the birth, ministry, death, and resurrection of Jesus, who himself engages in laudatory

---

1. Laudatory worship refers to an "expression of worship which recognizes and acknowledges God as the ultimate source and giver of all good gifts. In the Bible it encompasses a number of elements [such as, praise, thanks, blessing, as well as glorifying, magnifying, singing]. Scholars discuss nuances of difference among the various terms, but they clearly belong to the same semantic field" (Guinan, "Praise," 1076). "God's faithful people clearly are the prime actors in the praise of God, but all peoples are expected to join it.... Everything created by God is invited to join in jubilant praise of God" (Endres, "Praise," 579).

2. "God's benefactions, together with human petitions for them, and ardent praise of God for blessings received are reciprocal actions in the biblical economy of divine providence" (McBride, "Bless," 476). "God, angels, and humanity may bless; God, humanity, animals, and inanimate objects can be blessed.... Blessing is a performative utterance, or speech act, that brings good upon someone or something" (Magdalene, "Bless," 192).

3. "But the Lukan narrative does not completely equate joy and praise. In some cases, joy and praise appear together. However on other occasions, characters express joy in response to events in the story, but they do not explicitly praise God (or, they praise God but do not express joy).... In several cases, joy and praise of God signify the same narrative act (joyful praise), but in others, joy does *not* represent a positive response to God" (De Long, *Surprised by God*, 8; emphasis original).

worship, and God's activity in bringing all kinds of people to faith in Jesus, provide a focus and foundation for Christian laudatory worship.

Praise to God and/or the Divine Lord Jesus in Luke

The Lukan Infancy Narrative

In response to the supplicatory worship of the childless priest Zechariah (Luke 1:7-9), and implicitly that of the people (1:10), the angel Gabriel (1:19) informed him that in answer to his prayer his wife Elizabeth will bear him a son whom he is to name John (1:13). The angel raised the expectation of future laudatory worship of God for this birth as he announced that Zechariah will have joy and gladness, and many will rejoice at the birth of John (1:14).[4] But this joyful laudatory worship will be delayed, since Zechariah will be struck silent and unable to speak because he did not believe the words of Gabriel (1:20). Once the mute and deaf Zechariah (1:62) wrote on a tablet the name of his son as John (1:63) in faithful obedience to the words of Gabriel (1:13), immediately his mouth was opened and his tongue freed, enabling him to engage in laudatory worship, as he spoke, blessing God (1:64).

Then Zechariah, filled with the Holy Spirit, prophesied (1:67), as he elaborated his "blessing" (εὐλογῶν) in joyful praise of God (1:64): "Blessed [εὐλογητός] be the Lord God of Israel, for he has visited and brought redemption to his people" (1:68). He initially praised God not for his son John but for Jesus, as he continued, "for he has raised up a horn of salvation for us in the house of David his servant" (1:69; cf. 1:27, 32).[5] By saying "he raised" (ἤγειρεν) up, Zechariah refers here to the birth of Jesus, but the Lukan audience, already instructed about Jesus (1:4), can appreciate an allusion also to God's future raising of Jesus from the dead. Indeed, a refrain of six occurrences in Acts of the expression God "raised" (ἤγειρεν) Jesus (3:15; 4:10; 5:30; 10:40; 13:30, 37; cf. Luke 9:22; 24:6, 34) follows the first and only occurrence of this verb form in Luke.[6] God raised up Jesus as a

---

4. "In the infancy narrative, joy in response to God's saving action is praise, and praise of God is joyous" (De Long, *Surprised by God*, 147).

5. "'Horn' (v. 69) is a Hebrew metaphor for power and might (Deut 33:17; Ps 75:10); 'horn of salvation' thus connotes the power of salvation (2 Sam 22:3; Ps 18:3[2])" (Edwards, *Gospel According to Luke*, 62).

6. "The word ἤγειρεν ('he has raised up') indicates the appearance of an agent of divine deliverance here, as in Judg 2:16, 18; cf. Acts 13:22. This verb also later refers to Jesus' resurrection (e.g., Acts 3:15; 5:30), a nuance that might be heard by a Christian auditor who knows the whole story" (Carroll, *Luke*, 59n19). See also Dillon,

horn of salvation from our enemies (1:71, 74), in accord with past promises (1:70, 72-73), so that we might without fear "serve/worship" (λατρεύειν) him (1:74) in holiness and righteousness before him all our days (1:75).[7]

Zechariah then prophesied that his own son John will be called prophet of the Most High, for he will go before the Lord Jesus (cf. 1:43) to prepare his ways (1:76; cf. 1:15-17; 3:4). He will give his people knowledge of salvation through the forgiveness of their sins (1:77), the salvation from enemies (1:71) God brought about by raising up Jesus as a horn of salvation (1:69).[8] John will do this on account of the tender mercy of our God, by which the "dawn" (ἀνατολή) from on high will visit us (1:78), a reference to the messianic "dawn" or "branch" that God promised to raise up for David (LXX Jer 23:5; cf. Zech 3:8; 6:12).[9] Since the basic meaning of ἀνατολή is "rising," it provides another allusion, in addition to God having "raised" up Jesus to be a horn of salvation (Luke 1:69), to the resurrection of Jesus from the dead as the Davidic messiah (Acts 13:34). That Jesus as the messianic "dawn/branch/rising" will shine on those who sit in darkness and in the shadow of death (cf. LXX Isa 9:1; Acts 2:24), to guide our feet into the way of peace (Luke 1:79), confirms these allusions.

Zechariah's hymnic blessing began with how God "visited" (ἐπεσκέψατο) us (1:68) in "raising" up Jesus (1:69). It concluded with how the "rising" of Jesus "will visit" (ἐπισκέψεται) us (1:78) and shine on us who sit in darkness and in the shadow of death (1:79).[10] Zechariah's joyful hymn of laudatory worship of God (1:68-79) speaks not only for himself but for and to the Lukan communal audience of believers as the people of God. It abounds with communal references, with terms such as "people" (1:68,

---

"Benedictus," 476-77.

7. "'To serve' or 'to worship' is used to clarify the nature of the redeemed people, a community whose practices were to be formed in their worship of the Lord God. Thus, the freedom to worship without fear refers to much more than spiritual or cultic practices. Worship or service embraces the whole way of communal life of those who have been delivered" (Green, *Gospel of Luke*, 117).

8. "When Zechariah forecasts his son's role, he does not mention what will be its defining symbol, baptism, but he does address the *point* of the ritual: forgiveness of sins" (Carroll, *Luke*, 60; emphasis original).

9. "The word translated 'dawn' (ἀνατολή) can refer to the sprouting up of a plant and the rising of a star, and its usage gave it a messianic connotation of 'branch'" (Garland, *Luke*, 108). See also Fitzmyer, *Gospel According to Luke I–IX*, 387; Gathercole, "Heavenly ἀνατολή," 471-88; Lanier, "'From God,'" 121-27.

10. "Within the hymn, the repetition of ἐπεσκέψατο in 1:68 and ἐπισκέψεται in 1:78 makes it clear that God's visitation comes in Messiah's visitation" (Bock, *Luke 1:1—9:50*, 178-79). On the significance of the divine visitation for laudatory worship in the Lukan infancy narrative, see De Long, *Surprised by God*, 152-78.

77), "us" (1:69, 71, 78), and "our" (1:71, 72, 73, 75, 78, 79).[11] It invites the audience to join Zechariah in joyfully praising God not only for the birth of his son John but for the salvation God has brought to us in raising up Jesus to be born as the Davidic messiah and in raising Jesus from the dead for our salvation from darkness and the shadow of death.

After Zechariah's wife Elizabeth conceived (1:24), she implicitly praised God when she declared, "So has the Lord done for me in the days when he looked upon me to take away my disgrace among people" (1:25).[12] She then indirectly praised God when she acknowledged that God has blessed Mary and her son Jesus: "Blessed [εὐλογημένη] are you among women, and blessed [εὐλογημένος] is the fruit of your womb!" (1:42).[13] Gabriel told Zechariah that he will have joy and "gladness" (ἀγαλλίασις) at the birth of John (1:14). But, ironically, the unborn John leaped in "gladness" (ἀγαλλιάσει) when Elizabeth heard Mary's greeting (1:44; cf. 1:41), adding to her joyful praise. When Elizabeth gave birth to John (1:57), her neighbors and relatives heard that the Lord had magnified his mercy toward her, and they "rejoiced with" (συνέχαιρον) her (1:58), fulfilling Gabriel's promise that many "will rejoice" (χαρήσονται) at the birth of John (1:14).[14] This invites the audience likewise to join Elizabeth in her joyful praise of God not only for the birth of John but for blessing Mary in becoming the mother of the "Lord" Jesus (1:43).[15]

Before the angel Gabriel informed Mary that she is to give birth to a son whom she will name Jesus (1:31), he greeted her with an exhortation: "Rejoice [χαῖρε], favored one, the Lord is with you!" (1:28).[16] After

11. See also Dillon, "Narrative Analysis," 253–59.

12. "Elizabeth acknowledges God's mercy, so perhaps her speech should be understood as praise, even if it is not explicitly described as such. Later, she and her neighbors rejoice because God has shown mercy (ἔλεος) to her (1:58)" (De Long, *Surprised by God*, 167n83).

13. "Blessedness is a condition for which God alone is responsible" (Just, *Luke 1:1—9:50*, 76).

14. "The description of vv. 57–58 may foreshadow the Christian community, for the fulfillment of God's promises is a source of joy to others no less than to the specific recipient(s) of the promise" (Edwards, *Gospel According to Luke*, 57). "Joy and praise are strains that run through the infancy narrative (1:14, 64; 2:10, 14, 28), and rejoicing with others in community is a theme that runs throughout the gospel" (Garland, *Luke*, 104).

15. "Taking into account Luke's frequent use of κύριος [Lord] for the God of Israel and the movement of the Lukan narrative, it becomes possible to draw the conclusion that the dramatic moment of 1:43 in the narrative bespeaks a kind of unity of identity between YHWH and the human Jesus within Mary's womb by means of the resonance of κύριος" (Rowe, *Early Narrative*, 45).

16. "[I]t seems best to understand the angel's address to Mary as playing upon the dual sense of χαῖρε: it serves as a greeting (albeit an unusual one in the narrative world

Elizabeth declared Mary "blessed" (μακαρία) for believing that what the Lord spoke to her would be fulfilled (1:45), Mary responded to her and to Gabriel's exhortation to rejoice with a hymnic act of laudatory worship: "My soul magnifies the Lord, and my spirit rejoices [ἠγαλλίασεν] in God my savior" (1:46–47).

She went on to praise the God who "has thrown down rulers from thrones and exalted [ὕψωσεν] the humble [ταπεινούς]" (1:52). This refers to how God, as the Mighty One, has done great things for her (1:49), when he looked upon her "humble state [ταπείνωσιν]" (1:48). But it also prepares for the teaching uttered twice by Jesus, which he later exemplified by his death and resurrection, namely, that everyone who "exalts" [ὑψῶν] himself will be "humbled" (ταπεινωθήσεται) by God (divine passive), but the one who "humbles" (ταπεινῶν) himself "will be exalted" (ὑψωθήσεται) by God (14:11; 18:14). Peter confirmed this teaching and example of Jesus, when he declared after the Pentecost event in Jerusalem that Jesus, "exalted" (ὑψωθείς) at the right hand of God, and having received the promise of the Holy Spirit from the Father, has poured it forth (Acts 2:33).[17] And again Peter declared that the Jesus whom the Jewish leaders subjected to a very humiliating death by hanging him on a tree (5:30) God "exalted" (ὕψωσεν) at his right hand as leader and savior (5:31).[18]

From now on not only Elizabeth but all generations "will call blessed" (μακαριοῦσίν) Mary (Luke 1:48b). In Mary, God has helped the people of Israel, remembering his "mercy" (1:54), the "mercy" that is from generations to generations for those who revere him (1:50). Mary's Magnificat hymn (1:46–55) invites the audience to revere God by joining her in joyfully praising God by calling her blessed to be the mother of Jesus, the holy Son of God (1:35).[19]

---

of Luke-Acts) but also imparts an underlying meaning of joy. . . . Gabriel both hails Mary and exhorts her, personally, to rejoice" (De Long, *Surprised by God*, 141, 142).

17. "Peter's interpretation of the story of Jesus in the Pentecost speech places primary emphasis on Jesus' resurrection and exaltation" (Tannehill, *Narrative Unity*, 2.37).

18. "Implying an allusion to Deut 21:22–23, Peter accuses the Jewish leaders of having treated Jesus as a dangerous criminal, as someone who is under God's curse and must be eliminated from God's people. In the Second Temple period Jews used the expression 'hang on a tree' for crucifixion" (Schnabel, *Acts*, 312). On the crucifixion of Jesus as humiliation and his resurrection as exaltation, see also Phil 2:8–9: Jesus "humbled [ἐταπείνωσεν] himself, becoming obedient to the point of death, even death on a cross, and as a result God exalted [ὑπερύψωσεν] him and gave him the name that is above every name."

19. "There is an invitation here to Israel (and subsequently to members of the Church) to join her in her song, to make her experience of salvation their own" (Byrne, *Hospitality*, 26). "The reader is to identify with Mary's confidence, her faith, and her sense of joy" (Bock, *Luke 1:1—9:50*, 161). "Mary's Song is not a revolutionary call to

When the angel of the Lord appeared to the shepherds (2:9), he proclaimed to them good news of great joy (2:10), because in the city of David a savior has been born for them who is Christ the Lord (2:11; cf. 1:43). Then suddenly with the angel there was a multitude of heavenly hosts "praising" God (2:13) with an act of laudatory worship: "Glory to God in the highest and on earth peace among people with whom he is pleased!" (2:14).[20] After the shepherds saw Mary and Joseph and the infant lying in the manger (2:16), and made known the message told them about the child (2:17), they returned and joined the angels in their laudatory worship, as they were "glorifying" and "praising" God for all they had heard and seen, just as it had been told to them (2:20). The laudatory worship by the angels and the shepherds invites the audience to join them in joyfully praising and glorifying God for the "peace" that will result from the birth of a savior, Christ the Lord. He will guide those who sit in the shadow of death into the way of "peace" (1:79), a peace implicitly resulting from Jesus' resurrection from death.[21]

The Holy Spirit revealed to the righteous and devout Simeon, who was awaiting the consolation of Israel (2:25), that he would not see death until he had seen the Lord's Christ (2:26). When in the Spirit he came into the temple (2:27), he received the child Jesus into his arms.[22] He then performed an act of hymnic laudatory worship as he "blessed" (εὐλόγησεν) God, beginning with the words (2:28), "Now release your servant, Master, in peace, according to your word [cf. 1:38]" (2:29).[23] Simeon thus acknowledged that now God can release him to see "death" in the "peace" associated with the hope of being raised from death, the way of "peace" into which Jesus, as the "rising" from on high (1:78), will guide us, as he visits us to shine on those

---

human action but a celebration of God's action" (Green, *Gospel of Luke*, 100).

20. "The distance that separates heaven and earth from each other is removed for a moment; the earth becomes the place of the heavenly praise of God and humans become its earwitnesses" (Wolter, *Luke*, 128). "The meaning seems to be . . . that at the birth of the Saviour God's peace rests on those whom he has chosen in accord with his good pleasure" (Metzger, *Textual Commentary*, 111).

21. "[T]he messianic peace he [Jesus] brings is ultimately the gift of heaven" (Byrne, *Hospitality*, 33). "Zechariah's song pictured peace as one of the aims of divine visitation (1:79); the declaration of praise in 2:14 names peace as heaven's desire for human beings, matching God's glory in heaven" (Carroll, *Luke*, 79).

22. Note the wordplay: Simeon "received" (ἐδέξατο) the child Jesus as the personified consolation of Israel for which he was "awaiting" (προσδεχόμενος) in hope; Edwards, *Gospel According to Luke*, 85.

23. "What follows is a hymn of prophetic praise to God for the joy of seeing the Messiah in fulfillment of God's word. Simeon's reception of Jesus is intended to picture the arrival of messianic hope for Israel. The prophet represents the nation and, beyond that, all humanity" (Bock, *Luke 1:1—9:50*, 241).

Laudatory Worship

who sit in the darkness and shadow of "death" (1:79).[24] The association of "peace," the heavenly "peace" now on earth (2:14) at the birth of Christ the Lord (2:11), with resurrection from death is confirmed by the final, climactic occurrence of the term in Luke when the risen Lord Jesus stood in the midst of his disciples and proclaimed, "Peace be with you" (24:36).[25]

Simeon continued his laudatory blessing of God, as he proclaimed, "For my eyes have seen your salvation" (2:30). Simeon can now see death in peace (2:26, 29) because he has seen God's "salvation" (σωτήριόν), personified in the child Jesus (2:27–28), the "horn of salvation [σωτηρίας]" God "raised" up for us (1:69; cf. 1:71, 77), referring to Jesus' birth but also hinting at his resurrection from the dead.[26] Jesus represents the salvation God has prepared before all peoples (2:31), as a "light" (φῶς) for revelation to the gentiles and glory for his people Israel (2:32). Later, appearing to Paul on his way to Damascus as "light" (φῶς), the risen Jesus revealed the resurrection from the dead not only to the Jew Paul (Acts 9:3; 22:6, 9, 11, 13) but told Paul that he has appointed him to be a minister and witness of what he has seen of the risen Jesus to the gentiles to open their eyes that they may turn from darkness to "light [φῶς]" (26:17–18). Paul then told King Agrippa (26:19) that, as the first to rise from the dead, the Christ would proclaim "light" (φῶς) both to our people and to the gentiles (26:23; cf. 13:47).[27]

The "glory" (δόξαν) for Israel, an implicit fulfillment of the "consolation" of Israel for which Simeon is awaiting (Luke 2:25) in hope, emerges later before Paul as "the glory of the light" (τῆς δόξης τοῦ φωτός) of the risen Jesus (Acts 22:11), who embodies the "hope" of Israel for resurrection from the dead. Near the conclusion of Acts the imprisoned Paul in Rome told the leaders of the Jews (28:17) that it is on account of the "hope" of

---

24. "In view of the Spirit's promise mentioned in v. 26, release from the master's service is also an image for release to death, to a death in peace. Simeon thus takes his place among the favored ones who experience the peace being brought by the divine visitation announced in Zechariah's song (1:79)" (Carroll, *Luke*, 77).

25. "Coming from Jesus, this greeting of peace packs more punch since he has come to guide our feet into the way of peace and actually brings peace to people's lives (1:79; 2:14, 29; 7:50; 8:48; 19:38, 42). But his way of peace is frightening since it requires self-sacrifice and even death" (Garland, *Luke*, 965). "Within the Third Gospel, 'peace' is metonymic for 'salvation,' so that, in this co-text, Jesus' greeting takes on an enlarged meaning" (Green, *Gospel of Luke*, 854).

26. "In seeing the Christ child, Simeon sees everything that God ordains pertaining to salvation" (Edwards, *Gospel According to Luke*, 86).

27. "Verse 23 wraps up the speech tidily by associating the words 'resurrection' (v. 8) and 'light' (vv. 13, 18)" (Pervo, *Acts*, 635). "The reference to light should remind Luke's readers of the words of Simeon in Luke 2:32, who said, with the newborn Jesus in his arms, that Jesus is God's salvation and 'a light for revelation to the gentiles, and the glory of your people Israel'" (Schnabel, *Acts*, 1014).

Israel that he wears this chain (28:20). Previously to King Agrippa (26:2), Paul declared that he is on trial because of his "hope" in the promise made by God to his Jewish ancestors (26:6). The twelve tribes of Israel "hope" to obtain that promise, and concerning this "hope" Paul is accused by Jews (26:7), namely, the hope that God raises the dead (26:8). Paul told the governor Felix (24:3) that he has the same "hope" as the Jews that there will be a resurrection of the righteous and the unrighteous (24:15). And Paul cried out before the Sanhedrin that he is on trial concerning "hope" in the resurrection of the dead (23:6; cf. 2:26–27).[28]

Continuing his laudatory worship, Simeon implicitly praised God when he "blessed" (εὐλόγησεν) the parents of Jesus and told Mary that Jesus is destined (by God, divine passive) for the falling and rising of many in Israel and to be a sign that will be contradicted (Luke 2:34). The "falling and rising" of many refers generally to the division between nonbelievers and believers that Jesus will cause.[29] But the "rising" (ἀνάστασιν) of many in Israel alludes more specifically to the "resurrection" from the dead (Luke 20:27, 33, 35, 36; Acts 1:22; 2:31; 4:2, 33; 17:18, 32; 23:6, 8; 24:15, 21; 26:23) that Jesus' resurrection begins, as the "hope of Israel" (Acts 28:20). That Jesus will be a sign that will be "contradicted" (ἀντιλεγόμενον) anticipates his controversy with the Sadducees as those "contradicting resurrection" (ἀντιλέγοντες ἀνάστασιν) in general and implicitly that of Jesus (Luke 20:27).[30] It also anticipates the division among the Athenians, some of whom mocked Jesus' "resurrection" (ἀνάστασιν) from the dead, while others were open to hearing more about resurrection from the dead (Acts 17:32; cf. 17:18).

Simeon's exuberant laudatory worship (Luke 2:28–34) invites the audience to join him in blessing and praising God not only for the birth but for the resurrection of Jesus from the dead. Like Simeon, each member of the audience can face his or her inevitable death in peace, consoled by the hope of being raised from death because of the resurrection of Jesus from the dead. The audience can join Simeon in blessing and praising God for the birth and resurrection of Jesus from the dead, as the embodiment of

---

28. "Here Paul implies that *the hope of the resurrection of the dead* belongs to all true Israelites. This is an important foundation for arguing that Israel's hope is fulfilled in the resurrection of Jesus, making it possible for all who call on his name to share in the promised resurrection from the dead (cf. 4:10–12; 5:30–32; 13:30–37)" (Peterson, *Acts*, 616–17; emphasis original).

29. It is "likely that 'falling and rising' should be understood here as a description of two opposite consequences that the activity and proclamation of Jesus in Israel will draw after it" (Wolter, *Luke*, 143).

30. For the preference of the reading ἀντιλέγοντες rather than λέγοντες for Luke 20:27, see Metzger, *Textual Commentary*, 145–46.

Laudatory Worship

salvation for all peoples (2:30–31), who sit in the darkness and shadow of death, as proclaimed by Zechariah in his Benedictus (1:79). As salvation personified, Jesus represents the light that reveals resurrection from death to the gentiles and the glory that fulfills the hope of the people of Israel for resurrection from the dead (2:32). As Paul declared to King Agrippa, the Christ, as the first to rise from the dead, would proclaim the "light" that symbolizes the resurrection from the dead to the people of Israel and to the gentiles (Acts 26:23).

The prophetess and elderly widow Anna from one of the twelve tribes of Israel (Luke 2:36) never left the temple, with prayer and fasting "worshiping night and day [λατρεύουσα νύκτα καὶ ἡμέραν]" (2:37). She exemplifies how the twelve tribes "night and day worship" (νύκτα καὶ ἡμέραν λατρεῦον) in hope of attaining the promise of the resurrection of the dead (Acts 26:7; cf. 23:6; 24:15; 28:20).[31] Coming forward at that very hour, she performed an act of laudatory worship, as she "thanked" God and spoke about Jesus to all who were "awaiting" (προσδεχομένοις) the redemption of Jerusalem (Luke 2:38).[32] This resonates with Simeon "awaiting" (προσδεχόμενος) the consolation of Israel (2:25). Awaiting the "redemption" (λύτρωσιν) of Jerusalem alludes to the hope for the resurrection of the dead, as it recalls Zechariah's praise of God, who brought "redemption" (λύτρωσιν) for his people (1:68) when he "raised" up Jesus in birth and from the dead (1:69). Anna's praise invites the audience to join her in thanking God for the birth of Jesus, which will lead to their redemption from death.[33]

When the shepherds saw the infant Jesus lying in a manger, they made known the word told them by the angel (2:16–17), the word of the birth of Jesus as a savior, Christ the Lord (2:11). While all who heard it were amazed (2:18), Mary kept these things, reflecting on them in her heart (2:19). Hinting at the suffering and death of Jesus, Simeon prophesied that a metaphorical sword will pierce Mary's "soul" (2:35), the "soul" that magnified the Lord (1:46) in laudatory worship.[34] After the young Jesus was found in the temple, he told Mary that it was divinely "necessary" (δεῖ) that he be "in the things

---

31. "Anna embodies worship in the temple, the tribes of Israel, the prophetic ministry, and the prayer and praise of Israel" (García Serrano, "Anna's Characterization," 479). "The tribes give constant worship to God for the hope of resurrection. Anna in Luke 2:37b was an example of this hope" (Bock, *Acts*, 714)." See also Keener, *Acts*, 4.3501.

32. The Greek word for "thanked" (ἀνθωμολογεῖτο), "occurring only here in the Greek Bible, means to thank publicly" (Edwards, *Gospel According to Luke*, 89n96).

33. "Whereas the shepherds' proclamation was about the birth of Jesus, Anna's is about the death of Jesus, his 'redemption of Jerusalem'" (Just, *Luke 1:1—9:50*, 125).

34. "Mary . . . will be pierced at the cross as she watches her son die the humiliating death of crucifixion" (Just, *Luke 1:1—9:50*, 124).

of his Father" (2:49). This foreshadows that according to his Father's will it is "necessary" (δεῖ) for him to undergo suffering and death before being raised from the dead (9:22; 17:25; 24:7, 26, 44).[35] Mary again kept all these things in her heart (2:51; cf. 2:19). Mary thus indicates to the audience how their joyful laudatory worship is to include the praise of God not only for the birth but for the resurrection of Jesus, as they keep in their hearts the divine necessity for Jesus' suffering, death, and resurrection.

The Ministry of Jesus

The shepherds were "glorifying" (δοξάζοντες) and praising God for all they had heard and seen regarding the birth of Jesus, just as it had been told them by the angel (2:20; cf. 2:9–12). But when Jesus was teaching in the synagogues of Galilee (4:14), he himself became an object of laudatory worship, as he was being "glorified" (δοξαζόμενος) by all (4:15). When Jesus proclaimed the fulfillment in him of the scripture he read in the Nazareth synagogue (4:16–21), this favorable response continued, as all were bearing witness to him and marveling at the words of grace coming from his mouth (4:22). But when Jesus insinuated that they were going to reject him as a prophet in his native place (4:24), they indeed did exactly that, as they attempted to kill him (4:29), but he escaped (4:30). This foreshadows the eventual death of Jesus as a prophet in accord with God's scriptural plan (13:33). It underscores for the audience how Jesus is worthy of being glorified in laudatory worship not only for his teaching but for his fulfillment of the divine necessity that he be killed by his people before being raised from the dead.[36]

When Jesus saw the faith of those who lowered a paralytic through the roof to reach him (5:19), he said to the paralytic, "Your sins are forgiven [ἀφέωνταί] for you [by God, divine passive]" (5:20). After the scribes and Pharisees raised the question of who can forgive sins but God alone (5:21), Jesus pointed out that both healing and forgiveness involve divine authority (5:22–23). But that they may know that he, as the Son of Man, has the divine heavenly authority on earth to forgive sins, he pronounced the healing of the paralytic (5:24), who then performed an act of laudatory worship

---

35. With his first fateful words (Luke 2:49), "Jesus was darkly alluding to his future passion and Resurrection in the Holy City" (McHugh, *Mother of Jesus*, 124).

36. "All those glorifying him in Galilee for his teaching may be paired with the centurion who 'began to glorify God' when he saw what happened in his death on the cross (23:47). The glory that ultimately counts ... is the glory that comes from the giving of his life, which is tied to the eternal glory that is to come (9:26; 21:27; 24:26)" (Garland, *Luke*, 195).

as he was "glorifying" (δοξάζων) God (5:25). Then astonishment seized all who witnessed this, and they too "glorified" (ἐδόξαζον) God, and they were filled with awe, saying, "We have seen surprising things [παράδοξα] today" (5:26).[37] This scene invites the members of the audience likewise to join the paralytic in this communal glorifying of God for giving Jesus the divine authority not only to heal diseases but to forgive sins, so that they may experience divine salvation "through the forgiveness [ἀφέσει] of their sins" (1:77).

After Jesus told a widow at Nain, whose only son had died, not to weep (7:11–13), he commanded the dead young man, "I say to you, be raised [ἐγέρθητι; by God, divine passive]" (7:14). Then the dead man sat up and began to speak, and Jesus gave him to his mother (7:15). Awe seized all who witnessed it, and they performed an act of laudatory worship as they "glorified" (ἐδόξαζον) God, saying, "A great prophet has been raised [ἠγέρθη] among us!" and "God has visited his people!" (7:16). This recalls Zechariah's hymnic laudatory worship when he blessed the Lord the God of Israel "for he has visited and brought redemption to his people; he has raised up [ἤγειρεν] a horn of salvation for us in the house of David his servant" (1:68–69). The audience can again appreciate the double meaning. The great prophet Jesus "has been raised" among us by being born and by being raised from the dead. The Jesus who told the dead young man to "be raised" will himself be raised by God to eternal life. This scene invites the audience likewise to glorify God for "raising up" Jesus for our eschatological salvation.[38]

In her laudatory hymn Mary declared that her spirit "rejoices" (ἠγαλλίασεν) in God her savior (1:47). Echoing this, Jesus himself performed an act of laudatory worship when he "rejoiced" (ἠγαλλιάσατο) in the Holy Spirit and said, "I praise [ἐξομολογοῦμαί] you, Father, Lord of heaven and earth, because you have hidden these things from the wise and intelligent and revealed them to the childlike. Yes, Father, for thus has been your good pleasure" (10:21). He then proclaimed that all things have been handed over to him by his Father (cf. 4:6; 10:18), and no one knows who the Son is except the Father, and who the Father is except the Son and anyone to

---

37. "The narrative sets up the reader to expect healing, but instead Jesus forgives *and* heals. Thus in this scene, Jesus surprises readers and characters alike, and when the religious authorities voice praise for παράδοξα, they acknowledge the divine origin of these unexpected words and actions of Jesus" (De Long, *Surprised by God*, 186; emphasis original). "The crowd knew it was dealing with God's surprising presence" (Bock, *Luke 1:1—9:50*, 487).

38. "The exclamation of the people in v. 16 is a *confession of faith* that, in the raising of the boy in Nain, this prophet from Capernaum is the fulfillment of the longing of Israel for God's eschatological intervention of salvation" (Edwards, *Gospel According to Luke*, 216; emphasis original). On Luke 7:11–17 as a prefiguration of the resurrection of Jesus, see De Santis, "La visita," 49–74.

whom the Son wishes to reveal him (10:22). The members of the audience are to identify with the childlike disciples to whom Jesus has revealed the Father and the knowledge of the mysteries of the Kingdom of God (10:23; cf. 8:10). They are invited to join Jesus in praising his Father for revealing him as the Son, an agent of divine revelation, and thus worthy to be an object of laudatory worship as the divine Son of his divine Father.[39]

After Jesus healed a woman, severely crippled for eighteen years, in a synagogue on the Sabbath (13:10-12), she performed an act of laudatory worship as she "glorified" (ἐδόξαζεν) God (13:13).[40] When the leader of the synagogue objected to this being done on the Sabbath (13:14), the "Lord" Jesus, as "Lord" of the Sabbath (6:5), declared that it was divinely "necessary" (ἔδει) for this "daughter of Abraham," a representative of the people of Israel, whom Satan has bound for eighteen years, to be freed from this bondage on the day of the Sabbath (13:16).[41] When he said this all his adversaries were put to shame, but all the crowd complemented the woman's laudatory worship as they "rejoiced" (ἔχαιρεν) at all the "glorious" (ἐνδόξοις) things done by him (13:17), implying that he, like God, is worthy to be glorified.[42] This scene invites the audience to join the healed woman and all the crowd in glorifying not only God but the divine Lord Jesus for not only healing this woman on the Sabbath but for all of the glorious things done by him for the salvation of his people.[43]

39. "What the Father has hidden from the wise and understanding is that Jesus is his Son" (Just, *Luke 9:51—24:53*, 445). "This indeed is a strong description of the Son's central, mediatorial role in salvation. He functions like the Father" (Bock, *Luke 9:51—24:53*, 1012). "Jesus offers this praise right after his critique of the disciples' incorrect joy (10:20). Thus while Jesus' praise implies that his disciples are the 'children' who will see, his words are proleptic: the disciples are not *yet* the children who see (Lk 18:34) nor have they yet offered (proper) praise" (De Long, *Surprised by God*, 219; emphasis original).

40. "Praise or glorification of God is a signature Lukan characteristic, in every instance coming from those whose afflictions or social conditions place them on the margins of or outside the circle of Jewish ritual cleanness" (Edwards, *Gospel According to Luke*, 395–96).

41. "It was not coincidental but 'necessary' that Jesus should free a woman bound by Satan, and to do so *on the Sabbath*, for Jesus, who is Lord of the Sabbath, must complete his mission of redemption on Sabbath, just as God completed his mission of creation on Sabbath" (Edwards, *Gospel According to Luke*, 397; emphasis original).

42. "The crowd adds to the woman's praise of God with rejoicing, the proper response to what God is doing through Jesus" (Garland, *Luke*, 550).

43. "Jesus' description of her as a 'daughter of Abraham' adds to the sense that the woman is emblematic of the restored community. . . . This healing story suggests that the woman's transformation represents the eschatological visitation of divine mercy upon Israel, marked by praise of God" (De Long, *Surprised by God*, 202–3). The healed woman is "a model for everyone who responds correctly to Jesus" (O'Toole, "Some

Laudatory Worship

When a Samaritan leper realized that he had been healed by Jesus, he returned to him and began to perform an act of laudatory worship, with a loud voice "glorifying" (δοξάζων) God (17:15). He continued his laudatory worship as he fell upon his face at the feet of Jesus in a posture for worship (cf. 5:12; 8:41), "thanking" (εὐχαριστῶν) him (17:16). Jesus pointed out that although ten were cleansed of their leprosy (17:17) none but this "foreigner" (ἀλλογενής) has returned to give "glory" (δόξαν) to God (17:18).[44] In thanking Jesus the Samaritan leper gave glory to God, continuing the implication that God is uniquely at work in Jesus so that both are worthy objects of laudatory worship.[45] Jesus dismissed the Samaritan with the words, "Your faith has saved [σέσωκέν] you" (17:19; cf. 7:50; 8:48), indicating that his faith has not only brought him healing but eschatological salvation.[46] The healed Samaritan leper serves as a model for all people, no matter their ethnic origin, to have the faith to give glory to God by thanking Jesus for his divine authority not only to heal but to bring them eschatological salvation.[47]

Jesus answered the prayer of the blind beggar at Jericho to regain his sight (18:35–41) with the words, "Have sight; your faith has saved you" (18:42; cf. 7:50; 8:48; 17:19), affirming not only his healing but his eschatological

---

Exegetical Reflections," 99). See also Hamm, "Freeing of the Bent Woman," 23–44; May, "Straightened Woman," 245–58; Ryan, "Jesus and Synagogue Disputes," 41–59.

44. "This statement of Jesus includes a christological assumption not found on the lips of Jesus anywhere else in all of Luke-Acts, namely, that his presence is the place to give glory to God. Indeed, the Lucan Jesus here accepts the worshipful behavior of the healed Samaritan as appropriate. . . . In a narrative whose language is already steeped in the atmosphere of worship, for Jesus to refer to this Samaritan at his feet as 'this ἀλλογενής' is to suggest that this person, who belongs to the group included among those officially excluded from the worship space in Jerusalem has, ironically, found the right place to glorify God" (Hamm, "What the Samaritan Leper Sees," 284–85).

45. "The irony here is this: the ten lepers were happy to journey to the temple with the expectation that they would be cleansed, but only one leper, *after the cleansing*, was willing to return to give glory to God—God in the person of Jesus, whose presence in the world and whose sacrifice on the cross would bring an end to temple worship" (Just, *Luke 9:51—24:53*, 653; emphasis original).

46. "The Greek verb used here, σῳζω, is a flexible word that can refer to a whole spectrum of rescues, from disease and enemies, the usual reference in the OT, to eschatological salvation. Since, in this case, all ten experienced physical healing, the salvation that the tenth leper came to know must have something to do with his recognition that the presence of Jesus is the place to acknowledge the work of God" (Hamm, "What the Samaritan Leper Sees," 285).

47. "The careful nuancing of vocabulary for the healing and the sequence of action and speech suggest that the faith that 'has saved [delivered]' includes the return to thank Jesus and honor God" (Carroll, *Luke*, 344).

salvation.⁴⁸ He then followed Jesus, performing an act of laudatory worship, as he was "glorifying" (δοξάζων) God, and when all the people saw it, they joined his laudatory worship, as they "gave praise" (ἔδωκεν αἶνον) to God (18:43; cf. 17:18). Similar to the tax collector Levi (5:27), who left everything behind and "followed" (ἠκολούθει) Jesus (5:28) as a disciple, the beggar left behind his begging (18:35) and "followed" (ἠκολούθει) Jesus. In contrast to the Twelve, who did not understand/see that Jesus was going up to Jerusalem to suffer, be killed, and raised (18:31-34), the beggar was given the sight and insight to follow Jesus, and thus to deny himself and take up his cross (9:23).⁴⁹ This laudatory worship by the beggar and all the people invites the audience to have the faith likewise to glorify and praise God for the insight to follow God's agent, Jesus, and receive eschatological salvation.⁵⁰

When Jesus, mounted on a colt (19:35), was approaching the slope of the Mount of Olives, the whole multitude of the disciples, "rejoicing" (χαίροντες), began to "praise" (αἰνεῖν) God with a loud voice for all the "mighty deeds" (δυνάμεων) they had seen (19:37; cf. 13:17). In contrast to the Galilean villages that failed to repent at the "mighty deeds" (δυνάμεις) Jesus did among them (10:13), the whole multitude of disciples performed an act of joyful laudatory worship, as they climactically praised God for all the mighty deeds of Jesus' ministry. The comprehensive praise of God by the *whole* "multitude" of disciples for *all* they had seen Jesus do complements that of the shepherds, who were glorifying and "praising" (αἰνοῦντες) God for all they had heard and seen regarding the birth of Jesus (2:20), as well as that of the "multitude" of heavenly host with the angel, who were likewise "praising" (αἰνούντων) God (2:13).⁵¹ This leads the audience to praise God joyfully not only for the birth of Jesus but for all of the mighty acts God has enabled Jesus to perform for their salvation.⁵²

---

48. "'Your faith has saved you' emphasizes that opened eyes enable both physical and *spiritual* sight. This man has received eternal salvation" (Just, *Luke 9:51—24:53*, 708; emphasis original).

49. "A healed blind man, an outsider beside the way, fulfills the ideal of insider disciples by 'following Jesus and praising God' (v. 43); he 'sees' what the Twelve do not" (Edwards, *Gospel According to Luke* 527). "The blind man is presented as the foil to the uncomprehending Twelve" (Fitzmyer, *Gospel According to Luke X–XXIV*, 1214).

50. "As is typical in Lukan accounts of healing, people attribute restorative power to God, even while recognizing Jesus as the one through whom that power is manifest. Jesus is thus identified as the authorized agent of God" (Green, *Gospel of Luke*, 665).

51. "Luke's unique reference to praise fits his emphasis, since αἰνέω (to praise) is used elsewhere by him five times (Luke 2:13, 20; Acts 2:47; 3:8, 9) but only twice in the rest of the NT (Rom. 15:11; Rev. 19:5)" (Bock, *Luke 9:51—24:53*, 1557).

52. "Praising God for his wondrous works is typically associated with Jesus' miraculous deeds in Luke-Acts, and joy is regularly associated with divine intervention.

Laudatory Worship

In their laudatory worship the whole multitude of disciples proclaimed: "Blessed [εὐλογημένος] is the king who comes in the name of the Lord! Peace in heaven and glory in the highest [δόξα ἐν ὑψίστοις]!" (19:38). This serves as a preliminary anticipation of the laudatory worship Jesus predicted that the people of Jerusalem will proclaim after Jesus has abandoned their temple and they see him when he comes again: "Blessed [εὐλογημένος] is he who comes in the name of the Lord!" (13:35).[53] Although the disciples address Jesus as "the king," they do not yet understand how he will become "the king" in the kingdom of God (cf. 19:11–27), namely, by the divine necessity of his death and resurrection (18:31–34).[54] Their laudatory acclamation complements that of the angels at the birth of Jesus: "Glory in the highest [δόξα ἐν ὑψίστοις] to God and peace on earth!" (2:14).[55] The audience, however, can appreciate that God and Jesus are to be praised with joy for bringing about the kingdom of God for the salvation of all people (2:29–32; 3:6) through mighty deeds to be climaxed by the death and resurrection of Jesus.

The Death and Resurrection of Jesus

At the death of Jesus darkness came over the whole land for three hours (23:44), and the veil of the sanctuary in the temple was torn down the middle (23:45). Then in a loud voice Jesus called out in prayer, quoting LXX Ps 30:6, "Father, into your hands I entrust my spirit," and when he said this he

---

Jesus' 'powerful deeds' appear repeatedly in Luke-Acts, and the Evangelist habitually interprets them theocentrically: In them we discern God at work through Jesus, who is thus identified as the divinely authorized and empowered agent of salvation" (Green, *Gospel of Luke*, 686–87).

53. "Jesus anticipates that at some point, Jerusalem *will* truly see Jesus and will offer the very words that appear in the disciples' praise in Lk 19:37–38" (De Long, *Surprised by God*, 231; emphasis original).

54. "Jesus is for the first time rightly acclaimed as 'the king who comes in the name of the Lord,' even though the crowds do not understand—and cannot until the cross—the full meaning of his kingship" (Edwards, *Gospel According to Luke*, 548). "Jesus as the eschatological king . . . brings divine peace and glory from heaven" (Garland, *Luke*, 771).

55. "Whereas in Lk 2:14, divine beings laud God for 'peace on earth,' in Lk 19:38, earthly beings exalt God for 'peace in heaven.' In Luke's hands, the praise as Jesus approaches Jerusalem becomes an earthly counterpart to the heavenly praise of the angels at his birth. This pair of complementary praise responses frames Jesus' life in the Gospel: the first praise response following his birth (angels) and the last praise response (by someone other than Jesus) prior to his death (disciples)" (De Long, *Surprised by God*, 226–27). "This is a foretaste of the peace of the atonement, a proleptic announcement of the peace whose source is Christ's death and resurrection" (Just, *Luke 9:51—24:53*, 748).

expired (23:46). When the centurion saw what had happened, he performed an act of laudatory worship, as he "glorified" (ἐδόξαζεν) God, saying, "Certainly this man was righteous!" (23:47).[56] The centurion thus acknowledged that Jesus died as the suffering "righteous one [δίκαιος]" (cf. LXX Ps 30:19; Acts 3:14; 7:52; 22:14), with full confidence in God.[57] That Jesus was "righteous" means that he died not only innocently but in accord with what God's will commanded for him.[58] The centurion's praise reaffirmed Jesus' previous prayer: "Father, if you are willing, take this cup away from me, yet not my will but yours be done" (22:42). The centurion's laudatory worship invites the audience to join him in glorifying God for Jesus' accomplishment of God's salvific will in and through his death as God's "righteous one."[59]

The risen Jesus told his disciples to stay in Jerusalem, because he is going to send "the promise of my Father upon you," and they will be "clothed with power from on high" (24:49), the Holy Spirit (Acts 1:4–5, 8). He then led them out as far as Bethany, and lifting up his hands, he performed an act of laudatory worship, as he "blessed" (εὐλόγησεν) them (Luke 24:50), implicitly praising God for what he had done for them in raising Jesus from the dead and in anticipation of their being given the Holy Spirit.[60] While he was "blessing" (εὐλογεῖν) them he parted from them and was taken

---

56. "The centurion joins a medley of those who witness God's mighty salvific deeds worked through Jesus and praise God [Luke 2:20; 5:25–26; 7:16; 13:13; 17:15; 18:43]" (Garland, *Luke*, 929). "This praise marks the first positive response to Jesus' death in the narrative, in contrast with the disciples, who remain silent throughout the Passion Narrative. . . . In the praise in the infancy narrative, Simeon anticipates a 'revelation to the gentiles.' Now, in the praise of a gentile centurion—who 'sees' the significance of Jesus' identity in the events surrounding his death—we hear an early note of the fulfillment [of] Simeon's prediction, which will arrive fully in Acts" (De Long, *Surprised by God*, 240–41).

57. "In the psalm Jesus has just uttered in his plea to God, the psalmist identifies himself as 'righteous' (Ps 31:18 [30:19, LXX])" (Garland, *Luke*, 929).

58. That Jesus "certainly" or "really" (ὄντως) was "righteous" aligns him with those who, like Zechariah and Elizabeth, were "righteous" before God, following all the commandments and ordinances of the Lord blamelessly (Luke 1:6), and it differentiates him from those who only think or pretend that they are "righteous" (18:9; 20:20).

59. "Whether or not this gentile centurion had access to all the interpretive clues available to Luke's audience and thus could discern the depth of his own christological statement, it is nevertheless clear that, in his response to Jesus' death, he recognizes the salvific hand of God at work in Jesus" (Green, *Gospel of Luke*, 827).

60. On Luke 24:50–53 as an allusion to Sir 50:20–21, see Hamm, "Tamid Service," 217–20. "Although not a priest and therefore not bestowing a priestly blessing, Jesus nevertheless offers his followers a gesture that brings completion to an intended act of blessing the people that the priest Zechariah was (implicitly) unable to pronounce, after he was rendered speechless by the angel Gabriel (1:21–22)" (Carroll, *Luke*, 495–96).

up into heaven (24:51) by God.⁶¹ After "worshiping" (προσκυνήσαντες) him, the disciples complemented his praise, as they returned to Jerusalem with great joy (24:52), and they were continually in the temple "blessing" (εὐλογοῦντες) God (24:53).⁶² This final, climactic scene of laudatory worship in Luke invites the audience likewise to bless God for exalting Jesus to heaven to be an object of worship and source for the gift of the Holy Spirit to all believers, as promised by John the Baptist (3:16; Acts 2:33).⁶³

Praise to God in Acts

Peter proclaimed to the Jewish people in Jerusalem that although they killed Jesus (Acts 2:23), God raised him from the dead (2:24). He then quoted LXX Ps 15:8–11, as spoken originally by David but now by Jesus (Acts 2:29–31), in which Jesus, in view of his resurrection, performs an act of joyful laudatory worship, when he declares, "My heart has been glad and my tongue rejoiced. . . . You will not abandon my soul to the netherworld, nor permit your holy one to see corruption. . . . You will fill me with gladness in your presence" (LXX Ps 15:9–11 in Acts 2:26–28).⁶⁴ That Jesus' heart has been glad and his tongue "rejoiced" (ἠγαλλιάσατο) in joyful praise of the God who will raise him from the dead complements his previous act of laudatory worship when he "rejoiced" (ἠγαλλιάσατο) in the Holy Spirit and said, "I

---

61. "For Jesus to bless his disciples is for him to bestow upon them a new status. They are now designated as recipients of his grace and eschatological blessings. They are set apart as a worshiping community" (Just, *Luke 9:5—24:53*, 1056).

62. "Following the resurrection, Jesus receives the worship due to God alone, for he is the glorified Son of God. . . . The disciples return to Jerusalem in great joy. Their joy implies a major transition in their understanding of Jesus. His earlier appearances and disappearances evoked confusion and fear (vv. 37–38). The disciples now experience the great joy proclaimed by the angel at Jesus' birth (2:10), for his bodily departure portends their spiritual empowerment from on high (v. 49)" (Edwards, *Gospel According to Luke*, 741–42). The disciples "'bless God'—that is, render to God thankful praise for the manifestation of his salvific purpose" (Green, *Gospel of Luke*, 862). On Luke 24:53, see also Hamm, "Praying," 50–52.

63. "Jesus was for Luke the culmination of Israel's life and worship" (Hamm, "Tamid Service," 220). "The disciples' terror and doubts (24:37) have been replaced by faith that leads to worship. As a divine being, the worship of Jesus is appropriate and praising God is necessary" (Garland, *Luke*, 970). "Luke's final note is that, as the disciples await the arrival of the Father's promise, God is to be praised for his work in Jesus Christ the exalted Lord" (Bock, *Luke 9:51—24:53*, 1946).

64. "Peter's speech links joy in Ps 15 with anticipation of Jesus' resurrection (LXX Ps 15:8–11; Acts 2:25–31). Thus joyful praise by members of the expanding restoration community—which follows shortly thereafter—is presented in the narrative as echoing a prophetic psalm (Acts 2:42–47)" (De Long, *Surprised by God*, 247).

praise you, Father, Lord of heaven and earth" (Luke 10:21). Jesus' laudatory worship invites the audience to join him in joyfully praising God for raising Jesus from the dead to be a source of the divine giving of the Holy Spirit to all believers (Acts 2:33, 38).[65]

Although the angel Gabriel told Zechariah that he will have joy and "gladness" (ἀγαλλίασις), and many will rejoice at the birth of his son John (Luke 1:14), it was the unborn infant John who leaped "in gladness" (ἐν ἀγαλλιάσει) when his mother Elizabeth heard Mary's greeting (1:44), thus adding a note of joy to her laudatory worship (1:42). Similarly, the Christian community in Jerusalem added a note of joy to their prayerful worship (Acts 2:42), as daily they ate their meals "in gladness [ἐν ἀγαλλιάσει]" (2:46).[66] At the birth of Jesus the angels were "praising" (αἰνούντων) God (Luke 2:13) and the shepherds were glorifying and "praising" (αἰνοῦντες) God (2:20). For all the mighty deeds done by Jesus the whole multitude of disciples began "to praise" (αἰνεῖν) God (19:37). Complementing this laudatory worship, the believers in Jerusalem were "praising" (αἰνοῦντες) God (Acts 2:47), implicitly for the gift of the Holy Spirit given them by the risen Jesus (2:1–11, 33). They thus serve as a model for the audience likewise to praise God with joy for their reception of the Holy Spirit through the risen Jesus.[67]

In the name of Jesus Christ, which connotes his power as risen Lord (cf. 4:7, 10), Peter told a lame man at the temple gate (3:2) to rise and walk (3:6). Then taking him by his right hand, he raised him, and immediately his feet and ankles were strengthened (3:7).[68] The man entered the temple,

---

65. "The theme of joy surrounds momentous events in the infancy narrative (Luke 1:14, 44, 47, 58; 2:10); miracle working (10:17; 13:17); suffering in hope of divine vindication (Luke 6:23; Acts 5:41); and celebrating eternal life (Luke 10:20; Acts 8:8, 39; 13:48, 52; 16:34), others' conversions (Luke 15:5–10, 32; Acts 11:21–23; 15:3), and other good news (Acts 12:14; 15:31). It could be empowered by the Holy Spirit (Luke 10:21; Acts 13:52) and is associated with resurrection in Luke 24:41, 52" (Keener, *Acts*, 1.948).

66. "Prayer typifies the Christian community in Acts, which replicates the practice of Jesus" (Holladay, *Acts*, 109). "Their *gladness* was doubtless motivated by more than the provision of daily needs. They were aware that God was at work in their midst in a new way and that they were enjoying the benefits of the messianic salvation" (Peterson, *Acts*, 163; emphasis original).

67. This "group of new believers move from amazement (Acts 2:12) to belief in Jesus' identity by hearing a message about the meaning of Jesus' death, resurrection, and exaltation (2:22–35). In response, they share food joyously and constantly voice praise, both in the temple and at home (2:46). The narrative depicts this praise as growing each day (2:47)" (De Long, *Surprised by God*, 247). "Luke affirms the internal fellowship, intimacy, and engagement of the community. This positive activity is accompanied by joy and glad hearts, and their worship and praise of God are ongoing" (Bock, *Acts*, 154).

68. That Peter took the man by his "right" (δεξιᾶς) hand when he raised him (3:7)

performing an act of laudatory worship, as he was walking and leaping and "praising" (αἰνῶν) God (3:8). All the people saw him "praising" (αἰνοῦντα) God (3:9).[69] That Peter "raised" (ἤγειρεν) the lame man carries a double meaning for the audience. The man was not only healed but was "saved [σέσωται]" (4:9), implying his eschatological salvation (2:21, 40, 47; 4:12), in the name of Jesus Christ, whom God "raised" (ἤγειρεν) from the dead (3:15; 4:10), establishing the hope for resurrection from the dead (4:2; cf. 23:6; 24:15; 26:6–8; 28:20).[70] That Peter "raised" the lame man thus points to his future participation in the resurrection of the dead. The laudatory worship of the "raised" lame man (3:6–8) invites the audience to join him in praising God not only for his healing but for the salvific hope of being raised from the dead.

"All the people" who saw the "raised" lame man walking and "praising" (αἰνοῦντα) God (3:9), complemented his laudatory worship, as they appropriately "glorified" (ἐδόξαζον) God (4:21), who "glorified" (ἐδόξασεν) Jesus (3:13) by raising him from the dead (3:15), for the man on whom this sign of healing had been done was over forty years old (4:22).[71] The healing of the lame man was thus considered a "sign" (cf. 4:16), which indicated to "all the people" that it was in the name of the risen Jesus Christ that the man was healed (4:10). It also pointed to and established a hope for an eschatological salvation that goes beyond this healing, as to "the people" the

resonates with what Jesus declared as the speaker of LXX Ps 15:8–11 in Acts 2:25: "I saw the Lord ever before me, for he is at my "right" [δεξιῶν]," which gave Jesus the hope of being raised from the dead (2:26–32).

69. "Luke describes the complete cure of the beggar and his consequent reaction in almost the same way that Isaiah once proclaimed the restoration of Zion: 'Then shall the lame one leap like a deer' (Isa 35:6). The allusion to Isaiah makes it clear that Luke sees this miracle as a fulfillment of the prophet's utterance, an event of salvation history" (Fitzmyer, *Acts*, 279). "By repetition and visual detail, the narrator amplifies the individual praise response in this story; the reader is meant not to miss it" (De Long, *Surprised by God*, 193). See also Hamm, "Acts 3:1–10," 305–19.

70. "The perfect passive verb 'was healed' (σέσωται), which describes a continuous state of affairs, can be understood in the sense of being cured from an illness, but it can also be understood in the sense of being saved from eternal death or, positively, of receiving messianic salvation" (Schnabel, *Acts*, 238).

71. "Luke as narrator calls the result 'this sign of healing' (τὸ σημεῖον τοῦτο τῆς ἰάσεως) from God. The phrase appears emphatically at the end of the verse in Greek and is combined with the pluperfect γεγόνει to highlight the abiding result" (Bock, *Acts*, 199). "The genitive 'of healing' (ἰάσεως) is epexegetical: the healing was a 'sign' (σημεῖον) of the reality of the power of Jesus, who was crucified but who had been raised from the dead" (Schnabel, *Acts*, 247). "That the man disabled from birth (3:2) was more than forty (4:22) heightens the magnitude of the miracle, eliciting the crowd's praise. His disability had been neither temporary nor partial and was widely known (3:10), and thus the healing was impossible to deny" (Keener, *Acts*, 2.1163–64).

apostles were proclaiming in Jesus the resurrection of the dead (4:2).[72] The laudatory worship of the "raised" lame man as well as that of all the people invite the audience to join them in praising and glorifying God not only for the continuing healing activity of the risen Jesus, but for the hope of a future resurrection from the dead for all people, based on the resurrection of Jesus from the dead.

Peter's speech to the God-fearing gentile centurion, Cornelius (10:1–2), and those gentiles gathered in his house (10:24, 27), emphasized the resurrection of Jesus: "This man [Jesus] God raised on the third day and granted that he be visible to us . . . who ate and drank with him after he rose from the dead. . . . The one appointed by God as judge of the living and the dead" (10:40–42). While Peter was speaking, the Holy Spirit came down on all listening to the word (10:44). The circumcised believers who had accompanied Peter were amazed that even upon the gentiles the gift of the Holy Spirit had been poured out (10:45). They heard them performing an act of laudatory worship, as they were "magnifying" (μεγαλυνόντων) God (10:46).[73] Their praise of God for being given the Holy Spirit by the risen Jesus (2:33) complements that of Mary, who was to give birth to Jesus by the Holy Spirit (Luke 1:35), and declared that her soul "magnifies" (μεγαλύνει) the Lord (1:46).[74] This laudatory worship invites the audience to praise God for the gift of the Holy Spirit even to gentiles and thus to all peoples.

After "those of the circumcision," Jewish Christians, criticized Peter for eating with uncircumcised people (Acts 11:2–3; cf. 10:1–48), he explained to them how the Holy Spirit came down on these uncircumcised people just as it had on the circumcised in the beginning (11:15; cf. 1:8; 2:1–4), and he thus could not hinder God (11:17). When they heard this, they performed an act of laudatory worship, as they "glorified" (ἐδόξασαν) God, saying, "Then even to the gentiles God has given the repentance that leads to life!" (11:18).[75] They complemented all the people who "glorified"

---

72. "[I]t is clear from the context that the lame man is a symbol of hope for Israel as a whole" (Peterson, *Acts*, 196).

73. "Like the praise of healed people in Luke-Acts, the praise of the gentiles responds directly to their experience of divinely-empowered transformation, indicating their salvation by God and receipt of the Holy Spirit" (De Long, *Surprised by God*, 253).

74. "Praise of God is the purpose for which they are endowed with the Spirit" (Fitzmyer, *Acts*, 467). "In the context of Peter's sermon, the praise directed to God would have acknowledged and celebrated God's mighty acts in Jesus' ministry (vv. 36–39), Jesus' death and resurrection (vv. 39–41), the possibility of salvation through Jesus, and the reality of the divine forgiveness of sins and justification in view of the day of judgment (vv. 42–43)—available not only to Jews but to people in every nation who fear God (v. 35) and believe in Jesus (v. 43)" (Schnabel, *Acts*, 505).

75. "Those of the circumcision party in Jerusalem accept the salvation of the gentiles

(ἐδόξαζον) God for the healing of a Jewish lame man (4:21), and the Spirit-given gentiles who "magnified" God (10:46).⁷⁶ God exalted Jesus to his right hand to give "repentance" not only to Israel (5:31) but even to the gentiles.⁷⁷ They were given the repentance that leads to "life," the eternal "life" that follows upon resurrection from the dead (2:27–28; 13:46, 48). This laudatory worship invites the audience to glorify God for giving the repentance that leads to eternal life to all peoples, based on Jesus' resurrection to eternal life.⁷⁸

In his sermon on a Sabbath in the synagogue in Pisidian Antioch (13:14), Paul emphasized God's gift of eternal life in raising Jesus from the dead: "God raised him from the dead . . . raising up Jesus . . . and he raised him from the dead never to return to corruption. . . . The one God raised up did not see corruption" (13:30, 33, 34, 37). But on the following Sabbath the Jews contradicted Paul (13:44–45). Since the Jews rejected the word of God and condemned themselves as unworthy of eternal life, Paul and Barnabas will now turn to the gentiles (13:46). The gentiles responded with an act of laudatory worship, as they rejoiced and "glorified" (ἐδόξαζον) the word of the Lord, and all who had been appointed for eternal life believed (13:48).⁷⁹ The gentiles in Pisidian Antioch thus complemented the Jews in Jerusalem who also "glorified" (ἐδόξασαν) God for giving the repentance that leads to eternal life even to the gentiles (11:18). This reinforces how the audience

---

in Caesarea as the work of God and—like the witnesses in the healing stories—they signal their acceptance of this new moment in the process of divine salvation through praise" (De Long, *Surprised by God*, 255–56).

76. "Luke likes to recount people's recognition of God's works and hence that, as here they 'glorified' God (Luke 2:20; 5:25–26; 7:16; 13:13; 17:15; 18:43; 23:47; Acts 13:48; 21:20; cf. 4:15)" (Keener, *Acts*, 2.1827–28).

77. "Reference to *the gentiles*, rather than simply to Cornelius and his household, indicates that the wider implications of this event have been clearly understood" (Peterson, *Acts*, 349–50; emphasis original).

78. "'Life' is shorthand for 'eternal life' (Luke 10:25; 18:18, 30; Acts 13:46, 48; in the shorthand form, see Acts 5:20; cf. 2:28; 3:15). . . . The vast majority of its occurrences are in Jewish sources, beginning with Dan 12:2, where it refers to the life inherited at the resurrection of the dead; at that time the righteous would be 'raised up to eternal life'" (Keener, *Acts*, 2.1828–29).

79. "This instance of the praise motif combines joy with praise of the 'word of the Lord' . . . unique as the object of a praise verb in Luke-Acts. . . . It praises God for what God has *done*. . . . The gentiles glorify God (implicitly) because God is the source of the saving word . . . leading to eternal life" (De Long, *Surprised by God*, 257–58; emphasis original). "The Jews 'rejected the word of God' and judged themselves 'unfit for eternal life'; in contrast, the gentiles show that they are destined for eternal life by 'glorifying' this same 'word of the Lord'" (Johnson, *Acts*, 242).

likewise may glorify God with joy for his word about the eternal life granted to all who believe in the risen Jesus.

The Roman jailer in Philippi, a pagan rather than God-fearing gentile, "rejoiced" (ἠγαλλιάσατο) that he had come to believe in God together with his whole household (16:34). He thus performed an act of implicit laudatory worship, joyfully praising God for the gift of faith by which he and his household received the eschatological salvation (16:30–32) that includes eternal life for believers (13:48). His implicit laudatory worship echoes that of Jesus as the speaker of LXX Ps 15:8–11, who declared to God his praise in hope of being raised from the dead to eternal life: "My heart was glad and my tongue rejoiced [ἠγαλλιάσατο], my flesh too will dwell in hope, because you will not abandon my soul to the netherworld, nor will you permit your holy one to see corruption. You have made known to me the paths of life, you will make me full of gladness with your presence" (Acts 2:26–28; cf. Luke 10:21).[80] The gentile jailer's laudatory worship invites the audience of believers to join him in joyfully praising God for the gift of faith that brings salvation to eternal life based on Jesus' resurrection from the dead.[81]

When Paul returned to Jerusalem (Acts 21:17), he visited James with all the elders of the Jerusalem church present (21:18). After greeting them, he reported in detail what God had done among the gentiles through his ministry (21:19). When they heard this, they performed an act of laudatory worship, as they "glorified" (ἐδόξαζον) God (21:20), bringing to a climax all of the previous instances in Luke-Acts of "glorifying" God (Luke 2:20; 5:25–26; 7:16; 13:13; 17:15; 18:43; 23:47; Acts 4:21; 11:18; 13:48). They thus complemented the laudatory worship of the gentiles in Pisidian Antioch who "glorified" (ἐδόξαζον) God and believed, demonstrating their worthiness to receive salvation to eternal life (13:48; cf. 13:46–47). They also complemented the laudatory worship of the Jewish Christians in Jerusalem who "glorified" (ἐδόξασαν) God for what he had done through the ministry of Peter in granting the repentance that leads to eternal life even to the gentiles (11:18).[82] This laudatory worship invites the audience to likewise

---

80. "The verb ἀγαλλιάω ('rejoice') is used by Luke for specifically religious responses to God's visitation (Luke 1:47; 10:21; Acts 2:26)" (Johnson, *Acts*, 301). "That the jailer 'rejoiced' fits a Lukan motif for a response to God's works, including conversion, both for those receiving it (Luke 8:13; Acts 8:39; cf. Acts 8:8; Luke 10:20) and for those learning of it (Luke 15:5–10, 32; Acts 11:23; 15:3)" (Keener, *Acts*, 3.2514).

81. "Joy is a sign of the presence of both salvation and faith. Faith in Jesus, the Lord who saves, triggers joy at the presence of the Lord" (Schnabel, *Acts*, 693). "Belief in the Lord Jesus Christ (v. 31) is equated with belief in the one true God (v. 34)" (Peterson, *Acts*, 470).

82. "Finally, the praise of the saved gentiles in Pisidian Antioch is echoed by the important witnesses of the Jerusalem leadership, who—as in Acts 11 and in the healing

glorify God for giving Jews as well as gentiles the faith that brings believers salvation to eternal life.

When Paul finally arrived in Rome (28:14), completing his divinely appointed ministry (19:21; 23:11), "the brothers," that is, fellow Christian believers, came out to meet him and his companions, which prompted Paul to perform the final, climactic act of laudatory worship in Luke-Acts, as he "gave thanks" (εὐχαριστήσας) to God and took courage (28:15).[83] Paul then met with the leaders of the Jews (28:17) and told them that he has arrived in Rome as a prisoner on account of the "hope of Israel" (28:20), that is, the hope for the resurrection from the dead (23:6; 24:15; 26:6–7), and thus for salvation to eternal life (13:46–48), based on Jesus' resurrection from the dead. While Paul's preaching about Jesus (28:23) persuaded some Jews, others did not believe (28:24), and so Paul declared that this salvation of God has been sent to the gentiles, and they will listen (28:28). Paul's climactic act of laudatory worship invites the audience to likewise give thanks to God not only for those among Jews as well as gentiles who have already become believers but for all those who are yet to listen and believe.[84]

Summary

Zechariah's joyful hymn of laudatory worship addressed to God (Luke 1:68–79) speaks not only for himself but for and to the audience of believers as the people of God. It abounds with references to "people," "we," "us," and "our." It invites the audience to join Zechariah in joyfully praising God not only for the birth of his son John but for the salvation God has brought to us in raising up Jesus to be born as the Davidic messiah and in raising Jesus from the dead for our salvation from the shadow of death (1:79).

When Zechariah's wife Elizabeth gave birth to John (1:57), her neighbors and relatives heard that the Lord had magnified his mercy toward her,

---

miracle stories—validate Paul's ministry and demonstrate their recognition and acceptance of the divine visitation to the gentile people who have responded to his message. Praise then opens and closes Paul's ministry to the gentiles, just as praise opened and closed Jesus' healing ministry" (De Long, *Surprised by God*, 264).

83. "The delegation's coming to meet him relieved any concerns of Paul's that Christians might avoid him because of his chains, a mark of shame" (Keener, *Acts*, 4.3711). A discussion of the occurrences of the verb "to give thanks" (εὐχαριστέω) in Luke 22:17, 19 and Acts 27:35 will be included as part of the ritual worship in the chapter on Meals and the Eucharist below (ch. 7).

84. "At the end of Acts, Paul arrives in Rome to find that there are believers already there, which elicits his praise of God.... In this way, the two-volume work frames the entire story (from Jerusalem to Rome) with expressions of praise" (De Long, *Surprised by God*, 265).

and they "rejoiced with" her (1:58), fulfilling Gabriel's promise that many "will rejoice" at the birth of John (1:14). This invites the audience likewise to join Elizabeth in her joyful praise of God not only for the birth of John but for blessing Mary in becoming the mother of the divine "Lord" Jesus (1:42–43).

Before the angel Gabriel informed Mary that she is to give birth to a son whom she will name Jesus (1:31), he greeted her with an exhortation: "Rejoice, favored one, the Lord is with you!" (1:28). After Elizabeth declared Mary "blessed" for believing that what the Lord spoke to her would be fulfilled (1:45), Mary responded to her and to Gabriel's exhortation to rejoice with a hymnic act of laudatory worship: "My soul magnifies the Lord, and my spirit rejoices in God my savior" (1:46–47). She praised God for looking upon her "lowliness" (1:48a), as an instance of how God has exalted the "lowly" (1:52). From now on not only Elizabeth but all generations "will call blessed" Mary (1:48b). In Mary God has helped the people of Israel, remembering his "mercy" (1:54), the "mercy" that is from generations to generations for those who revere him (1:50). Mary's hymn invites the audience to revere God by joining her in joyfully praising God by calling her blessed to be the mother of Jesus, the holy Son of God (1:35).

When the angel of the Lord appeared to the shepherds (2:9), he proclaimed to them good news of great joy that will be for all the people (2:10), because in the city of David a savior has been born for them who is Christ the Lord (2:11; cf. 1:43). Then suddenly with the angel there was a multitude of heavenly hosts "praising" God (2:13) with an act of laudatory worship: "Glory to God in the highest and on earth peace among people with whom he is pleased!" (2:14). After the shepherds saw Mary and Joseph and the infant lying in the manger (2:16), and made known the message told them about the child (2:17), they returned and joined the angels in their laudatory worship, as they were "glorifying" and "praising" God (2:20). The laudatory worship by the angels and the shepherds invites the audience to join them in joyfully praising and glorifying God for the "peace" that will result from the birth of a savior, Christ the Lord, who will guide those who sit in the shadow of death into the way of "peace" (1:79).

Simeon's exuberant laudatory worship (2:28–34) invites the audience to join him in blessing and praising God not only for the birth but for the resurrection of Jesus from the dead. Like Simeon, each member of the audience can face his or her inevitable death in peace, consoled by the hope of being raised from death because of the resurrection of Jesus from the dead. They can join Simeon in blessing and praising God for the birth and resurrection of Jesus, as the embodiment of salvation for all peoples (2:30–31), who sit in the darkness and shadow of death (1:79). As salvation personified, Jesus represents the light that reveals resurrection from death to the gentiles and the glory that fulfills the hope of the people of Israel for resurrection from the dead (2:32; cf. Acts 22:11; 26:23).

The prophetess and elderly widow Anna from one of the twelve tribes of Israel (Luke 2:36) never left the temple, with prayer and fasting "worshiping night and day" (2:37). She exemplifies how the twelve tribes "night and day worship" in hope of attaining the promise of the resurrection of the dead (Acts 26:7; cf. 23:6; 24:15; 28:20). Coming forward at that very hour, she performed an act of laudatory worship, as she "thanked" God and spoke about Jesus to all who were awaiting the "redemption" of Jerusalem (Luke 2:38). This alludes to the hope for the resurrection, as it recalls Zechariah's praise of God, who brought "redemption" for his people (1:68) when he "raised" up Jesus in birth and death (1:69). Anna's praise invites the audience to join her in thanking God for the birth of Jesus, which will lead to their redemption from death.

After the young Jesus was found in the temple, he told Mary that it was divinely "necessary" that he be "in the things of his Father" (2:49). This foreshadows that according to his Father's will it is "necessary" for him to undergo suffering and death before being raised from the dead (9:22; 17:25; 24:7, 26, 44). Mary again kept all these things in her heart (2:51; cf. 2:19). Mary thus indicates to the audience how their joyful laudatory worship is to include the praise of God not only for the birth but for the resurrection of Jesus, as they keep in their hearts the divine necessity for Jesus' suffering, death, and resurrection.

When Jesus was teaching in the synagogues of Galilee (4:14), he became an object of laudatory worship, as he was being "glorified" by all (4:15). But when in Nazareth he insinuated that they were going to reject him as a prophet in his native place (4:24), they attempted to kill him (4:29), but he escaped (4:30). This foreshadows the eventual death of Jesus as a prophet in accord with God's scriptural plan (13:33). It underscores for the audience how Jesus is worthy of being glorified in laudatory worship not only for his teaching but for his fulfillment of the divine necessity that he be killed by his people before being raised from the dead.

Jesus pronounced the forgiveness of sins (5:20) and the healing of a paralytic (5:24), who then performed an act of laudatory worship as he was "glorifying" God (5:25). Then astonishment seized all who witnessed this, and they too "glorified" God (5:26). This scene invites the members of the audience likewise to join the paralytic in this communal glorifying of God for giving Jesus the divine authority not only to heal diseases but to forgive sins, so that they may experience divine salvation "through the forgiveness of their sins" (1:77).

After Jesus raised from death the only son of a widow at Nain (7:11–15), those who witnessed it performed an act of laudatory worship as they "glorified" God, saying, "A great prophet has been raised among us!" and "God has visited his people!" (7:16). This recalls Zechariah's hymnic laudatory worship when he blessed the Lord the God of Israel "for he has visited and brought redemption to his people; he has raised up a horn of salvation for us in the house of David his servant" (1:68–69). The audience can again appreciate the double meaning. The great prophet Jesus "has been raised" among us by being born and by being raised from the dead. The Jesus who told the dead young man to "be raised" will himself be raised by God to eternal life. This scene invites the audience likewise to glorify God for "raising up" Jesus for our eschatological salvation.

Jesus performed an act of laudatory worship when he "rejoiced" in the Holy Spirit and said, "I praise you, Father, Lord of heaven and earth, because you have hidden these things from the wise and intelligent and revealed them to the childlike. Yes, Father, for thus has been your good pleasure" (10:21). He then proclaimed that all things have been handed over to him by his Father (cf. 4:6; 10:18), and no one knows who the Son is except the Father, and who the Father is except the Son and anyone to whom the Son wishes to reveal him (10:22). The members of the audience are to identify with the childlike disciples to whom Jesus has revealed the Father and the knowledge of the mysteries of the Kingdom of God (10:23; cf. 8:10). They are invited to join Jesus in praising his Father for revealing him as the Son, an agent of divine revelation, and thus worthy to be an object of laudatory worship as the divine Son of his divine Father.

After Jesus healed a severely crippled woman in a synagogue on the Sabbath (13:10–12), she performed an act of laudatory worship as she "glorified" God (13:13). When the leader of the synagogue objected to this being done on the Sabbath (13:14), the "Lord" Jesus, as "Lord" of the Sabbath (6:5), declared that it was divinely "necessary" for this "daughter of Abraham," a representative of the people of Israel, to be freed from this bondage on the day of the Sabbath (13:16). When he said this, all the crowd complemented the woman's laudatory worship as they "rejoiced" at all the "glorious" things done by him (13:17), implying that he, like God, is worthy to be glorified. This scene invites the audience to join the healed woman and all the crowd in glorifying not only God but the divine Lord Jesus for not only healing this woman on the Sabbath but for all of the glorious things done by him for the salvation of his people.

A Samaritan leper, healed by Jesus, began to perform an act of laudatory worship, with a loud voice "glorifying" God (17:15). He then fell upon his face at the feet of Jesus in a posture for worship, "thanking" him (17:16).

Jesus pointed out that although ten were cleansed (17:17) none but this foreigner has returned to give "glory" to God (17:18). In thanking Jesus the Samaritan leper gave glory to God, continuing the implication that God is uniquely at work in Jesus so that both are worthy objects of laudatory worship. Jesus dismissed the Samaritan with the words, "Your faith has saved you" (17:19), indicating that his faith has not only brought him healing but eschatological salvation. The healed Samaritan leper serves as a model for all people, no matter their ethnic origin, to have the faith to give glory to God by thanking Jesus for his divine authority not only to heal but to bring them eschatological salvation.

Jesus answered the prayer of the blind beggar at Jericho to regain his sight (18:35–41) with the words, "Have sight; your faith has saved you" (18:42), affirming not only his healing but his eschatological salvation. He then followed Jesus, performing an act of laudatory worship, as he was "glorifying" God, and when all the people saw it, they "gave praise" to God (18:43). In contrast to the Twelve, who did not understand/see that Jesus was going up to Jerusalem to suffer, be killed, and raised (18:31–34), the beggar was given the sight and insight to follow Jesus, and thus to deny himself and take up his cross (9:23). This laudatory worship by the beggar and all the people invites the audience to have the faith likewise to glorify and praise God for the insight to follow God's agent, Jesus, and receive eschatological salvation.

When Jesus, mounted on a colt (19:35), was approaching the slope of the Mount of Olives, the whole multitude of the disciples, "rejoicing," began to "praise" God with a loud voice for all the "mighty deeds" they had seen (19:37). The whole multitude of disciples thus performed an act of joyful laudatory worship, as they climactically praised God for all the mighty deeds of Jesus' ministry. This leads the audience to likewise praise God joyfully for all of the mighty acts God has enabled Jesus to perform for their salvation.

Before his death Jesus called out in prayer, quoting LXX Ps 30:6, "Father, into your hands I entrust my spirit" (23:46). The centurion who saw this performed an act of laudatory worship, as he "glorified" God, saying, "Certainly this man was righteous!" (23:47). The centurion thus acknowledged that Jesus died as the suffering "righteous one" (cf. LXX Ps 30:19; Acts 3:14; 7:52; 22:14), with full confidence in God. That Jesus was "righteous" means that he died not only innocently but in accord with what God's will commanded for him. The centurion's laudatory worship invites the audience to join him in glorifying God for Jesus' accomplishment of God's salvific will in and through his death as God's "righteous one."

The risen Jesus led his disciples out as far as Bethany, and lifting up his hands, he performed an act of laudatory worship, as he "blessed" them

(Luke 24:50), implicitly praising God for what he had done for them in raising Jesus from the dead and in anticipation of their being given the Holy Spirit (24:49; Acts 1:4-5, 8). While he was "blessing" them he parted from them and was taken up into heaven (Luke 24:51) by God. After "worshiping" him, the disciples complemented his praise, as they returned to Jerusalem with great joy (24:52), and they were continually in the temple "blessing" God (24:53). This final, climactic scene of laudatory worship in Luke invites the audience likewise to bless God for exalting Jesus to heaven to be an object of worship and source for the gift of the Holy Spirit to all believers, as promised by John the Baptist (3:16; Acts 2:33).

"All the people" who saw the lame man, whom Peter had "raised" up (Acts 3:7), "praising" God (3:9), complemented his laudatory worship, as they appropriately "glorified" God (4:21), who "glorified" Jesus (3:13) by raising him from the dead (3:15). The healing of the lame man was considered a "sign" (4:22; cf. 4:16), which indicated to "all the people" that it was in the name of the risen Jesus Christ that the man was healed (4:10). It also pointed to and established a hope for an eschatological salvation that goes beyond this healing, as to "the people" the apostles were proclaiming in Jesus the resurrection of the dead (4:2). The laudatory worship of the "raised" lame man as well as that of all the people invite the audience to join them in praising and glorifying God not only for the continuing healing activity of the risen Jesus, but for the hope of a future resurrection from the dead for all people, based on the resurrection of Jesus from the dead.

After Jewish Christians criticized Peter for eating with gentiles (Acts 11:2-3; cf. 10:1-48), he explained to them how the Holy Spirit came down on these gentiles just as it had on the Jews in the beginning (11:15; cf. 1:8; 2:1-4). When they heard this, they performed an act of laudatory worship, as they "glorified" God, saying, "Then even to the gentiles God has given the repentance that leads to life!" (11:18). This laudatory worship invites the audience to glorify God for giving the repentance that leads to eternal life to all peoples.

In his sermon on a Sabbath in the synagogue in Pisidian Antioch (13:14), Paul emphasized God's gift of eternal life in raising Jesus from the dead (13:30, 33, 34, 37). But on the following Sabbath the Jews contradicted Paul (13:44-45). Since the Jews rejected the word of God and condemned themselves as unworthy of eternal life, Paul and Barnabas will now turn to the gentiles (13:46). The gentiles responded with an act of laudatory worship, as they rejoiced and "glorified" the word of the Lord, and all who had been appointed for eternal life believed (13:48). This reinforces how the audience likewise may glorify God with joy for his word about the eternal life granted to all who believe in the risen Jesus.

Laudatory Worship

Paul reported to James and the elders of the Jerusalem church what God had done among the gentiles through his ministry (21:17–19). When they heard this, they performed an act of laudatory worship, as they "glorified" God (21:20), bringing to a climax all of the previous instances in Luke-Acts of "glorifying" God. This laudatory worship invites the audience to likewise glorify God for giving Jews as well as gentiles the faith that brings believers salvation to eternal life.

When Paul was met by fellow Christian believers from Rome, he performed the final, climactic act of laudatory worship in Luke-Acts, as he "gave thanks" to God and took courage (28:15). After Paul met with the leaders of the Jews (28:17), some were persuaded, but others did not believe (28:24), and so Paul declared that this salvation of God has been sent to the gentiles, and they will listen (28:28). Paul's climactic act of laudatory worship invites the audience to likewise give thanks to God not only for those among Jews as well as gentiles who have already become believers but for all those who are yet to listen and believe.

6

Baptismal Worship

The verb "baptize" (βαπτίζω) in general means to wash ritually or ceremonially for the purpose of purification.[1] More specifically, the verb and noun "baptism" (βάπτισμα) refers to a ritual form of worship that involves the ceremonial use of water for the purpose of renewing or establishing a relationship with God.[2] In the Gospel of Luke, John proclaimed and performed a baptism that included repentance for the forgiveness of sins (3:3).[3] Jesus underwent John's baptism with the result of receiving the Holy Spirit (3:21–22), which would enable him to baptize with the Holy Spirit, as promised by John (3:16; cf. Acts 1:5; 2:33).[4] The baptism of John and of Jesus laid the foundation for the sacrament of baptism, which initiated people into the Christian community and empowered them to become witnesses of the risen Lord Jesus (Luke 24:46–48; Acts 1:8). The incidents in Luke-Acts involving the ritual worship of baptism have noteworthy ramifications for

---

1. BDAG, 164.

2. BDAG, 165.

3. "John may have taken two ideas from the OT: the idea of ethical purification under the image of purification with water (Isa 1:16ff) and the expectation that God himself will execute the great purification in the end time (Ezek 36:25; Zech 13:1). John connects these two ideas and puts them to use in the urgent appeal to adapt one's life toward the Messiah's work of judgment and purification in the renunciation of sin and reorientation toward God in ethical reform" (Bieder, "βαπτίζω," 193). "The necessity for repentance and forgiveness of sins (inward cleansing) in order to make ritual immersion (outer cleansing) effective would have distinguished John's baptism from other kinds of immersion practiced by 1st cent. Jews" (Taylor, "Baptism," 391–92).

4. "John's baptism is a prophetic eschatological washing; that is, it is a baptism of promise that looks to the greater baptism of the Spirit" (Bock, *Luke 1:1—9:50*, 289).

the audience composed of those already instructed and implicitly baptized and of those who may be preparing to be baptized (Luke 1:3–4).

Baptism in Luke

John, the son of Zechariah (3:2), went into all the region around the Jordan, proclaiming a "baptism of repentance for the forgiveness of sins" (3:3).[5] This begins to fulfill the prophecy of Zechariah that John would give knowledge of salvation to his people through the "forgiveness of their sins" (1:77). In accord with the words of the prophet Isaiah (LXX Isa 40:3–5), John was crying out for his people to "prepare the way of the Lord" (Luke 3:4), and all flesh will see the "salvation" (σωτήριον) of God (3:6). John's preaching of a baptism of repentance thus fulfills the prophecy of Zechariah that John would "go before the Lord to prepare his ways" (1:76) and of the angel Gabriel that he would "prepare a people fit for the Lord" (1:17). It resonates with and reinforces Simeon's blessing of God (2:28) when he declared, after seeing the infant Jesus, that "my eyes have seen your salvation [σωτήριον], which you prepared in the presence of all peoples, a light for revelation to the gentiles and for glory of your people Israel" (2:30–32).[6] The goal of John's baptism of repentance is the salvation of all peoples through the person of Jesus.[7]

John exhorted the crowds who came out to be baptized by him (3:7) to "produce good fruits" as evidence of their repentance (3:8), otherwise they will be "cut down and thrown into the fire" at God's final judgment (3:9). After the crowds asked what they should do (3:10), John told them that "whoever has two tunics should share with the one having none, and whoever has food should do likewise" (3:11).[8] This indicates to the audi-

---

5. "Repentance [μετάνοια] throughout Luke-Acts embraces a comprehensive spiritual change that includes sorrow for sin and conversion to a new way of life in Christ. Thus far more is involved than the 'change of mind' suggested by the etymology of the words" (Just, *Luke 1:1—9:50*, 149n5).

6. That the form σωτήριον for "salvation" occurs in Luke only in 2:30 and 3:6 enhances this connection. "The word for 'salvation,' σωτήριον, the same word used in Simeon's prophecy (2:30) and Acts 28:28, is an inclusion of Luke's two-volume work" (Edwards, *Gospel According to Luke*, 109).

7. "John's ministry may be more narrowly directed to Israel (cf. 1:16; 3:3), but it is part of God's larger project of bringing redemption to all humanity" (Green, *Gospel of Luke*, 172).

8. A tunic [χιτών] was "worn either against the bare skin or over a linen shirt . . . was made of linen or wool, reached to the ankles or knees, had long or half-sleeves, and was worn by both rich and poor" (Rebell, "χιτών," 468). "Here χιτών and βρώματα [food] stand as examples for the basic needs of human existence" (Wolter, *Gospel According to Luke*, 165).

ence that Christian baptism, prefigured by and built upon the foundation of John's baptism of repentance, is a form of ritual worship that includes an ethical dimension. All baptized Christians should complete and live out their ritual reception of the sacrament of baptism with their corresponding ethical behavior, demonstrating their repentance and transformed life with an active care and concern for the poor and less fortunate among them.

After "tax collectors" (τελῶναι), those engaged in a profession notorious for unfair practices and greediness, who came to be baptized by John asked him what they should do (3:12), he notably did not tell them to quit their questionable profession.[9] Rather, they are to be honest tax collectors who do not collect more than what is prescribed (3:13). And, similarly, after "soldiers" (στρατευόμενοι), most likely those serving in the military under the regime of Herod Antipas, the tetrarch of Galilee, asked what they should do, John did not tell them to quit their questionable profession.[10] Rather, they are not to practice extortion or falsely accuse anyone, and they should be satisfied with their wages (3:14). These examples remind the audience that baptized Christians, whatever their profession or way of life, need to live out their sacramental baptism with upright ethical practices to complement their ritual worship with ethical worship. They are to be honest in their dealings with others and not use others to advance and satisfy their own greediness.[11]

To all the people who were wondering whether John might be the Christ (3:15), John said, "I am baptizing you with water, but one more powerful than I is coming; I am not worthy to loosen the strap of his sandals;

---

9. "The prevailing system of tax collection afforded a collector many opportunities to exercise greed and unfairness. Hence tax collectors were particularly hated and despised as a class. . . . A strict Israelite was further offended by the fact that tax-collectors had to maintain continual contact with non-Israelites in the course of their work; this rendered an Israelite tax-collector ceremonially unclean" (BDAG, 999). See also Seo, *Luke's Jesus*, 68–72.

10. "Roman legions were not stationed in Palestine in the first century, and Palestinian Jews were exempt from serving in the Roman army. The 'soldiers' in v. 14 therefore may have been enlisted Jews in the service of Herod Antipas rather than Roman soldiers. This may be the reason why 'soldiers' (v. 14) is a Greek participle (στρατευόμενοι), meaning 'those in service,' rather than the noun στρατιῶται, which connoted '(Roman) soldiers'" (Edwards, *Gospel According to Luke*, 112). "The soldiers are assumed to belong to the corrupt system that tyrannized the people rather than fighting to defend them. With their weaponry and authority they could bully others and confiscate property to supplement their meager provisions or salaries" (Garland, *Luke*, 158).

11. "John's response to the three groups says to be compassionate, loving, and fair to fellow human beings and not to take advantage of another or leave another in destitution for one's own gain. Rather, one is to be content with what one has. Look to meet needs rather than to aggravate them" (Bock, *Luke 1:1—9:50*, 314).

he will baptize you with the Holy Spirit and fire" (3:16). After all the people were baptized and Jesus was baptized and praying, the heaven opened and the Holy Spirit descended upon him in bodily form like a dove, and a voice came from heaven: "You are my beloved Son; with you I am well pleased" (3:21–22). This indicates the transition from John's baptism of repentance to the baptism of Jesus, the Son of God, with the Holy Spirit.[12] Later, Jesus declared that "I have a baptism with which I am to be baptized, and how distressed I am until it is accomplished" (12:50). This metaphorical "baptism" refers to his divinely determined death before being raised (9:22).[13] It reminds the audience that Christian baptism with the Holy Spirit includes participation in the metaphorical baptism of Jesus by taking up the cross daily and following Jesus with a willingness to lose one's life in order to save it (9:23–24).[14]

Baptism in Acts

Before his ascension to heaven, the risen Jesus told his apostles (Acts 1:2) to wait for the "promise of the Father" (1:4), that is, being clothed with the Holy Spirit as a "power from on high" (Luke 24:49). John baptized with water, but in a few days they will be baptized with the Holy Spirit (Acts 1:5).[15] After his ascension, as they were gathered together on the day of Pentecost (2:1), suddenly there came from heaven a noise like a strong driving wind, and it filled the entire house where they were sitting (2:2). And tongues spreading out like fire appeared to them and came to rest on each one of them (2:3). All were filled with the Holy Spirit and began to speak in different tongues as the Spirit enabled them to speak out (2:4). Each of the Jewish pilgrims who had come to Jerusalem for the feast (2:5, 9–10) heard them speaking

---

12. "John's prediction that Jesus will baptize with the Holy Spirit (3:16) will be fulfilled after that Spirit is first poured forth upon Jesus" (Just, *Luke 1:1—9:50*, 159).

13. "Baptism" in Luke 12:50 "connotes a future occurrence, no longer an initiatory rite (so 3:21–22), but rather Jesus' death, which Luke also refers to as 'exodus' (9:31) or 'completion' in Jerusalem (18:31!). The use of 'baptism' as a metaphor of Jesus' impending death is evidence that he foresaw both his death in Jerusalem and its atoning significance" (Edwards, *Gospel According to Luke*, 384).

14. "Three baptisms are referred to in Luke's gospel: the baptism of John (3:3, 7, 12, 16; 7:29–30; 20:4), the baptism of Jesus by John (3:21), and Jesus' bloody 'baptism' on the cross (12:50). Acts will refer to Christian Baptism, which embraces all three Lukan baptisms" (Just, *Luke 1:1—9:50*, 149).

15. "John's water baptism foreshadows Jesus's greater baptism in fire and the Spirit" (Keener, *Acts*, 1.680). "Such a baptism will thus be the Spirit principle by which Jesus' followers will live their new lives and bear witness to the risen Lord. The Spirit will be the dynamo that activates their testimony" (Fitzmyer, *Acts*, 204).

in his own language (2:6) of the mighty acts of God (2:11). This baptism with the Holy Spirit by the risen Jesus (2:33) established the sacrament of Christian baptism, which brings with it the ability to communicate to others what God has done in raising Jesus from the dead (2:22-24).[16]

To the Jews staying in Jerusalem (2:14) for the feast of Pentecost, who heard the apostles, baptized with the Holy Spirit by the risen Jesus (2:33), speaking to them in different tongues, Peter declared that the whole house of Israel should know for certain that God has made this Jesus whom they crucified both Lord and Christ (2:36). When they heard this, they were pierced to the heart, and asked Peter and the rest of the apostles what they should do (2:37; cf. Luke 3:10, 12, 14). Peter told them, "Repent, and each one of you be baptized in the name of Jesus Christ for the forgiveness of your sins, and you will receive the gift of the Holy Spirit" (Acts 2:38).[17] Those who accepted Peter's word were baptized, and on that day about three thousand persons were added to the Christian community (2:41). This confirms for the audience how the Christian sacrament of baptism embraces and is founded upon John's baptism of repentance for the forgiveness of sins (Luke 3:3), but adds to it the gift of the Holy Spirit, which enables those baptized to become witnesses of God's raising Jesus from the dead (Acts 1:8, 22; 2:32).

After Philip went down to the city of Samaria (8:5), the crowds believed him as he was proclaiming the good news about the kingdom of God and the name of Jesus Christ, and men as well as women were baptized (8:12). Then the apostles in Jerusalem sent to them Peter and John (8:14), who went down and prayed for them so that they might receive the Holy

---

16. "In Acts the pouring out of the Holy Spirit therefore not only follows the death and resurrection of Jesus as the next stage in God's salvation-historical purposes, but Jesus himself, as the reigning Lord, is the one who pours out the Spirit" (Thompson, *Acts*, 129).

17. "In the present context, the baptismal washing that comes with repentance signifies an inner cleansing that allows the person to be indwelt by the Spirit" (Bock, *Acts*, 142). For how this relates to other baptismal texts in Acts, see Avemarie, *Tauferzählungen*. "Luke connects the reception of the Holy Spirit in various ways with immersion 'in the name of Jesus'—in v. 38 baptism in the name of Jesus seems to precede the reception of the Spirit (cf. 8:16); in 10:44-48 the gift of the Holy Spirit precedes baptism in the name of Jesus; in 19:5-6 baptism in the name of the Lord Jesus Christ is accompanied by the laying on of hands and the reception of the Spirit" (Schnabel, *Acts*, 164). "Christian baptism is virtually defined as being *in the name of Jesus Christ* (cf. 10:48). This expression may suggest that the person being baptized actually called upon Jesus as Lord and Christ, as a way of confessing faith in him (cf. 22:16). The *name* of Jesus represents his divine authority and power to grant the blessing of the Spirit and to save people from the coming judgment through the forgiveness of sins" (Peterson, *Acts*, 155; emphases original).

Baptismal Worship

Spirit (8:15). For it had not yet fallen on any of them, but they had only been baptized in the name of the Lord Jesus (8:16).[18] Then they laid hands on them and they received the Holy Spirit (8:17).[19] When Simon, who had been practicing magic in Samaria (8:9), saw that the Spirit was given through the laying on of the apostles' hands, he offered them money (8:18) and asked that he be given this same authority (8:19). But Peter told him, "May your silver perish with you, because you thought you could acquire the gift of God with money!" (8:20). This underscores for the audience that the Spirit cannot be purchased but rather is freely given by God to those who have believed, repented, and been baptized (2:38).[20]

An Ethiopian eunuch, an important court official, had come to Jerusalem to worship (8:27). As he was returning to Ethiopia, seated in his chariot, he was reading the prophet Isaiah (8:28) about someone who was unjustly slaughtered like a silent lamb, so that his life was taken from the earth (8:32–33; cf. LXX Isa 53:7-8). Prompted by the Spirit, Philip joined the chariot (8:29–31). On behalf of the slaughtered one who "did not open his mouth" (8:32), Philip "opened his mouth" and, beginning with the passage from Isaiah, proclaimed Jesus to him (8:35). After the eunuch requested to be baptized (8:36), they both went down into some water and Philip baptized him (8:38).[21] Then the Spirit of the Lord snatched Philip away and the eunuch saw him no longer, but went on his way rejoicing (8:39). Through his baptism the eunuch implicitly received the Spirit (2:38), enabling him to be a witness of Jesus in Ethiopia, an area included within the "end of the earth" (1:8).[22] He reminds the audience that their reception of the Spirit in

18. "Luke marks the delay of the reception of the Holy Spirit in v. 16 as extraordinary, stating that the Spirit had 'not yet' (οὐδέπω) come upon any of them. This explanation would be superfluous if Luke or his readers regarded an interval between baptism and the reception of the Spirit as normal" (Schnabel, *Acts*, 410).

19. "Why might this delay have occurred? The most common and plausible explanation is that God waited for apostolic ratification to maintain the unity of the Jerusalem and Samaritan churches" (Keener, *Acts*, 2.1523).

20. "Controlling the power of the Spirit is exclusively a divine prerogative, beyond the scope of human manipulation" (Spencer, *Journeying through Acts*, 98–99). "God withheld the gift for his own revelatory and salvific purpose, not because of an inadequate response on the part of the Samaritans. The apostles needed to be there as reliable witnesses on behalf of the Jerusalem church, not to impart the Spirit because of their office" (Peterson, *Acts*, 287). Luke "indicates that the believers in Samaria, like the later gentile Christians, become not mere beneficiaries of Jerusalem's ministry but themselves empowered agents for the spreading of the word" (Keener, *Acts*, 2.1527).

21. For the reasons to omit the variant reading regarding the eunuch's confession of faith in Acts 8:37, see Metzger, *Textual Commentary*, 315–16.

22. "The Ethiopian official continues his journey 'rejoicing,' a remark . . . implying that he had received the Holy Spirit" (Schnabel, *Acts*, 429). "The movement of this

baptism likewise empowers them to spread the Christian faith throughout the world.

On his way to Damascus to persecute Christians, Saul was blinded by his experience of the risen Jesus (9:1–9), who told Ananias, a disciple, to lay his hands on Saul so that he may see again (9:10–12). The Lord Jesus told Ananias that Saul "is a chosen instrument of mine to carry my name before gentiles, kings, and the people of Israel, for I will show him how much he must suffer for the sake of my name" (9:15–16). After Ananias laid his hands on Saul, he regained his sight, was filled with the Holy Spirit, and was baptized (9:17–18; cf. 22:16).[23] This enabled Saul to proclaim Jesus in the synagogues, that he is the Son of God (9:20). Despite Saul being empowered to prove to the Jews that Jesus is the Christ, they conspired to kill him, but he escaped (9:22–25). When he arrived in Jerusalem, Saul spoke out boldly in the name of the Lord and debated with the Hellenists, but they tried to kill him, so that he had to be sent to Tarsus (9:26–30). This indicates to the audience that although their reception of the Spirit in baptism empowers them to proclaim Jesus, they may, like Saul/Paul, encounter rejection and suffering.[24]

To the centurion Cornelius and his household of God-fearing gentiles in Caesarea (10:1–2), Peter referred to all the good that Jesus did (10:38) after the baptism of repentance for the forgiveness of sins that John preached (10:37; Luke 3:3). After Peter indicated that everyone who believes in the risen Jesus will receive forgiveness of sins through his name (10:43), the Holy Spirit fell on all those listening to the word (10:44). Since they could be heard speaking in tongues and glorifying God (10:46), like the Jews who had received the Spirit at Pentecost (2:1–11), Peter ordered that these gentiles be baptized in the name of Jesus Christ (10:47–48). Peter later recounted the

---

transformed, exuberant chamberlain ('he went on his way rejoicing', 8:39) from the desert back home to Ethiopia propels the gospel mission even further out from its Pentecostal epicenter in Jerusalem. Indeed, since ancient Ethiopia . . . was renowned in Greco-Roman lore as the farthest outpost of the known inhabitable world . . . the eunuch's journey may be regarded as the trailblazing expedition 'to the ends of the earth' in Acts (1:8)" (Spencer, *Journeying through Acts*, 101). See also Smit, "Negotiating a New World View," 1–22.

23. "Now liberated and prepared for his mission, Saul is baptized immediately, as the eunuch was. Next he will go out into Damascus and preach Jesus" (Bock, *Acts*, 362).

24. "And while not many Christian converts resemble Saul in that they are called to missionary ministry at the time of their conversion (although some are!), all believers in Jesus confess him as 'Lord' and thus his servants or 'slaves' totally devoted to him. This new commitment to Jesus is expressed in baptism . . . a challenge as conversion means total commitment to and consistent loyalty for Jesus throughout our lives" (Schnabel, *Acts*, 460). "Luke speaks of Spirit empowerment primarily in terms of empowerment for mission (1:8)" (Keener, *Acts*, 2.1662).

event to the church in Jerusalem, recalling how the Lord had said, "John baptized with water, but you will be baptized with the Holy Spirit" (11:16; cf. 1:5; Luke 3:16).[25] Since God had given the Spirit even to gentiles, Peter had them baptized (11:17).[26] This models how anyone can be baptized to whom God has given faith and the Spirit through the preaching of the gospel that begins with John's baptism of repentance for the forgiveness of sins.[27]

After Peter referred to John's baptism of repentance for the forgiveness of sins (10:37; Luke 3:3) and that everyone who believes in the risen Jesus will receive forgiveness of sins (Acts 10:43; cf. 5:31), Cornelius and his household became believers, as they were given the Holy Spirit and baptized (10:44, 47–48). The believers to whom Peter reported this in Jerusalem glorified God, saying, "God has then given the repentance that leads to life even to the gentiles" (11:18).[28] After Paul in the synagogue in Pisidian Antioch referred to John's baptism of repentance (13:24) and that forgiveness of sins through the risen Jesus is being proclaimed to them (13:37–38), the Jews contradicted what Paul said (13:45). But Paul and Barnabas told these Jews who judge themselves as unworthy of eternal life that they are now turning to the gentiles (13:46), who then glorified the word of the Lord and all who had been appointed by God for eternal life believed (13:48), and implicitly were baptized.[29] This indicates that God can give anyone the faith to receive the baptism that not only forgives sins but gives eternal life.

25. "In terms of narrative fulfillment, this reminiscence is significant because it shows that the risen Lord's promise is having a double fulfillment: at Pentecost with the conversion of Jews, and at Caesarea with the conversion of gentiles. The conversion of gentiles is not an afterthought but part of the risen Lord's original intention" (Holladay, *Acts*, 243).

26. "Nowhere else does Luke narrate an event in which the gift of the Holy Spirit comes prior to baptism.... Gentiles cannot be denied baptism because God has overtly and unmistakably included them" (Gaventa, *Acts*, 172). "Peter's statement confirms the norm of 2:38–39, which stated the association between baptism and the reception of the Holy Spirit. The dramatic outpouring of the Spirit (v. 44) commits Peter and believers from Joppa (vv. 45, 47), and eventually the church in Jerusalem (11:15–18), to accepting Cornelius and his gentile household into the congregation of the followers of Jesus immediately, without demanding circumcision and full submission to the Torah" (Schnabel, *Acts*, 506).

27. "Even after the gift of the Spirit, baptism remains an important means of calling upon the name of Jesus with repentance and faith and identifying with the community of believers. The initiation sequence is not complete without water baptism, because of its character as a public act of commitment and reception of the gospel promises" (Peterson, *Acts*, 340).

28. "'Life' is shorthand for 'eternal life.'... The vast majority of its occurrences are in Jewish sources, beginning with Dan 12:2, where it refers to the life inherited at the resurrection of the dead" (Keener, *Acts*, 2.1828–29).

29. "The concept of eternal life is mentioned only here [13:46] and in verse 48

In Philippi the Lord opened the heart of a woman named Lydia, a gentile worshiper of God, to pay attention to what Paul was saying (16:14). After she and her household were baptized, she urged Paul and his companions that if they consider her to be a believer in the Lord they should stay at her home, and so they did (16:15). Paul and Silas told the pagan gentile jailer to "believe in the Lord Jesus and you and your whole household will be saved" (16:31).[30] After he and all his family were baptized (16:33), he brought Paul and Silas into his house, provided a meal, and with his whole household rejoiced at having come to faith in God (16:34).[31] This develops the trend of baptism opening the way for Jews to associate with gentiles (cf. 10:28) that began when Peter and his companions stayed in the house of the gentile Cornelius after he and his household were baptized (10:48). These baptisms of a God-fearing man (Cornelius), woman (Lydia), and a pagan (jailer) along with their households indicate that baptism makes believers, whatever their ethnic origins or differences, full members of the Christian community.

In Corinth Paul, speaking in the synagogue every Sabbath, was attempting to convince Jews and Greeks (18:4). He testified to the Jews that Jesus was the Christ (18:5). When they opposed and reviled him, he told them that he is now going to the gentiles (18:6). Paul then left the synagogue and entered the house of a man named Titius Justus, a gentile who worshiped God (cf. 16:14), whose house was next to the synagogue (18:7). Crispus, the synagogue official, believed in the Lord together with his entire household, and many of the Corinthians who heard believed and were baptized (18:8; cf. 1 Cor 1:14).[32] This continues to develop the trend of entire households

---

(though cf. 5:20; 11:18). Although it may be taken as a broad equivalent for salvation or the kingdom of God, the idea that resurrection to eternal life is specifically the outcome of Christ's resurrection is suggested by 3:21; 4:2, 10–12; 17:18, and is implied by 13:32–37" (Peterson, *Acts*, 398).

30. "The inclusion of 'your household' echoes the story of Lydia (16:15) and of Cornelius (11:14)" (Johnson, *Acts*, 301).

31. "As elsewhere in Acts, baptism of the household reflects a culture in which the head (Cornelius, Lydia, the jailer) decides on behalf of all, and that all includes not only the immediate family but the extended family, as well as slaves and their families. The jailer then tends to other needs, in particular the need for food, which reflects the formation of community (see 2:42) and which extends the earlier motif of hospitality between believing Jews and gentiles (10:48)" (Gaventa, *Acts*, 240).

32. "This household conversion links Crispus with Cornelius (10.44–48; 11.14), Lydia (16.14–15), and the Philippian jailer (16.31–34). Remarkably, the messianic mission brings together people as diverse as synagogue rulers, Roman centurions, female purple-merchants, and prison wardens within the one household of God" (Spencer, *Journeying through Acts*, 189). "This scene concludes with the report that many Corinthians 'became believers and were baptized.' Presumably the many include both Jews

Baptismal Worship

of various sociological types believing and being baptized. Baptism has now brought into the church believers of entire households headed by a gentile God-fearing man (Cornelius), a gentile God-fearing woman (Lydia), a gentile pagan jailer, and a Jewish synagogue official. Christian baptism includes and embraces a wide variety of different kinds of people, uniting them within a community of those who believe in the Lord Jesus Christ.

In Ephesus Paul found some disciples (19:1) who had not yet received the Holy Spirit (19:2). They had been baptized only with the baptism of John (19:3; cf. 18:25). Paul informed them that John baptized with a baptism of repentance, telling the people to believe in the one who was to come after him, that is, in Jesus (19:4), who will baptize them with the Holy Spirit (Luke 3:16; Acts 1:5; 2:33). When they heard this, they were baptized in the name of the Lord Jesus (19:5). And when Paul laid his hands on them, the Holy Spirit came upon them, and they spoke in tongues and prophesied (19:6), just like those who received the Holy Spirit in Jerusalem at Pentecost (2:4, 11, 17–18).[33] This reinforces for the audience how John's baptism of repentance for the forgiveness of sins prepared for and was complemented by Christian baptism with the Holy Spirit (2:38).[34] The Holy Spirit that believers receive at Christian baptism inspires and empowers them to communicate and bear witness to the risen Lord Jesus to all the peoples of the world (Luke 24:46–49; Acts 1:4–5, 8; 13:47).[35]

---

and gentiles, since Paul is now teaching in the house of the gentile Titius Justus, and a synagogue leader is among those convinced" (Gaventa, *Acts*, 258). "Luke does not actually say that the household of Crispus was baptized, though it is a reasonable assumption" (Peterson, *Acts*, 512–13).

33. "But this separation of the gift of the Spirit from the water rite itself does not imply any sharp theological dissociation for it: the gift of the Spirit is always assumed to be part-and-parcel of the broader complex of 'conversion-initiation' even where there is modulation within the ordering of the constitutive elements. Faith and baptism which does *not* lead to the gift of the Spirit is regarded as an *anomalous* state of affairs to be corrected (8.14–17; 19:1–6)" (Turner, *Power*, 398; emphases original).

34. "John's baptism was good, but it was only preparatory to baptism in Jesus's name and the greater baptism in the Spirit (Acts 1:4–5; 2:38)" (Keener, *Acts*, 3.2820).

35. "[T]he nexus of believing in Jesus, being baptized in Jesus' name, and receiving the gift of the Spirit remain foundational for salvation and witness in Acts (cf. 2:38)" (Spencer, *Journeying through Acts*, 195). "They became Christians and were empowered for Christian life and ministry by a single endowment of the Spirit" (Peterson, *Acts*, 532).

Summary

Christian baptism, prefigured by and built upon the foundation of John's baptism of repentance, is a form of ritual worship that includes an ethical dimension. All baptized Christians should complete and live out their ritual reception of the sacrament of baptism with their corresponding ethical behavior, demonstrating their repentance and transformed life with an active care and concern for the poor and less fortunate among them (Luke 3:7–11). Baptized Christians, whatever their profession or way of life, are to be honest in their dealings with others and not use others to advance and satisfy their own greediness (3:12–14).

John declared, "I am baptizing you with water, but one more powerful than I is coming; I am not worthy to loosen the strap of his sandals; he will baptize you with the Holy Spirit and fire" (3:16). After all the people were baptized by John and Jesus was baptized and praying, the heaven opened and the Holy Spirit descended upon him in bodily form like a dove, and a voice came from heaven: "You are my beloved Son; with you I am well pleased" (3:21–22). This indicates the transition from John's baptism of repentance to the baptism of Jesus, the Son of God, with the Holy Spirit. Later Jesus declared that "I have a baptism with which I am to be baptized, and how distressed I am until it is accomplished" (12:50). This metaphorical "baptism" refers to his divinely determined death before being raised (9:22). It reminds the audience that Christian baptism with the Holy Spirit includes participation in the metaphorical baptism of Jesus by taking up the cross daily and following Jesus with a willingness to lose one's life in order to save it (9:23–24).

After Jesus' ascension, as the disciples were gathered together on the day of Pentecost (Acts 2:1), suddenly there came from heaven a noise like a strong driving wind, and it filled the entire house where they were sitting (2:2). And tongues spreading out like fire appeared to them and came to rest on each one of them (2:3). All were filled with the Holy Spirit and began to speak in different tongues as the Spirit enabled them to speak out (2:4). Each of the Jewish pilgrims who had come to Jerusalem for the feast (2:5, 9–10) heard them speaking in his own language (2:6) of the mighty acts of God (2:11). This baptism with the Holy Spirit by the risen Jesus (2:33) established the sacrament of Christian baptism, which brings with it the ability to communicate to others what God has done in raising Jesus from the dead (2:22–24).

Peter told the Jews in Jerusalem, "Repent, and each one of you be baptized in the name of Jesus Christ for the forgiveness of your sins, and you will receive the gift of the Holy Spirit" (2:38). Those who accepted Peter's word were baptized, and on that day about three thousand persons were added to the Christian community (2:41). This confirms for the audience how the Christian sacrament of baptism embraces and is founded upon John's baptism of repentance for the forgiveness of sins (Luke 3:3), but adds to it the gift of the Holy Spirit, which enables those baptized to become witnesses of God's raising Jesus from the dead (Acts 1:8, 22; 2:32).

The apostles in Jerusalem sent to the believers in Samaria (8:12) Peter and John (8:14), who went down and prayed for them so that they might receive the Holy Spirit (8:15). For it had not yet fallen on any of them, but they had only been baptized in the name of the Lord Jesus (8:16). Then they laid hands on them and they received the Holy Spirit (8:17). When Simon, who had been practicing magic in Samaria (8:9), saw that the Spirit was given through the laying on of the apostles' hands, he offered them money (8:18), and asked that he be given this same authority (8:19). But Peter told him, "May your silver perish with you, because you thought you could acquire the gift of God with money!" (8:20). This underscores for the audience that the Spirit cannot be purchased but rather is freely given by God to those who have believed, repented, and been baptized (2:38).

After Philip proclaimed Jesus to the Ethiopian eunuch (8:35), he requested to be baptized (8:36), and so he and Philip went down into some water and Philip baptized him (8:38). Then the Spirit of the Lord snatched Philip away and the eunuch saw him no longer, but went on his way rejoicing (8:39). Through his baptism the eunuch implicitly received the Spirit (2:38), enabling him to be a witness of Jesus in the distant land of Ethiopia, an area included within the "end of the earth" (1:8). He reminds the audience that their reception of the Spirit in baptism likewise empowers them to spread the Christian faith throughout the world.

After Ananias laid his hands on Saul, he regained his sight, was filled with the Holy Spirit, and was baptized (9:17–18; cf. 22:16). This enabled Saul to proclaim Jesus in the synagogues, that he is the Son of God (9:20). Despite Saul being empowered to prove to the Jews that Jesus is the Christ, they conspired to kill him, but he escaped (9:22–25). When he arrived in Jerusalem, Saul spoke out boldly in the name of the Lord and debated with the Hellenists, but they tried to kill him, so that he had to be sent to Tarsus (9:26–30). This indicates to the audience that although their reception of the Spirit in baptism empowers them to proclaim Jesus, they may, like Saul/Paul, encounter rejection and suffering.

After Peter indicated to the centurion Cornelius and his household of God-fearing gentiles in Caesarea (10:1–2) that everyone who believes in the risen Jesus will receive forgiveness of sins through his name (10:43), the Holy Spirit fell on all those listening to the word (10:44). Since they could be heard speaking in tongues and glorifying God (10:46), like the Jews who had received the Spirit at Pentecost (2:1–11), Peter ordered that these gentiles be baptized in the name of Jesus Christ (10:47–48). Peter later recounted the event to the church in Jerusalem, recalling how the Lord had said, "John baptized with water, but you will be baptized with the Holy Spirit" (11:16; cf. 1:5; Luke 3:16). Since God had given the Spirit even to gentiles, Peter had them baptized (11:17). This models how anyone can be baptized to whom God has given faith and the Spirit through the preaching of the gospel that begins with John's baptism of repentance for the forgiveness of sins.

After Paul in the synagogue in Pisidian Antioch referred to John's baptism of repentance (13:24) and that forgiveness of sins through the risen Jesus is being proclaimed to them (13:37–38), the Jews contradicted what Paul said (13:45). But Paul and Barnabas told these Jews who judge themselves as unworthy of eternal life that they are now turning to the gentiles (13:46), who then glorified the word of the Lord and all who had been appointed by God for eternal life believed (13:48), and implicitly were baptized. This indicates that God can give anyone the faith to receive the baptism that not only forgives sins but gives eternal life.

After Lydia, a gentile worshiper of God in Philippi (16:14) and her household were baptized, she urged Paul and his companions that if they consider her to be a believer in the Lord they should stay at her home, and so they did (16:15). Paul and Silas told the pagan gentile jailer to "believe in the Lord Jesus and you and your whole household will be saved" (16:31). After he and all his family were baptized (16:33), he brought Paul and Silas into his house, provided a meal, and with his whole household rejoiced at having come to faith in God (16:34). This develops the trend of baptism opening the way for Jews to associate with gentiles (cf. 10:28) that began when Peter and his companions stayed in the house of the gentile Cornelius after he and his household were baptized (10:48). These baptisms of a God-fearing man (Cornelius), woman (Lydia), and a pagan (jailer) along with their households indicate that baptism makes believers, whatever their ethnic origins or differences, full members of the Christian community.

Paul testified to the Jews in the synagogue in Corinth (18:4) that Jesus was the Christ (18:5). When they opposed and reviled him, he told them that he is now going to the gentiles (18:6). Paul then left the synagogue and entered the house of a man named Titius Justus, a gentile who worshiped God (cf. 16:14), whose house was next to the synagogue (18:7). Crispus, the synagogue official, believed in the Lord together with his entire household, and many of the Corinthians who heard believed and were baptized (18:8; cf. 1 Cor 1:14). This continues to develop the trend of entire households of various sociological types believing and being baptized. Baptism has now brought into the church believers of entire households headed by a gentile God-fearing man (Cornelius), a gentile God-fearing woman (Lydia), a gentile pagan jailer, and a Jewish synagogue official. Christian baptism includes and embraces a wide variety of different kinds of people, uniting them within a community of those who believe in the Lord Jesus Christ.

Paul found some disciples in Ephesus (19:1) who had not yet received the Holy Spirit (19:2), as they had been baptized only with the baptism of John (19:3; cf. 18:25). He informed them that John baptized with a baptism of repentance, telling the people to believe in the one who was to come after him, that is, in Jesus (19:4), who will baptize them with the Holy Spirit (Luke 3:16; Acts 1:5; 2:33). When they heard this, they were baptized in the name of the Lord Jesus (19:5). And when Paul laid his hands on them, the Holy Spirit came upon them, and they spoke in tongues and prophesied (19:6), just like those who received the Holy Spirit in Jerusalem at Pentecost (2:4, 11, 17–18). This reinforces for the audience how John's baptism of repentance for the forgiveness of sins prepared for and was complemented by Christian baptism with the Holy Spirit (2:38). The Holy Spirit that believers receive at Christian baptism inspires and empowers them to communicate and bear witness to the risen Lord Jesus to all the peoples of the world (Luke 24:46–49; Acts 1:4–5, 8; 13:47).

7

Meals and Eucharistic Worship

Theophilus represents the audience of Luke-Acts as those already instructed in the basics of the Christian faith (Luke 1:3–4; Acts 1:1). They are those already baptized or preparing to be baptized, and those who celebrate or are preparing to celebrate the ritual meal of the Lord's Supper, the Eucharist.[1] Acts provides the foundational model for the audience to engage in their eucharistic "breaking of the bread." After about three thousand persons were baptized to form the early community of believers in Jerusalem (Acts 2:41), "they were devoting themselves to the teaching of the apostles and to the fellowship, to the breaking of the bread and to the prayers" (2:42). "They were breaking bread from house to house, sharing their food with exultation and sincerity of heart" (2:46). In various ways each of the many different meal scenes throughout Luke-Acts, even though many may not be eucharistic meals in themselves, indicate to the audience, who may well be hearing Luke and Acts in the context of a eucharistic meal, some significant aspect relevant for their communal celebrations of the Eucharist.[2]

---

1. "Luke's Gospel is a book of the church, written for the church, to be used by the church in its proclamation of the Gospel to the unbaptized and the baptized. The community that receives Luke's Gospel is a catechetical and eucharistic body. His Gospel prepares the baptized for the Eucharist and catechizes the unbaptized" (Just, "Luke's Canonical Criterion," 256n26).

2. "The meal, therefore, bridges the earthly ministry of Jesus with the life of the community which gathers together in his name to listen to the presentation of his deeds and words and to break bread, as he told his disciples to do at the Last Supper. . . . Luke, unique among the evangelists, is aware of the potent significance of linking Jesus' earthly meals with the meal shared by the community for which he writes" (Esposito, *Jesus' Meals*, 363–64). "Every meal in Luke-Acts has dimensions that intimate the Eucharist"

Meals and Eucharistic Worship in Luke

After Jesus told Levi the tax collector to follow him (Luke 5:27), he left behind everything and became one of Jesus' disciples (5:28; cf. 3:12–13). Then Levi gave a great banquet in his house for Jesus, and a large crowd of tax collectors and others were reclining at the meal with them (5:29). The Pharisees and scribes complained to his disciples about their sharing of meal fellowship with tax collectors and sinners (5:30). Jesus told them that those who are well do not need a physician but the sick do (5:31). He has come not to call the righteous but the sinners to repentance (5:32).[3] This meal scene indicates to the audience that their eucharistic banquets celebrate their past repentance in being baptized (cf. 3:3, 8) and becoming followers of Jesus like Levi. It also reminds them that at the Eucharist they share meal fellowship with the Jesus who calls them to recognize their moral or spiritual "sickness" and need to further repent and be forgiven (cf. 5:17-26). Finally, it encourages them not to shun but to call their fellow sinful followers to likewise repent and be forgiven in anticipation of the eschatological banquet.[4]

At that same great banquet (5:29) the Pharisees and scribes continued their complaining. They pointed out that the disciples of John and of the Pharisees fast often and pray to supplicate and prepare for God's future salvation (cf. 2:37), as proclaimed by John (3:3–6), but the disciples of Jesus eat and drink, feasting rather than fasting (5:33).[5] Jesus then indicated that God's future salvation has begun to arrive with him as the "bridegroom" and his disciples as the "wedding guests" of the eschatological wedding banquet (5:34).[6] But the days are coming when Jesus will be taken away from them

---

(Pervo, *Luke's Story*, 58).

3. "The feast with Levi the tax collector is the first meal in Luke's gospel and is programmatic for all other meals. It introduces the major themes that will be associated with Luke's portrayal of Jesus' table fellowship matrix: the forgiveness of sins, the ministry to the outcasts, and the controversy with the religious establishment" (Just, *Luke 1:1—9:50*, 244).

4. According to LXX Isa 55:1-2, 7, sinners are invited to repent and receive God's abundant forgiveness in a great eschatological banquet offered by God: "You who are thirsty come to the water . . . drink wine and milk . . . eat good things. . . . Let the wicked leave behind his ways and the lawless man his plans and turn to the Lord, and receive mercy, for he will generously forgive your sins." "At the Last Supper, Jesus points to the future kingdom in which he will eat and drink with the disciples; the church's eucharistic celebrations are already a foretaste of the eschatological banquet" (Boring, "Messianic Banquet," 67).

5. "The thing for which hope is expressed in fasting is already present. . . . This is a time for feasting, not fasting!" (Green, *Gospel of Luke*, 249).

6. The eschatological banquet was sometimes pictured as a joyous wedding feast

through his death and resurrection, and then they will fast in supplication and preparation for the completion of God's salvation when Jesus comes again (5:35).[7] This indicates to the audience how their eucharistic meals are to celebrate the arrival of Jesus as the divine "bridegroom" in anticipation of the eschatological wedding banquet. But it also establishes for them a new kind of fasting that is a joyous anticipation of God's final fulfillment of the wedding feast that Jesus has already inaugurated.

Jesus justified allowing the disciples who were with him to do the work of satisfying their hunger on the Sabbath, just as those who were with David (6:1-4; cf. 1 Sam 21:2-7; Lev 24:5-9), with the pronouncement: "Lord of the Sabbath is the Son of Man!" (6:5).[8] That Jesus, as the heavenly Son of Man now on earth (cf. 5:24), is Lord of the Sabbath means much more than Jesus being an exception to, being above, or abrogating the law of the Sabbath. It means he has the divine authority to begin to fulfill the eschatological hope rooted in the original meaning of the Sabbath.[9] As a commemoration of the day on which God rested and set apart as sacred time after he completed the work of creation (Gen 2:1-3; Exod 20:8-11), every Sabbath anticipated the final, unending Sabbath, the sacred time of rest, relaxation, restoration, and refreshment, toward which all of creation was oriented as its consummation.[10] Their eucharistic celebrations of meal fellowship with Jesus thus enable the audience to experience and anticipate the restoration and refreshment that begins to fulfill the true meaning of the Sabbath.

Jesus' first meal with a Pharisee (7:36-50) presents the audience with a paradigm for their eucharistic meals. Although no eating is narrated in this scene, its meal context within a house, as well as its liturgical character, clearly orient it toward the audience's eucharistic meals celebrated "from house to house [κατ' οἶκον]" (cf. Acts 2:46).[11] After a Pharisee asked Jesus

---

(Isa 54:5-55:5), inasmuch as God was often portrayed as the bridegroom of his people (Hos 2:18, 21; Ezek 16:7-8; Isa 54:5-8; 62:5; Jer 2:2).

7. "With Jesus' departure, the totality of deliverance is still an awaited event for the church (Acts 3:12-26). Jesus' point is that fasting will again become appropriate and an option in this intermediate period, as the church longs for the return and final fulfillment" (Bock, *Luke 1:1—9:50*, 518).

8. On "Lord" (κύριός) in the emphatic first position and the significance of this for the divine identity of Jesus, see Rowe, *Early Narrative*, 105-11.

9. "The Sabbath was a day of eschatological significance . . . a sign of eschatological fulfillment" (Burer, *Divine Sabbath*, 119).

10. "When Jesus brought the kingdom, that to which the weekly Sabbath observation pointed *arrived*, and so the Sabbath was *fulfilled*" (Just, *Luke 1:1—9:50*, 255; emphases original).

11. "Luke makes subtle reference to the meal setting throughout the pericope. The words οἶκος and οἰκία occur three times (vv. 36, 37, 44), Jesus' entrance into the house

"to eat with him," Jesus entered the "house" of the Pharisee and "reclined at table" (Luke 7:36). A sinful woman, recognizing that Jesus was "reclining at table" in the "house" of the Pharisee, brought in an alabaster flask of ointment (7:37). She then performed a dramatic act of reverential worship of Jesus. She stood behind him at his feet weeping and with tears began to wet his feet and with the hair of her head wiped them and kissed and anointed his feet with the ointment (7:38). After Jesus pronounced the forgiveness of her sins (7:48), those "reclining with" him for the meal questioned his authority to do so (7:49; cf. 5:21–24). Jesus then gave the woman a liturgical sounding dismissal with the words: "Your faith has saved you; go in peace" (7:50).[12]

The sinful woman at the meal with Jesus provides a model for the audience. Like her they are to "recognize" (7:37) that at their eucharistic meals they encounter the Jesus who calls sinners to repentance (5:32) and has the divine authority and willingness to forgive their sins (5:24; 7:48–50), even and especially those who, like the woman, have many sins (7:40–43, 47).[13] As a demonstration of her repentance, faith, and great love, her extraordinary act of hospitably and reverently worshiping Jesus at the meal (7:38, 44–47) serves as both a supplication for forgiveness and anticipatory gratitude for the forgiveness and salvific peace she expects to receive through her faith (7:50).[14] Their eucharistic meals with Jesus likewise provide the members of the audience with the opportunity to encounter Jesus and his divine authority to forgive sins. They may not only demonstrate their repentance and pray for the forgiveness of their sins, no matter how great or how many, but also express their loving gratitude for the divine forgiveness and salvific peace they can expect to receive as believers.

Simon the Pharisee who invited Jesus to the meal provides a counter model for the audience. In contrast to him, they are to allow others, like the sinful woman, the opportunity to repent of their sinfulness, no matter

---

is recalled multiple times (vv. 36, 44, 45), and fellow diners [οἱ συνανακείμενοι] pop up suddenly near the end (v. 49)" (Esposito, *Jesus' Meals*, 202).

12. With regard to the sinful woman, "often overlooked is the liturgical significance of her actions and the sequence itself: not simply the washing, kissing, and anointing, but also her arrival, Jesus' reclining, his salvific (even sacramental) encounter with her, and her dismissal in peace (7:50), all of which suggest a liturgical context for the woman's actions and the meal itself" (Esposito, *Jesus' Meals*, 210). "The sinful woman goes in the peace of forgiveness, received at the table of Jesus" (Just, *Luke 1:1—9:50*, 330).

13. For the significance of the sinful woman's "recognizing" (ἐπιγνοῦσα) of Jesus at the meal, see Esposito, *Jesus' Meals*, 203–4.

14. On the woman's gesture with her hair as not sexually provocative but either an act of seeking or of gratitude for forgiveness, see Cosgrove, "Woman's Unbound Hair," 675–92.

how great, and receive God's forgiveness from Jesus at the celebration of the Eucharist. The figure of Simon the Pharisee calls for all in the audience to ask themselves whether they have a sinfulness of which they are unaware or refuse to acknowledge (7:40–47). Jesus invites Simon and the audience who share meal fellowship with Jesus at their eucharistic meals, once they have realized their need to be forgiven, to turn to Jesus with the faith that he can and will forgive them. Jesus' first meal with a Pharisee (7:36–50) ends without any indication of whether Simon recognized his need for repentance and without any narration of the actual eating of the meal. It prompts the audience to complete the open ending of the scene with the eating of their eucharistic meals as repentant sinners with faith in Jesus to forgive and dismiss them in salvific peace.[15]

Jesus' miraculously overabundant feeding of a large crowd (9:10–17) instructs the audience about their own eucharistic meals. The gestures of Jesus in taking the five loaves and the two fish, looking up to heaven, blessing and breaking them, and giving them to his disciples (9:16) establish the eucharistic character of this meal scene.[16] These gestures anticipate those of Jesus' last supper when he instituted the Eucharist (22:19; cf. Matt 26:26; Mark 14:22; 1 Cor 11:23–24) already celebrated by the audience, as those having been instructed in the words (Luke 1:4), in accord with Jesus' directive to "do this in memory of me" (22:19).[17] Jesus enabled the feeding not only to satisfaction but to overabundance of a large crowd of the people of Israel, who had reclined for the meal in groups of about fifty (9:14). This suggests to the audience that this miraculous meal in the desert (9:12; cf.

---

15. On the role of Simon the Pharisee as different than those Pharisees who rejected Jesus (cf. Luke 7:30), see Tannehill, "Should We Love," 424–33. "That Simon invites Jesus to a banquet suggests that he has not yet formed a negative opinion of Jesus" (Green, *Gospel of Luke*, 307). "The episode is open-ended. . . . What will Simon do? Will he repent too and show his overwhelming love for the forgiveness of his sins, or will he seethe because Jesus implies that he is on the same level before God as this scarlet woman?" (Garland, *Luke*, 331).

16. "The exactitude with which this verse was preserved in church tradition almost certainly resulted from the fact that the early church perceived a parallel between the accounts of the feeding of the five thousand and the Last Supper, both of which contain the fourfold word sequence: 'took (bread)/blessed/broke/gave'" (Edwards, *Gospel According to Luke*, 266).

17. "[T]he formulas used in all these passages are undoubtedly reflections of the early eucharistic liturgies" (Fitzmyer, *Gospel According to Luke I-IX*, 768). "This meal language links together the wilderness feeding, the Last Supper, and the meal at Emmaus, suggesting an interpretation of the feeding of the five thousand as an adumbration of the Last Supper, and the Last Supper as the precedent for the Lord's presiding at post-Easter meals, both the Emmaus meal and celebrations of the Lord's Supper in the church" (Just, *Luke 1:1—9:50*, 388).

LXX Exod 16:3; Ps 77:19-20) was a unique anticipation of the eschatological, messianic banquet, at which there was expected to be an overabundance of food (Isa 25:6-8; 55:1-2; Jer 31:14; Joel 2:24-26; Amos 9:13-15).[18]

Welcoming the crowds, Jesus, before he provided the meal, spoke to them about the kingdom of God, and cured those who had need of healing (Luke 9:11). This sets a pattern for the eucharistic celebrations of the audience, who likewise before the meal are to welcome and instruct participants about the kingdom of God anticipated by the eucharistic meal. Also before the meal those in need of the healing of the "sickness" of their sinfulness (cf. 5:17-32) are to be given the opportunity to repent and be forgiven.[19] With its eucharistic overtones Jesus' overabundant feeding of the people to satisfaction indicates to the audience how their eucharistic meals can similarly satisfy their spiritual hunger in anticipation of the eschatological banquet in the kingdom of God. But most of all, Jesus' enabling of his apostles, who did not think they could feed the crowds (9:12-13), to satisfy them with an overabundance so that there were twelve baskets of leftovers (9:17) indicates to the audience how their eucharistic meals likewise empower them to materially and spiritually feed hungry people to an overabundant satisfaction.[20]

As Jesus and his disciples were going to Jerusalem (10:38a; cf. 9:51) for his "exodus" through suffering and death to heavenly glory (9:31), he entered a village, and a woman by the name of Martha welcomed him (10:38b), which implied the hospitality of offering him a meal. She had a sister named Mary, who sat at the feet of the Lord, thus in the position of a disciple (cf. 8:35; Acts 22:3), and was "listening" (ἤκουεν) to his word (Luke 10:39).[21] She was obeying the command of God at the transfiguration

---

18. That Jesus enabled his disciples to feed five thousand men with five loaves and have leftovers (9:14-17) surpassed Elisha's enabling his servant to feed a hundred with twenty loaves and have leftovers (2 Kgs 4:41-44). That all ate and "were satisfied [ἐχορτάσθησαν]" (Luke 9:17) begins to fulfill for the hungry crowd what the audience heard Jesus promise in his beatitudes: "Blessed are those who hunger now, for you will be satisfied [χορτασθήσεσθε]" (6:21).

19. Jesus healed a man of his physical sickness as the equivalent of forgiving his sins (5:17-26) and he characterized sinners as those who are spiritually "sick" in need of the healing of forgiveness (5:31-32).

20. "The 'twelve baskets of leftovers' (v. 17) may symbolize the twelve tribes of Israel, a conjecture that is strengthened by the emphatic placement of δώδεκα, 'twelve,' as the final Greek word of the miracle. If so, 'twelve' is Luke's final reminder that the bread offered by Jesus not only feeds and satisfies a crowd of five thousand, but all Israel. At the same time, 'twelve' reminds the disciples how those sent in mission with a calculated deficit are not abandoned by Jesus but abundantly provided for" (Edwards, *Gospel According to Luke*, 267).

21. "Pupils 'sit at the *feet*' of the teacher" (Bergmeier, "πούς," 3.143; emphasis original). "Her position is that of a listening disciple" (Fitzmyer, *Gospel According to Luke*

of Jesus to "listen" (ἀκούετε) to him (9:35), in order to hear the necessity for his suffering, death, and resurrection (9:22, 44).[22] Martha, preoccupied over much "service" (διακονίαν) in preparing the meal, asked Jesus to tell Mary to help her with the "serving" (διακονεῖν) of the meal (10:40).[23] The Lord told her that she is worried and troubled over many things (10:41). But only one thing is necessary. In listening to Jesus, Mary has chosen the best portion of the meal, which will not be taken away from her (10:42).[24] This meal scene (10:38-42) indicates to the audience an element essential to their eucharistic meals.

Martha and her sister Mary present the audience with complementary models for a proper understanding of and participation in the Eucharist. Mary indicates that the one thing necessary and the best portion (10:42) offered at the eucharistic meal, hosted by Jesus rather than Martha, is to hear and understand that the eschatological banquet in the kingdom of God, anticipated by the Eucharist (cf. 9:10-17), is made possible through the divine necessity of the suffering, death, and resurrection of Jesus. Rather than being distracted in trying to serve many things (10:40-41), Martha and the members of the audience are, like Mary, to listen to the word of Jesus indicating the one thing necessary for their proper participation and service not only in the eucharistic meal but as Jesus' disciples.[25] Such service includes following Jesus by denying oneself and taking up one's cross daily in order to save one's life (9:23-25) and inherit the eternal life (10:25) of heavenly glory anticipated by the transfiguration of Jesus (9:29-31) and by the eucharistic meal, the goal of the best portion or part chosen by Mary and to be chosen by the audience.[26]

X-XXIV, 893).

22. Heil, *Transfiguration*, 287-88.

23. For the meal connotation of the Greek terms here, see BDAG, 229-30. But these terms can also refer to the more general service involved in discipleship; cf. Luke 22:26-27.

24. For the preference of this reading for Luke 10:41-42 over its variants, see Metzger, *Textual Commentary*, 129.

25. "The issue here is whether one is first to serve the Lord or first to be served by him. This is really a question of the proper approach to worship. Mary has the right liturgical theology. She sits at the feet of Jesus to receive divine service from him. Instead of trying to serve Jesus first, she allows Jesus first to serve her" (Just, *Luke 9:51—24:53*, 459).

26. "The word μερίς, 'part,' is used in the LXX for a portion of food (Gen 43:34; Deut 18:8; 1 Sam 1:4), but also for 'portion' in a higher sense (Pss 16:5; 119:57)" (Fitzmyer, *Gospel According to Luke X-XXIV*, 894). Mary's choice of the best portion that will not be taken away from her complements the lawyer's question to Jesus, "What must I do to inherit eternal life?" (10:25). The words "portion" or "part" and "inheritance" or "share" are often used together and synonymously in the biblical tradition to express

After Jesus made an appeal for people to repent (11:29–36), a Pharisee invited him to eat a meal with him, so he went in and reclined at table (11:37). The Pharisee was surprised that Jesus did not first wash before the meal (11:38), or literally, was not "baptized" (ἐβαπτίσθη) in preparation for the religious ritual of meal fellowship which was considered to take place in the presence of God.[27] But the Pharisees and the scholars of the law had rejected the plan of God for themselves, ironically by not being "baptized" (βαπτισθέντες) with John's "baptism" (βάπτισμα) of repentance (7:29–30; 3:3). Jesus then criticized the Pharisees (11:39–44) and the scholars of the law (11:45–52), indicating how they need repentance.[28] When Jesus went out from there, presumably without eating the meal, the scribes and the Pharisees, rather than repenting, became deeply hostile and interrogated him about many things, plotting to trap him in something he might say (11:53–54). This second meal of Jesus with the Pharisees (11:37–54), who fail to repent, thus serves as a counterexample for the eucharistic meals of the audience.

To the surprised Pharisee (11:38) the Lord Jesus pointed out the ironic contradiction that while the Pharisees cleanse the outside of the cup and of the dish used in the meal, the inside of their own persons is full of greed and wickedness (11:39). He then exhorted the Pharisees and the audience to a repentance that purifies externally and internally. They must give alms so that everything becomes clean for them (11:40–41). That their giving of alms includes sharing with those in need the food and drink that are inside their dishes and cups accords with John's exhortation to repent by sharing clothes and food with those who have none (3:8, 11). By giving alms to the poor, the Pharisees and the audience may cleanse themselves externally and internally, ritually and morally, by transforming their greed and wickedness into a selfless and compassionate concern for the needy. Jesus left the meal with the Pharisees, who failed to repent (11:53). By repenting and practicing almsgiving, the audience can properly and completely cleanse themselves so that Jesus will remain in union with them at their eucharistic meals.[29]

---

the acquisition of eschatological promises (LXX Ps 15:5). Mary is choosing the best "portion" to "inherit," that is, to acquire her portion or share of eternal life. See Heil, *Meal Scenes*, 76.

27. "Washing the hands at the table before the meal was a common practice of pagans as well as Jews, but it had been given special religious significance in Pharisaic Judaism" (Smith, "Meals," 875).

28. "While this pericope and others like it in the gospels will surely lead the Christian hearer to share at least some of Jesus' anger at the Pharisees, the hearer must remember that the hypocrisy of the Pharisees is symptomatic of the entire fallen world" (Just, *Luke 9:51—24:53*, 494).

29. "Almsgiving was considered meritorious in the OT and Jewish theology; it was

Addressing the Pharisees with "woes [οὐαί]" (11:42–44), which warn them of exclusion from eschatological salvation, Jesus continued to call them and the audience to repentance.[30] They should continue to pay tithes, which supported not only the temple for the worship of God but also the poor in the community.[31] But Jesus called them to convert by adding their personal commitment in working for social justice for the poor and loving God to their more impersonal paying of tithes (11:42).[32] Rather than seeking honor from others (11:43), they are to lead others to work for social justice and bring them to a sincere love of God. Ironically, the Pharisees, like unmarked tombs, are contaminating those who honor and greet them with their own hidden and deadly impurity (11:44). Jesus' woes to the Pharisees implicitly call the audience to repent by adding to their monetary donations their working for social justice and the love of God, and by seeking not adulation from others but authentic leadership of and service to others, in order to properly share a eucharistic meal with Jesus.

Jesus then directed woes to the scholars of the law or scribes (cf. 11:53), a group of experts in the law responsible for the details of Pharisaic piety Jesus just condemned. Unlike the scribes, who refuse to help those they burden with religious obligations, the audience must not only teach but compassionately assist others to fulfill their teachings (11:46). Unlike the Pharisees and scribes, the audience must learn to recognize, welcome, and heed the prophets or preachers of today who speak God's word to them (11:47–48). As disciples, members of the audience can expect to be rejected, persecuted, and even killed like Jesus, but they can be encouraged that God will ultimately vindicate them (11:49–51). Unlike the scribes, the audience must use the knowledge of God's will revealed to them by Jesus as a key to open the way for themselves and others into the kingdom of God (11:52) that Jesus is bringing about by his death and resurrection (11:53–54).[33]

---

thought to result in the forgiveness of sins (Prov 11:4; Dan 4:24, etc.), was regarded as a condition of salvation (Isa 58:6–12), and was equated with sacrifice (Tob 11:4; Sir 32:5)" (Staudinger, "ἐλεημοσύνη," 1.429). See also Reardon, "Cleansing through Almsgiving," 477–82.

30. Balz, "οὐαί," 2.540. "Again, the woes apply to the Pharisaic tendencies in all human beings" (Just, *Luke 9:51—24:53*, 491).

31. "The tithe was the donation of a tenth of one's material possessions for the nation, temple, or clergy" (Bock, *Luke 9:51—24:53*, 1115–16). "The purpose [of tithing] expressed in Deuteronomy is the support of the Levites and the poor in the land: sojourners, orphans and widows" (Johnson, *Luke*, 189).

32. On the meaning of "justice" for κρίσιν in Luke 11:42, see BDAG, 569.

33. "The intensity of the controversy between Jesus and the religious establishment outside of Jerusalem has reached a new level, and the fulfillment of 11:49 in Jesus' death now seems inevitable. . . . Jesus' woes are indictments of each of us, but also reminders

Such repentant behavior called for by the Jesus who left the meal with the unrepentant Pharisees will enable the audience to share a eucharistic meal with him.[34]

Jesus' third meal with the Pharisees (14:1-24) began when he went into the house of one of the leading Pharisees on a Sabbath to dine, literally "to eat bread," and they were watching him closely (14:1; cf. 6:9). The Sabbath setting, with its eschatological overtones of anticipating the final Sabbath rest, contributes to the eschatological tone of the entire meal scene.[35] In front of Jesus was a man suffering from dropsy or edema (14:2), a swelling of the body caused by an abnormal accumulation of fluids. It involved an unquenchable craving for drink, which only exacerbated the painful condition.[36] After the scholars of the law and the Pharisees remained silent when Jesus asked them if it was lawful to heal on the Sabbath or not, he healed and dismissed him, releasing him from the oppressive disease (14:3-6; cf. 13:15-16).[37] Jesus models for the audience how they are to have a compassionate care and concern for those who, like the man with dropsy, are in physical need, in order to celebrate appropriately their eucharistic meals as

---

that Jesus himself suffered the woes of God's wrath against all sin, and the plotting of the scribes and Pharisees played right into God's plan for the redemption of the world" (Just, *Luke 9:51—24:53*, 493-94).

34. "The sober conclusion, 'Jesus went outside' (v. 53), is both descriptive and symbolic, for even at table Jesus was an outsider among the scribes and Pharisees" (Edwards, *Gospel According to Luke*, 360). For a recent detailed discussion of Jesus' second meal with Pharisees (11:37-54), including the significance of the meal setting, see Esposito, *Jesus' Meals*, 211-73.

35. "Jesus enters the house of a leading Pharisee on the Sabbath 'to eat bread' [φαγεῖν ἄρτον]. These words serve a formative purpose within the entire 14:1-24 sequence.... An explicit reference back to v. 1 is found in v. 15, when one of the guests interjects a statement into what had been Jesus' monologue: 'Blessed is the one who eats bread in the Kingdom of God.' The phrase φαγεῖν ἄρτον links this verse, functioning as the introduction to the great banquet parable, with the meal setting prepared in v. 1. The guest's statement, like the sayings in vv. 11 and 14, elevate the pericopes to an eschatological level, with the result that the meal itself, outlined in v. 1, retrospectively assumes an eschatological tone and import" (Esposito, *Jesus' Meals*, 308).

36. Braun, *Feasting*, 32.

37. "Luke 14.1-6 illustrates how, in the central section of Luke, Jesus emerges as the definitive gatekeeper of speech in the narrative, and the leaders' identity shifts correlatively to those who cannot control others' speech, and whose own speech is rendered ineffectual" (Dinkler, *Silent Statements*, 163). "The Pharisees, who think Torah is honored by scrupulous adherence to its commands, ask what is *permitted* on Sabbath; Jesus, who is Lord of the Sabbath (6:5), asks what is *intended* by Sabbath. From the latter perspective, healing the man with edema is not simply permitted but *required* on Sabbath" (Edwards, *Gospel According to Luke*, 416; emphases original).

a prefigurement and anticipation of the eschatological banquet in the kingdom of God.

Dropsy often served as a metaphor for insatiable greed or craving desire.[38] The physically dropsical man in need of healing characterizes the morally dropsical Pharisees, also in need of healing by repenting of the greed and selfish desires of which Jesus has accused them (11:39, 43). With a poignant parable (14:8–11) Jesus calls those invited to the Sabbath meal (14:7) and the audience to humble themselves in dependence upon God in their social interaction to be cured of their dropsical self-seeking: "For everyone who exalts himself will be humbled, but the one who humbles himself will be exalted" (14:11). God will exalt them in places of honor at the eschatological banquet prefigured by their eucharistic meals. Similarly, Jesus invites the host of the Sabbath meal (14:12) and the audience to cure a dropsical, selfish craving for social honor by demonstrating a care and concern for the socially and economically unfortunate, represented by the poor, the crippled, the lame, the blind (14:13).[39] God will repay them in the eschatological resurrection of the righteous (14:14) anticipated by their eucharistic meals.[40]

The great dinner given by a certain man in Jesus' final parable during his third meal with Pharisees (14:16–24) characterizes the eschatological banquet in the kingdom of God (14:15) to which Jesus is inviting many to participate in by repenting. But in the parable a dropsical craving to acquire property and increase their wealth prevents those invited from attending. One purchased a field and must attend to it (14:18). Another purchased five yoke of oxen and must test his new acquisition (14:19). And another has married and thus acquired a wife, which involved accruing and maintaining additional wealth, and cannot come (14:20).[41] The economically lowly

---

38. For literary examples and a full discussion of the evidence, see Braun, *Feasting*, 22–42.

39. "[T]o exhort the Pharisee to provide hospitality to these groups is to imply that the Pharisee has overlooked Scripture, specifically, scriptural mandates for generosity to the poor, the blind, the lame" (Roth, *Blind*, 181–82).

40. "Jesus does not advise people to engage in guileless generosity *in order that* one might receive divine benefaction. Luke has already established that human generosity flows from an appreciation of the expansive mercy of God (6:36); to this he now adds that genuine, uncalculating generosity toward those of low status will not go unrewarded" (Green, *Gospel of Luke*, 554).

41. "Especially among the wealthy elite, primary among the motives for marriage was the generation of legitimate sons as heirs to ensure that property remained in the family.... It is fair to say that acquiring a wife in the first place was governed more by forces that regulated the flow of wealth than by noble fancies for friendship" (Braun, *Feasting*, 77).

and humble poor and disabled are invited instead (14:21), and even social outcasts are forced to come, so that there is no room for those originally invited (14:22–24). The parable reinforces for the audience their need to humble themselves (14:11) by rejecting a dropsical craving for wealth, in order to be exalted and blessed by God to dine at the eschatological banquet in the kingdom of God (14:15) foreshadowed by their eucharistic meals.[42]

The Pharisees and scribes kept grumbling against Jesus, saying, "This man welcomes sinners and eats with them" (15:2; cf. 5:30). Jesus then told three parables in which he explained that he eats with sinners not to condone their sinfulness but to celebrate their repentance. After the parable about rejoicing with the man who left ninety-nine sheep and found the one lost (15:3–6), Jesus said there will be more joy in heaven over one sinner who repents than over ninety-nine righteous who have no need of repentance (15:7). Similarly, a woman who found a lost coin invited others to rejoice with her, and in the same way there is joy among the angels of God over one sinner who repents (15:8–10). After the younger, prodigal son repented of his sinfulness in squandering the property of his father in the third parable (15:11–23), the father, representing God, declared, "Let us eat and celebrate, for this son of mine was dead but has come back to life, he was lost but has been found" (15:24). This reminds the audience that their eucharistic meals are opportunities to celebrate with Jesus the repentance and forgiveness of sinners.[43]

In the third parable the older son, characterizing the Pharisees and the scribes (15:2), refused not only to join the meal celebrating the repentance of the younger son (15:28), but to recognize him as his brother (15:30). The older son was relating to his father (God) more as a slave serving a strict and demanding master than as the son of a loving and compassionate father (15:29). The father then pointed out to him that everything he has was always available to him as his son (15:31), and he urged him to recognize the younger son as his brother: "But it was necessary to celebrate and rejoice, for this brother of yours was dead but has come to life, and he was lost but has been found" (15:32).[44] The parable concludes open-endedly with no

---

42. For a recent detailed discussion of Luke 14:1–24, see Esposito, *Jesus' Meals*, 275–339.

43. "Now the prodigal is like the newly baptized who has received the kiss of peace (reconciliation), the robe of righteousness, and now is ready to join in the eucharistic feast of the Father" (Just, *Luke 9:51—24:53*, 603). "The father's invitation of the unworthy to his banquet table is a foreshadowing of the invitation of the unworthy to the table of the Eucharist" (Edwards, *Gospel According to Luke*, 446).

44. "The older brother's bitter complaint serves as an occasion for the father to explain the acceptance of his wayward son and his joy in receiving him, just as the Pharisees' complaint served as an occasion for Jesus to explain God's acceptance of sinners"

response from the older son. It invites the audience to provide the response by realizing their need to repent (15:7) and relate to God as children of a compassionate and forgiving Father, and by recognizing repentant sinners forgiven by the Father as their fellow brothers and sisters. This will enable them to celebrate God's forgiveness of them and their fellow sinners at the Eucharist.[45]

In the parable of the rich man and Lazarus (16:19-31) the poor, hungry man Lazarus, who was denied food from the extravagant banquets of the rich man (16:21), after his death received a place of honor at the bosom of Abraham in the eschatological banquet (16:22).[46] The rich man, who found himself tormented in Hades after his death (16:23), continued to disrespect Lazarus by treating him as his servant. He implored Abraham to send Lazarus to soothe his torment, but it was impossible (16:24-26). He then begged Abraham to send Lazarus to his five brothers to warn them of his fate, pleading that if someone from the dead goes to them, they will repent (16:27-30). But Abraham replied that if they do not listen to Moses and the prophets, not even if one were to rise from the dead will they be convinced (16:31).[47] The parable calls for the audience to be convinced by the resurrection of Jesus to assist the poor with compassion for them as unfortunate fellow human beings. This will help to ensure that their eucharistic

---

(Garland, *Luke*, 632). "The older brother referred to his brother dismissively as 'this your son' (v. 30), but the father sets the record straight, 'This *your* brother was dead and is alive again; he was lost and is found' (v. 32)" (Edwards, *Gospel According to Luke*, 447; emphasis original). "Because of the several parallels between the two sons, the parable is about two lost sons, one who wanted to be a servant and the other who felt like one, but the father insisted that both are sons *and brothers* to each other" (Snodgrass, *Stories with Intent*, 140; emphasis original).

45. On the correspondence between the father in the parable and God as Father in the wider context of Luke's Gospel, see Burke, "Parable of the Prodigal Father," 217-38.

46. "The bosom [κόλπος] of Abraham is clearly an image of honor and may also point to intimacy (as in John 1:18), but most likely Luke intends his reader to think of the eschatological banquet (13:28-29) and of Lazarus having the place of honor at the table next to Abraham (cf. John 13:23)" (Snodgrass, *Stories with Intent*, 425). See also BDAG, 556-57.

47. "Abraham's comment clearly alludes to Jesus' approaching resurrection" (Bock, *Luke 9:51—24:53*, 1377). "Jesus is clearly alluding to his own resurrection from the dead" (Just, *Luke 9:51—24:53*, 637). "For the Christian reader of the Lucan Gospel, the reference to Jesus' own death and resurrection is obvious" (Fitzmyer, *Gospel According to Luke X-XXIV*, 1134). "The verb 'rise' (ἀνίστημι) [in 16:31] is one used frequently by Luke for the resurrection of Jesus (9:22; 18:33; 24:9, 46; Acts 2:24, 32; 3:22, 26; 13:32). . . . The statement points beyond the parable to Jesus as the prophet whom God raised up, proclaimed in the narrative of Acts" (Johnson, *Luke*, 253).

meals, as celebrations of the resurrection of Jesus, become a foretaste of the eschatological banquet.[48]

Jesus was passing through Jericho (19:1), a turning point on his way up to Jerusalem (18:31), meaning that his predicted suffering, death, and resurrection in Jerusalem was now imminent. A man named Zacchaeus, a chief tax collector and rich man, was seeking to see who Jesus was (19:2–3). Jesus told him that "today I must stay at your house" (19:5), which implied the hospitality of a meal.[49] Zacchaeus welcomed him, rejoicing (19:6).[50] After grumblings that Jesus has gone in to lodge, and thus share a meal, with a sinner (19:7), Zacchaeus declared his repentance. Half of his possessions he will give to the poor and he will repay fourfold all those he has extorted (19:8).[51] Because of his repentance and welcoming of Jesus, salvation has arrived in his house (19:9). Jesus serves as a model for the audience to call people to repent in order to share a eucharistic meal with Jesus. And Zacchaeus serves as a model for the audience to repent of their sinfulness, especially their neglect of the poor and wrongdoing toward others in order to celebrate at the Eucharist the salvation Jesus offers them through his death and resurrection.[52]

---

48. For a treatment of Luke 16:19–31 as one of seven "money-lover" parables in the Lukan travel narrative, which aim to persuade the rich to repentance, see Szukalski, *Tormented in Hades*.

49. "Although the story of Zacchaeus makes no explicit references to a meal or to the act of eating, μεῖναι ('abide') [19:5] and καταλῦσαι ('lodge') [19:7] strongly suggest that Jesus will eat a meal with Zacchaeus at his home. To spend the night at someone's house implies that a meal would be eaten" (Just, *Luke 9:51—24:53*, 720).

50. That Zacchaeus "welcomed him" (ὑπεδέξατο αὐτόν) as he finally nears Jerusalem reminds the audience how Martha likewise "welcomed him" (ὑπεδέξατο αὐτόν, 10:38) earlier on this same journey to Jerusalem. Just as the welcome of the journeying Jesus by Martha and her sister Mary into the hospitality of their home involved the preparation of a meal for their guest (10:38–42), so also Zacchaeus's welcome of Jesus into his home implies the hospitality of a meal. That these are the only occurrences in Luke-Acts of "welcomed him" enhances this connection. "Zacchaeus's rejoicing (χαίρων) lets the reader see joy from the perspective of the one who is lost and is found. The joy is also expressed in a meal, which becomes a celebration (15:22–24, 32)" (Garland, *Luke*, 748).

51. For the reasons to interpret Zacchaeus's declaration as repentance and a reference to his future behavior rather than as a defense of his past behavior, see Garland, *Luke*, 748–50.

52. On Luke encouraging the audience to identify with the sinner Zacchaeus by portraying him as such a vivid and memorable character, see Sick, "Zacchaeus," 229–44. On the audience seeing the events of this passage through the eyes of Zacchaeus and thus experiencing Jesus' concluding words to Zacchaeus as if they were addressed directly to them, see Yamasaki, "Point of View," 89–105.

When the feast of the Passover was drawing near (22:1), there came the day on which it was necessary that the Passover lamb be sacrificed (22:7).⁵³ So Jesus sent Peter and John to "go and prepare [ἑτοιμάσατε] for us to eat the Passover meal [τὸ πάσχα]" (22:8) at which Jesus will institute the Eucharist (22:19–20).⁵⁴ This recalls John the Baptist's command to "prepare" (ἑτοιμάσατε) the way of the Lord (3:4) by repenting (3:3). As "teacher" (3:12), John instructed the crowds, soldiers, and tax collectors how to repent (3:7–14). Similarly, "the teacher" Jesus (22:11) instructed Peter and John where to go that "we might prepare" (ἑτοιμάσωμεν) the Passover meal (22:9), the room where they are to "prepare" (ἑτοιμάσατε) it (22:12).⁵⁵ Obeying his instructions, they went out and found the place just as he had told them, and "they prepared" (ἡτοίμασαν) the Passover meal (22:13).⁵⁶ This indicates how the audience can properly prepare to eat the new Passover meal of the Eucharist by following not only the Baptist's teaching of repentance but all that Jesus, "the teacher," has taught them about God's way of salvation.⁵⁷

That "it was necessary" (ἔδει) for the Passover lamb "to be sacrificed [θύεσθαι]" (22:7) places the death of the Passover lamb within the framework of the divine necessity of God's plan of salvation as prescribed in scripture

---

53. This places the events of Jesus' suffering, death, and resurrection within not only the temporal but the interpretive context of the Passover, the great Jewish pilgrimage feast that centered upon a ceremonial meal in Jerusalem as a ritual remembrance of God's saving events in the exodus from Egypt. The feast began with the eating and drinking of the Passover meal, including the eating of the Passover lamb, and continued with the eating of only unleavened bread for the seven days of the festival. By this ritual eating and drinking the Jewish people not only relived and made present their past salvific exodus from Egypt, in which God liberated them from slavery and death by "passing over" their houses sprinkled with the blood of the Passover lamb (Exod 12:1–30; Deut 16:1–8), but also anticipated their share in God's future and final salvation. See also Patsch, "πάσχα," 3.50; Bubbers, *Scriptural Theology*, 57–75.

54. "τὸ πάσχα, depending on context, can refer to the Passover lamb, the Passover meal, or the festival of Passover" (Green, *Gospel of Luke*, 755n30). See also BDAG, 784–85.

55. "Their preparations give a new twist on what it means to go before the Lord 'to prepare his ways' (1:76; see 3:4). These two disciples are not simply preparing for a religious rite but for Jesus' sacrificial death" (Garland, *Luke*, 853).

56. "Jesus involves his disciples in the preparations. As leaders in the early church, they will be called upon by their Lord to make preparations for worship each Lord's Day, including worship and the Breaking of the Bread—Holy Communion (Acts 20:7; cf. Acts 2:42, 46)" (Just, *Luke 9:51—24:53*, 818).

57. The reference to Jesus as "the teacher" (ὁ διδάσκαλος) in 22:11 serves as the final climactic occurrence of this term in Luke after Jesus has repeatedly been referred to as a "teacher" (7:40; 8:49; 9:38; 10:25; 11:45; 12:13; 18:18; 19:39; 20:21, 28, 39; 21:7) who "teaches" the way of God (20:21; cf. 4:15, 31; 5:3, 17; 6:6; 11:1; 13:10, 22, 26; 19:47; 20:1; 21:37; 23:5).

(Exod 12:6, 21; Deut 16:2, 5–6).[58] This associates the sacrificial death of the Passover lamb with the sacrificial death of Jesus.[59] Jesus disclosed to his disciples his deep desire to eat "this" (emphatic τοῦτο) particular Passover meal "with you" before he "suffers [παθεῖν]" (22:15). This recalls that it is divinely "necessary" (δεῖ) that he "suffer" (παθεῖν) much on his way to death and resurrection (9:22; 17:25) according to God's scriptural plan (18:31). His deep desire to share the special meal fellowship of this Passover with his disciples indicates its great importance for closely uniting the disciples with Jesus before he suffers a necessary sacrificial death like that of the Passover lamb. This impresses upon the audience how their eucharistic meals unite them with Jesus as the new sacrificial Passover lamb, who effects salvation not just for the people of Israel but for all peoples (2:30–32; 3:6).[60]

With his pronouncement that he will never eat the Passover meal again until it is fulfilled in the kingdom of God (22:16), Jesus indicated that this particular Passover meal is not only the last that he will share with his disciples before his death, but also the one that anticipates the eschatological banquet in the kingdom of God (cf. 13:29; 14:15). He reinforced this when he said that from now on he will never again drink from the fruit of the vine with them until the kingdom of God comes (22:18).[61] He climaxed these promises as he told his disciples, who have remained with him throughout his trials (22:28), that they may eat and drink at his table in his kingdom

---

58. Moses instructed the elders of Israel to "sacrifice" (θύσατε) the Passover lamb (LXX Exod 12:21) and to tell their children that "this is the Passover sacrifice [θυσία] of the Lord, as he passed over the houses of the Israelites in Egypt; when he struck down the Egyptians, he saved our houses" (LXX Exod 12:27). See also LXX Deut 16:2, 4–6.

59. "Luke introduces Jesus' last meal with the statement that it 'was *necessary* to sacrifice the Passover lamb.'... Luke portrays Jesus' death as a matter of divine necessity (9:22; 13:33; 22:37; 17:25; 24:7, 26, 44; Acts 1:16; 17:2–3), and this reference to the necessity of the Passover sacrifice anticipates and parallels the necessity of Jesus' sacrificial death" (Garland, *Luke*, 852; emphasis original).

60. "Luke points to Jesus' death as the sacrificial Passover lamb who fulfills and renders obsolete the sacrifices of the OT.... The Passover lamb whose blood atones for all is Jesus.... The disciples prepared for this meal with expectations of celebrating another Jewish Passover with its fixed ritual of remembering God's gracious deliverance out of Egypt. But what the disciples experienced on this night in which Jesus was betrayed was not another Jewish Passover, but *Jesus' Passover*, in which he took the fixed ritual of the Passover Seder and gave everything in this meal new meaning" (Just, *Luke 9:51—24:53*, 817–18; emphasis original).

61. "Fruit of the vine" as an expression for wine made from grapes occurs in LXX Deut 22:9; Isa 32:12 as well as in the blessing over the cup at the Passover meal; see Johnson, *Gospel of Luke*, 338. "These words are neither an avowal of abstention nor a vow taken by Jesus against the drinking of wine. The drinking of wine is parallel to the eating of the Passover meal/lamb of v. 16" (Fitzmyer, *Gospel According to Luke X–XXIV*, 1398).

(22:30). The table fellowship that unites the disciples to the sacrificial death of Jesus at his last supper will reach its fulfillment in the table fellowship that will reunite the persevering disciples with the risen Jesus triumphantly exalted in his eschatological kingdom.[62] This reinforces for the audience, who are to persevere through their trials as followers of Jesus (cf. 8:13–15), that their eucharistic meals are celebratory anticipations of the final banquet in the kingdom of God.

The gestures Jesus performed in serving the bread as host of his new Passover meal—"taking bread," "giving thanks" for it, "breaking" it, and "giving" it to his disciples (22:19)—recall the overabundant meal with eucharistic overtones that Jesus shared with his disciples and the crowd (9:10–17). Similarly, "taking" the five "loaves" and the two fish, and looking up to heaven, he "blessed" them, "broke" them, and "kept giving" them to his disciples to set before the crowd (9:16). By miraculously multiplying five loaves and two fish, Jesus not only served the food to his twelve apostles but empowered them in turn to serve it to the crowd and to future crowds, as indicated by the overabundance of leftovers (9:17). Jesus not only empowered his disciples to feed the large crowd with the abundant bread he kept giving them, but he gave them the command for the ritual repetition of his new Passover meal (22:19), the Eucharist. This indicates that they and the audience are not only to keep sharing among themselves the bread that he gave them as his sacrificial body, but also to feed others with it continually in the future.

The bread of his last Passover meal that Jesus gave thanks to God for and broke he gave to his disciples with a new symbolic interpretation: "This is my body which is being given for you" (22:19). In identifying the bread as his "body" (σῶμά), that is, his whole person, his entire self, Jesus further associated his death with the sacrificial death of the Passover lamb, whose entire body was to be eaten roasted whole and without a bone broken, together with the unleavened bread and bitter herbs (Exod 12:8–9, 46; Num 9:11–12; Deut 16:2–3). The eating of the unleavened bread and the roasted body of the Passover lamb enabled the participants of the meal to experience in the communion of table fellowship the salvation God effected by the sacrificial death of the Passover lamb. So now in the same way the eating of the bread identified as the very body of Jesus in the Eucharist, their new Passover meal, enables the audience to experience in the communion of

---

62. "The eschatological dimension of this table fellowship of Jesus with his disciples links this section to the eschatological prospect of 22:16, 18 and earlier words about eating in the kingdom of God (13:29–30 and the beatitude of 14:15)" (Just, *Luke 9:51—24:53*, 848).

table fellowship the eschatological salvation God effected by the sacrificial death of Jesus.[63]

Jesus instructed his disciples to "keep doing this," to continue as a regularly repeated ritual the sharing of bread designated as his sacrificial body (22:19), just as the Passover meal was to be continually celebrated as a perpetual institution (Exod 12:17, 24; 13:10).[64] They are to keep doing this in "remembrance" (ἀνάμνησιν) of the Jesus who is giving himself in sacrificial death for their salvation (22:19), just as the Israelites were to keep eating the Passover meal as a continual "memorial" (μνημόσυνον) of their salvation (LXX Exod 12:14; 13:9).[65] For the Israelites to "remember" the exodus event meant not simply recalling it as a past event but reliving it, making it present for them again, and experiencing its salvific benefits in the communion with God and one another created by the fellowship of the Passover meal. Likewise, for the audience to "keep doing this in remembrance of me" means that, by repeatedly sharing the bread designated as Jesus' body in their eucharistic meals, they not only recall the significance of Jesus' sacrificial death for them, but also continue to share its salvific benefits.[66]

As he did with the bread, Jesus gave the after-dinner cup to his disciples with a new symbolic interpretation: "This cup is the new covenant in my blood which is being poured out for you" (22:20). In identifying this cup of wine as the new covenant "in my blood," Jesus exploited the ability of wine, often described as the "blood" of grapes (LXX Gen 49:11; Deut 32:14;

---

63. "The vicarious gift of himself is the Lucan Jesus' intention in reinterpreting the Passover offering of old; it implies the soteriological aspect of his life and death" (Fitzmyer, *Gospel According to Luke X–XXIV*, 1401).

64. "With these words Jesus institutes the Sacrament of the Lord's Supper *to be repeated* by the church until his return" (Just, *Luke 9:51—24:53*, 823; emphasis original).

65. "[B]oth the Passover practice that, according to Exod 12, reiterated the experience of the night in which the Israelites left Egypt and the Lord's Supper practice that developed out of this Last Supper experience share the same pattern: the originating occasion anticipated the saving event, while the ongoing celebration looked back to the saving event" (Nolland, *Luke 18:35—24:53*, 1048).

66. "This 'remembrance' (ἀνάμνησιν) of Jesus is not a reminder or commemoration of him, as one might find on tomb inscriptions, but, like the Passover meal, a re-presentation that proclaims the saving significance of his sacrificial death until he comes (1 Cor 11:26).... As the Passover remembers God's deliverance of Israel from the bondage of Egypt (Exod 12:14; 13:3, 8; Deut 16:3), so the re-presentation of this meal remembers God's deliverance of all believers through the cross of Jesus, giving them salvation" (Garland, *Luke*, 856). "The purpose of remembrance was not simply to recall the past, but to *represent* the past in order to participate in it and extend its effects into the present.... The imperative of Jesus, 'Do this in remembrance of me,' resulted in the Eucharist as the backbone of early Christian worship" (Edwards, *Gospel According to Luke*, 629; emphasis original).

Sir 39:26; 50:15), to symbolize his own blood, that is, his actual life.[67] He thus further interpreted his imminent death as a sacrificial offering to God of his total person, symbolized both by the bread that is his own body (self) and the wine that is his own blood (life). Both the body and blood of the sacrificed Passover lamb were instrumental in effecting God's salvation of the Israelites in the exodus event (Exod 12:7, 13, 22–23). Similarly, both the sacrificial body and blood of Jesus were instrumental in making his death a new event of God's salvation for his people, a salvation made present for the audience in their eating the bread/body and drinking the wine/blood of Jesus at their eucharistic meals.

The cup of wine Jesus designated as "the new covenant [διαθήκη]" in his blood (22:20) recalls the hope for a new covenant, after the establishment of the old Sinai covenant through the sacrificial "blood of the covenant" (Exod 24:6–8), by which God promises his new, definitive, eschatological forgiveness of sins (Jer 31:31–34).[68] That the cup of wine designated as the covenantal blood of Jesus "is being poured out [ἐκχυννόμενον] for you" (22:20) not only expresses Jesus' death by violent murder (cf. 18:32–33), but also underscores the sacrificial character of his death as an atonement for sins.[69] As the Levitical priest "pours out" (ἐκχεεῖ) the blood of sacrificed animals on the altar as a sin offering to atone for the sins of the people (LXX Lev 4:7, 18, 25, 30, 34), so the sacrificial blood of Jesus "is being poured out" in death to establish the new covenant that definitively unites God to his people through his forgiveness of their sins.[70] This indicates to the audience that in their eucharistic meals they are drinking the wine/blood of Jesus that effects and makes available for them God's forgiveness of their sins.[71]

---

67. "Blood is viewed as the carrier of life" (Böcher, "αἷμα," 1.37).

68. "With the wording 'this cup is the new covenant in my blood,' undoubtedly there is an allusion to Jer 31:31–34 (LXX 38:31–34), where Yahweh announces that he will 'make a new covenant with the house of Israel,' one that is totally different compared with the Sinai covenant (v. 32): now the covenant of obligation will be replaced by a covenant of promise. Yahweh promises the forgiveness of sins" (Hegermann, "διαθήκη," 1.300).

69. On Jesus' blood being poured out as expressive of both his murderous and his sacrificial death, see Untergassmair, "ἐκχέω," 1.424.

70. "Jesus' blood becomes a means of expiation provided by God" (Carpinelli, "Do This as *My* Memorial," 88).

71. "The blood of the new covenant is applied to those who drink it in the cup. They are brought into the covenant and receive all its benefits made possible by the sacrifice of Jesus.... Luke stresses the 'new' testament. 'New' is unique to Luke (and 1 Cor 11:25) and alludes to the promise of a new covenant in passages such as Is 42:9–10; 43:18–21; 55:3; 61:8; and Jer 31:31–34, which Jesus fulfills by the shedding of his blood so that sins may be remembered no more" (Just, *Luke 9:51—24:53*, 835).

With a startling transition, "But behold!," Jesus shocks the audience by introducing a dramatic contrast to the intimate meal fellowship he is sharing with his disciples at his last supper, as he then pronounced that "the hand of the one betraying me is with me at the table" (22:21). The repetitive stress on "me" highlights the treacherous incongruity of the one betraying *me* also sharing *with me* "at the table."[72] He continued his prediction by declaring that, as the Son of Man, he indeed goes "as it has been determined" by God (divine passive), but to that man by whom he is being betrayed he pronounced a condemnatory woe (22:22). This triggered in the disciples a questioning among themselves as to which one of them it could be who was going to do this (22:23). So uncertain are they of their own commitment and faithfulness that they readily accept Jesus' prediction without protesting it. The only question is which one of them will betray him. Their uncertainty serves as a poignant warning to the audience that their participation in the Eucharist does not guarantee that any one of them will not betray Jesus.[73]

There then arose an incongruous quarrel among the disciples as to which of them seemed to be greatest (22:24; cf. 9:46). In response, Jesus pointed to those who appear to be great in society: "The kings of the gentiles rule over them and those in authority over them are called benefactors" (22:25). He then issued a stern injunction for them not to strive for this kind of greatness. Rather, the greatest among them must become as the youngest (cf. 9:47-48), and the leader as one who serves (22:26). After inducing them to agree that the one who reclines at a meal is surely greater than the one who serves it, Jesus continued his paradoxical reversal and transformation of what constitutes the greatness of leadership, as he shockingly stated that he is among them as the one who serves (22:27).[74] Jesus thus indicated to his disciples and the audience that the new Passover meal of the Eucharist he has given them should issue in a leadership that imitates his humble life and

72. The word "table" (τράπεζα) often refers to the meal itself and here emphasizes the table fellowship involved; see *EDNT* 3.367; BDAG, 1013.

73. "Luke warns his community that everyone who partakes of the Eucharist is capable of betraying the Lord. Mere presence at the Eucharist is no assurance of perseverance. Indeed, only Jesus' intimates can betray him!" (Matera, *Passion Narratives*, 163). "Participation in the Lord's Supper is no guarantee that a disciple will not betray his Lord" (Fitzmyer, *Gospel According to Luke X-XXIV*, 1409).

74. "Luke says nothing about what Jesus does to serve the disciples at table. His service must refer to his pouring out his life's blood for others (vv. 19-20). Jesus therefore demonstrates what it means to be a true benefactor. By giving his life, he bestows benefits (salvation) on all humankind" (Garland, *Luke*, 867). "Jesus' life (and his coming passion and death) are thus interpreted as service, and it is all to be taken as the norm of apostolic ministry. No matter what rank the disciple or apostle may achieve in human eyes and by human estimate, their role as Christians is to serve in a lowly, humble way" (Fitzmyer, *Gospel According to Luke X-XXIV*, 1418).

sacrificial death, a leadership concerned not with the greatness of public acclaim but with the paradoxical greatness of lowly, selfless service of others.

The risen Jesus interpreted for the two Emmaus disciples, who did not yet recognize him, the things concerning himself in fulfillment of what was prophesied in *all* the scriptures (24:27). These things include the suffering, death, and resurrection of Jesus as the messianic, rejected prophet (24:19-21, 26). Invited to be the guest of the Emmaus disciples, Jesus took on the role of the host of the meal as he performed the familiar eucharistic gestures (9:16; 22:19)—"taking bread, he blessed it and breaking it, he was giving it over to them" (24:30). As soon as they recognized the risen Jesus, he disappeared from them (24:31). Before the disciples' eyes could be "opened" (διηνοίχθησαν) by God for them to recognize the risen Jesus, he had to "open" (διήνοιγεν) for them the scriptures concerning himself (24:27, 32). The Emmaus disciples' experience of the risen Jesus in both his scriptural teaching and breaking of the bread is paradigmatic for the audience's experience of the invisible risen Jesus in both their scriptural teaching and breaking of the bread whenever they celebrate the Lord's supper at the Eucharist.[75]

The risen Jesus then appeared to the entire assembly of disciples in Jerusalem (24:36). By asking his disciples to give him something to eat (24:41), Jesus continued to demonstrate that he is capable of resuming the eucharistic meal fellowship he enjoyed with his disciples before his death (cf. 24:30). That they gave over to him a piece of baked fish (24:42) recalls and complements how Jesus kept giving them broken bread and fish at the overabundant meal with eucharistic overtones (9:16).[76] At his last Passover supper before his death Jesus solemnly declared: "How eagerly I have desired to eat [φαγεῖν] this Passover meal with you before I suffer! For I say to you that I will never eat [φάγω] it again until it is fulfilled in the

---

75. "Luke's summary of the entire Emmaus episode lays the foundation for early Christian worship: 'And they were expounding the things in the way and how he was known to them in the breaking of the bread' (24:35). *This is the pattern preserved in the Divine Service: the Service of the Word followed by the Liturgy of the Lord's Supper*" (Just, *Luke 9:51–24:53*, 1014; emphasis original). "The revelatory effect of the meal at Emmaus (vv. 30-31), following immediately on the interpretative teaching of Jesus that all the Scriptures anticipate his person and ministry (vv. 25-27), foreshadows the ministries of Word and Sacrament" (Edwards, *Gospel According to Luke*, 724). "Jesus, who is now physically absent, becomes spiritually present among the community of believers through the breaking of bread" (Garland, *Luke*, 957). On the communal liturgy as the locus for the recognition of the glorified Jesus, see Bucur, "Blinded by Invisible Light," 685-707.

76. "This episode forms a parallel with the revelatory meal of Jesus with the Emmaus pair (v. 30), both of which complement the Feeding of the Five Thousand (9:16)" (Edwards, *Gospel According to Luke*, 732).

kingdom of God" (22:15-16). That Jesus actually "ate" (ἔφαγεν) with his disciples after his death (24:43) greatly bolsters the audience's hope of sharing meal fellowship with him at the final banquet in the future kingdom of God (14:15; 22:16-18, 29-30).[77] This hope is nourished for the audience whenever they celebrate Jesus' last Passover supper in remembrance of him at the Eucharist.[78]

Meals and Eucharistic Worship in Acts

Those who were baptized and received the gift of the Spirit after repenting at the preaching of Peter (Acts 2:37-38, 41) were devoting themselves not only to the teaching of the apostles, the fellowship, and the prayers, but also to "the breaking of the bread" (2:42).[79] Jesus' deliberate gesture of "the breaking of the bread" was a noteworthy feature of his meals with his disciples. He "broke into pieces" the bread and fish that he gave to his disciples (Luke 9:16). At his last supper he "broke" the bread he gave to his disciples as "my body which is being given for you" (22:19). When the risen Jesus "broke" the bread and gave it to the Emmaus disciples, they immediately recognized him (24:30). They recounted to the disciples in Jerusalem how he was made know to them in "the breaking of the bread" (24:35).[80] The devotion of the Jerusalem believers to "the breaking of the bread" (Acts 2:42), then, indicates

77. "For the first and only time, in a Gospel replete with meal scenes, Jesus' actual eating of food is the primary focus" (Carroll, *Luke*, 491-92). "A meal shows that it is Jesus and not a phantom, and it also indicates table fellowship and oneness" (Bock, *Luke 9:51—24:53*, 1935).

78. "Jesus' action at the table (24:41-43) is reminiscent of other table scenes in Luke. While here it is the risen Jesus who takes and eats before them, the matrix of fellowship at the table involves teaching and eating in the presence of God, who is present in Jesus. They give to him the fish (recalling the feeding of the five thousand), and taking it, he eats it in their presence, at their table. Later these eyewitnesses of the resurrection will testify to their ongoing table fellowship, saying that Jesus was manifest 'to us who ate and drank with him after he rose from the dead' (Acts 10:41)" (Just, *Luke 9:51—24:53*, 1046).

79. "While many scholars suggest the phrase ['the breaking of bread'] refers to the celebration of the Lord's Supper, i.e., remembering Jesus' last supper with his disciples, and while others argue that this is a reference only to ordinary meals, there is a distinct possibility that it refers to both. The 'breaking of the bread' is best understood as a reference to the ordinary meals that the believers regularly shared, during which they remembered Jesus' death on the cross for the forgiveness of sins and for the establishment of the new covenant, linked with the command to remember Jesus and his sacrifice during meals (cf. Luke 22:14-22)" (Schnabel, *Acts*, 179).

80. "'The breaking of the bread,' known from Luke 24:30, 35, is the abstract formulation that becomes the usual way Luke refers to the eucharistic celebration among early Christians" (Fitzmyer, *Acts*, 269).

that their communal meal fellowship included the eucharistic breaking of the bread that Jesus instructed them to do in remembrance of him as a way of uniting them to his death and resurrection.[81]

The Jerusalem believers had all things in common (2:44) and were sharing their property and possessions with one another, "as any had need" (2:45). They were "breaking bread in their houses" and "sharing food with gladness and generosity of heart" (2:46). This serves as a model for the eucharistic celebrations of the audience. Now that the risen Jesus has ascended to heavenly exaltation and is no longer visibly present, their eucharistic breaking of the bread is a way of uniting them to the salvific benefits of his sacrificial death and invisible presence as the risen and ascended Lord (Luke 24:30-35, 41-43; Acts 1:4). Their eucharistic meal fellowship should result in a glad and generous sharing of their food and possessions with one another, especially those who are most needy among them. By practicing and promoting eucharistic celebrations that lead them to selflessly serve one another in imitation of Jesus himself (Luke 22:24-27), rather than seeking individualistic honors and social repayment (14:7-14), they assure their inclusion in the eschatological banquet of the kingdom of God (14:15-24).

The ideal meal fellowship of the Jerusalem believers demonstrated one of the ways in which they were witnesses for the mission of proclaiming repentance for the forgiveness of sins to all nations beginning from Jerusalem (Luke 24:47-48; Acts 1:8). Their glad and generous eucharistic meal fellowship, in which they celebrated the joy of their own repentance for the forgiveness of sins (2:38), attracted the favor of the people. "Daily [καθ' ἡμέραν] the Lord was adding those who were being saved [σῳζομένους] to the community" (2:47) in correspondence to their "daily" (καθ' ἡμέραν) meal fellowship (2:46) and to Peter's exhortation that those in Jerusalem "be saved [σώθητε] from this crooked generation" (2:40). Likewise, through the eucharistic meal fellowship by which they celebrate their being saved by their own repentance and the forgiveness of sins, the members of the audience can be witnesses who attract others to be saved by repenting and being forgiven, and so share in the joy and generosity of their communal meal fellowship.[82]

---

81. "On a literary level, the breaking of bread here very likely alludes to and includes the Lord's Supper (Luke 22:19; cf. 24:30). If, for Luke, the Lord's Supper represented a meal believers shared together in memory of what Jesus had done for them (22:19), then ideally all early Christian meals together may have represented the Lord's Supper" (Keener, *Acts*, 1.1003-4). See also Walton, "Spirituality," 196-97.

82. "Luke has included this description of early Christian life as an ideal that he would desire to be characteristic of all Christians. It may be an idyllic description, but it highlights the elements that should be part of genuine Christian life: harmony, reverent care for one another, formal and informal prayer in common, and celebration of the

Saul, converted after persecuting the believers at Damascus and informed by Ananias that he is to be filled with the Holy Spirit (9:17), was baptized (9:18) and, "taking food" (λαβὼν τροφήν), was strengthened (9:19). This recalls that after the addressees of Peter repented, were baptized, and received the gift of the Holy Spirit (2:37-38, 41), they were "sharing food" (μετελάμβανον τροφῆς) with gladness and generosity of heart (2:46), while devoting themselves to the eucharistic breaking of the bread in their houses (2:42, 46).[83] Recalling how an angel appeared in answer to the prayer of Jesus, spiritually "strengthening" (ἐνισχύων) him (Luke 22:43), Saul was not only physically but spiritually "strengthened" (ἐνίσχυσεν) after taking food suggestive of a Eucharist (Acts 9:19).[84] That Saul was spiritually strengthened was confirmed when he began to proclaim in the synagogues that Jesus was the Son of God (9:20), and he was all the more "strengthened [ἐνεδυναμοῦτο]" (9:22).[85] This suggests to the audience that eucharistic meal fellowship is a source of spiritual strength for their apostolic mission.

After Peter commanded that the household of Cornelius be baptized, they invited him, the representative leader of Jewish believers (cf. 10:45), to stay for some days and share meal fellowship with these gentiles, who have now become believers (10:48).[86] That Peter stayed in this gentile household for "some days" (ἡμέρας τινάς) recalls how Saul not only took the food he was offered in meal fellowship in the house of Judas, but continued to accept the meal hospitality of the disciples in Damascus as he stayed with them for "some days [ἡμέρας τινάς]" (9:19).[87] Saul's meal fellowship with the Damascus disciples for some days implied his sharing in their eucharistic meals, since the meal fellowship of an ideal believing community includes regular devotion to the eucharistic breaking of the bread (2:42, 46). Similarly, Peter's meal fellowship with the newly baptized gentiles in the household of

Lord's Supper" (Fitzmyer, *Acts*, 269).

83. The next reference to the taking of "food" (τροφή) in Acts after 2:46 is in 9:19, enhancing this connection.

84. "An allusion to the Eucharist is perhaps present here" (Matson, *Household Conversion*, 99). That these are the only two occurrences of ἐνισχύω in Luke-Acts enhances this connection.

85. "That Paul engages in such preaching immediately after taking food suggests that more than physical strength is in view. The verb used at 9:22 to describe Paul's strengthening (ἐνεδυναμόω) is used primarily of religious and spiritual strength" (Matson, *Household Conversion*, 99n58). See also Paulsen, "ἐνεδυναμόω," 1.451.

86. "The singular personal pronoun (αὐτόν) refers to Peter, as does the discussion in 11:3; it can be assumed, however, that the believers from Joppa stayed in Caesarea as well" (Schnabel, *Acts*, 507n81).

87. The next reference to "some days" (ἡμέρας τινάς) in Acts after 9:19 is in 10:48, enhancing this connection.

Cornelius for some days implies their sharing of the Eucharist.[88] This serves as a model for the audience to share the Eucharist with the newly baptized in celebration of their full entrance into the community of believers.

Saul's meal fellowship with the Damascus disciples for "some days [ἡμέρας τινάς]" (9:19) and Peter's meal fellowship with the gentile household of Cornelius for "some days [ἡμέρας τινάς]" (10:48) implied their sharing of eucharistic meals. So the staying of Paul and his companions for meal fellowship with the newly baptized gentile household of Lydia (16:15), a worshiper of God (16:14), at Philippi for "some days [ἡμέρας τινάς]" (16:12) implies their sharing of the Eucharist.[89] The way Paul's meal fellowship with the household of Lydia resonates with Jesus' eucharistic breaking of bread for the Emmaus disciples (Luke 24:28–35) strengthens its eucharistic implications. After the Emmaus disciples "prevailed upon" (παρεβιάσαντο) Jesus, he entered to stay with them (24:29). Similarly, Lydia "prevailed upon" (παρεβιάσατο) Paul and his companions to enter her house and stay (Acts 16:15).[90] This reinforces for the audience how their own eucharistic meals can be celebrations of God's salvation for newly baptized believers regardless of their ethnic origin or gender.

The converted pagan Roman jailer at Philippi set a "table" (τράπεζαν) for Paul and Silas (16:34).[91] This recalls the special eucharistic "table" (τραπέζης) fellowship of Jesus' last supper (Luke 22:21), which anticipates the final "table" (τραπέζης) fellowship with Jesus at the eschatological banquet (22:30).[92] That the meal was the setting at which the newly baptized

88. "[I]t is more than likely, given Luke's interest in the symbolic power of food, that the table fellowship enjoyed by Peter and the newly converted household assumed a eucharistic character. It is scarcely conceivable that Luke did not intend the reader to see in this table-fellowship over the course of 'some days' a reference to the Lord's Supper" (Matson, *Household Conversion*, 116).

89. "'Worshiper of God' (σεβομένη τὸν θεόν, Acts 16:14) identifies her as a gentile who has been attracted to Jewish life and worship" (Carroll, *Luke*, 321). "As in the story of Cornelius, the meals celebrated in the house of Lydia no doubt involved the Eucharist" (Matson, *Household Conversion*, 148).

90. That these are the only two occurrences of the verb "prevail upon" (παρεβιαζομαι) in Luke-Acts (as well as in the NT) enhances this connection. The parallels between the Emmaus account and the story of Lydia "suggest that Paul's eating in the house of Lydia was similarly eucharistic in nature" (Matson, *Household Conversion*, 148–49).

91. "This is not explicitly described as a eucharist, but the allusions are plain. Every meal in Luke-Acts has dimensions that intimate the Eucharist" (Pervo, *Luke's Story*, 58).

92. That among the four Gospels only Luke employs the word "table" (τράπεζα) at Jesus' institution of the Eucharist (Luke 22:21, 30) enhances the connection and thus the eucharistic connotation of the Roman jailer's "table" (Acts 16:34). "Every meal in Luke and Acts is a proleptic celebration of the coming kingdom of God, including that

jailer and his household (Acts 16:33) "rejoiced" (ἠγαλλιάσατο) at coming to believe in God (16:34) echoes how the newly baptized believers in Jerusalem were sharing food and the eucharistic breaking of bread with "gladness [ἀγαλλιάσει]" (2:46).[93] Just as the Jerusalem believers celebrated their salvation with eschatological joy at eucharistic meals (2:42, 46), so the rejoicing jailer and his household in coming to the faith that means their salvation (16:30–31) imbues their special meal with a eucharistic association. This reinforces for the audience how at the Eucharist they celebrate God's salvation made available for and experienced presently by all the baptized in anticipation of its fullness at the eschatological banquet in the heavenly kingdom of God.

Paul's miraculous restoration to life of Eutychus, who fell from a third floor window after falling asleep and was taken up dead (20:9–10), took place "on the first day of the week," that is, on a Sunday, "when we gathered to break bread" (20:7; cf. 20:11), and thus within the context of the Eucharist.[94] The Emmaus disciples had experienced in the eucharistic breaking of the bread (24:30–35) the Jesus who died as the "living" (ζῶντα) one (Luke 24:5; cf. Acts 1:3). The community at Troas had another life-from-death experience during the eucharistic breaking of the bread, as they took the Eutychus who had died away "living [ζῶντα]" (Acts 20:12).[95] The eucharistic breaking of the bread empowered Paul to extend the life-giving effects of the death and resurrection of Jesus, continually commemorated at the Eucharist

---

of the jailer and his household" (Matson, *Household Conversion*, 164).

93. "The description of the jailer's joy with this unusual and strong verb (it and the related noun occur in Acts only in 2:46; 16:34; and in a Scripture quotation in 2:26) links the jailer with the early converts in Jerusalem. . . . In both the early Jerusalem church and in the jailer's house this exultation accompanies a meal that is evidently a celebration of salvation" (Tannehill, *Narrative Unity*, 2.200).

94. "When we gathered to break bread" is an expression that "notes an early Christian liturgical gathering on a Sunday to celebrate the Eucharist or Lord's Supper" (Fitzmyer, *Acts*, 669). "For all of its brevity and lively humor, this story provides a capsule description of an early Christian meeting, with distinctive features or activities that one might encounter as part of such a group: a Sunday night meeting in a private home, thus as a house church; a communal meal, 'breaking bread,' that easily acquires a eucharistic character; extended discussion, conversation, and discourse led by Paul or some other prominent teacher; a miracle or some other dramatic display of power. Some elements are missing, for example, singing and praying, but these have been mentioned earlier (2:42; 16:25)" (Holladay, *Acts*, 392).

95. "The life of the resurrected one means, most importantly, that he again has a physical life, like that of Tabitha or Eutychus after they were miraculously raised from the dead (Acts 9:41; 20:12)" (Schottroff, "ζῶ," 2.108). "Eutychus (whose Greek name means 'lucky one') is aptly named by Luke, who depicts him restored to 'life' in the context of a eucharistic 'breaking of bread'" (Fitzmyer, *Acts*, 667–68).

(Luke 22:19–20), to an individual member of the community.[96] But there were also communal consequences. Not only was Eutychus restored to life, but those who took him away alive "were encouraged immeasurably" (Acts 20:12), after Paul had assured them that "his life is in him" (20:10).[97]

Paul's eucharistic meal with the community at Troas (20:7–12) develops for the audience the life-giving and salvific benefits of their communal celebrations of the Eucharist in three notable ways: First, by identifying with Eutychus, the members of the audience gain a deeper appreciation of the life-giving effects of the Eucharist for their own lives. The miraculous revival of Eutychus from death, as a consequence of Jesus' resurrection from the dead commemorated and made present at the Eucharist, invites the audience to celebrate the Eucharist as a hopeful anticipation of their own ultimate participation in the eternal life of the risen Jesus at the eschatological banquet in the heavenly kingdom of God.

Second, by identifying with the community at Troas, the members of the audience gain a deeper appreciation of the life-giving effects of the Eucharist for the fellow members of their own community. That Eutychus was restored to life at the Eucharist "immeasurably encourages" (20:12) and comforts the audience that their fellow members who have died will ultimately share in the life of the risen Jesus at the eschatological banquet. And third, by identifying with Paul, the members of the audience gain a deeper appreciation of the life-giving effects of the Eucharist for its pastoral leadership. The missionary Paul's revival of Eutychus's physical life and his spiritual encouragement of the community at his farewell eucharistic breaking of the bread serve as a model for the audience's eucharistic celebrations. The Eucharist empowers the audience, like Paul, to apply the life-giving effects of the death and resurrection of Jesus to both the physical and spiritual needs of the members of the community.[98]

Paul repeatedly encouraged all on board the ship destined to be destroyed in a sea storm to share food for their salvation—not only immediately from death at sea but ultimately for their eschatological salvation

---

96. "The passage has clear symbolic features. To deny that a short pericope describing a celebration of the Eucharist in an upper room on Sunday that climaxes in the return of a dead person in the morning has any symbolic reference would border on absurdity" (Pervo, *Acts*, 513).

97. "The customary response to a miracle comes, not immediately after Eutychus is restored to life, but at the very conclusion of the event, after Paul has broken bread and after he has finished instruction, further reinforcing the communal significance of the event" (Gaventa, *Acts*, 280).

98. On the portrayal of Paul's authority in this story, see Glavic, "Eutychus," 179–206.

Meals and Eucharistic Worship

(27:33–34).⁹⁹ Paul then "took bread," "thanked" God before all, and "broke" it before he began to eat (27:35), meal gestures reminiscent of previous eucharistic meals with Jesus (Luke 9:16; 22:19; 24:30).¹⁰⁰ Whereas Paul's eating of the Eucharist at Troas led to the encouragement of believers (Acts 20:12), his eating of a meal with eucharistic associations on the ship encouraged even and especially nonbelievers (27:35–36). Because of Paul's eating of a eucharistic meal, which led to all on the ship being satisfied and thus strengthened with food (27:36–38), eventually, although the ship itself was lost as Paul predicted (27:22), "all" who had remained united by sharing food on the ship were "saved" on the land (27:44). Paul's eating of a eucharistic meal thus made the salvific, life-giving effects of the death and resurrection of Jesus present and active for all on the ship, even nonbelievers.¹⁰¹

Paul's eating of a eucharistic meal before and on behalf of all on the ship (27:33–38) has the following ramifications for the audience: The eating of the Eucharist can empower the audience, like it did Paul, to extend the life-giving, salvific effects of the death and resurrection of Jesus, commemorated and made present at the Eucharist, to both believers and nonbelievers. The celebration of the Eucharist not only anticipates future eschatological salvation at the eschatological banquet, but can have salvific and life-giving effects in present situations of distress and despair. Their eating of the Eucharist can strengthen the individual members of the audience, like it did Paul, to encourage, help, and rescue all who are in need. And finally, the celebration of the Eucharist can unite the audience, like all of those on the ship with Paul, not only with their fellow believers but with nonbelievers to work together for the present and future salvation of all peoples to be completed at the eschatological banquet in the heavenly kingdom of God.

---

99. Salvation here "is not only the hope of those in a storm at sea but the purpose of God for all humanity, as announced at the beginning of Luke (2:30–32; 3:6). The emphasis on salvation in Luke-Acts gives to the emphasis on salvation in this sea voyage a second, symbolic sense" (Tannehill, *Narrative Unity*, 2.336–37).

100. "In Christian usage 'breaking of bread' took on the specific sense of 'eucharistic' breaking of bread.... According to Acts 27:35 Paul acted in accordance with Jewish table customs. For Luke, however, an allusion to the nearness of the Lord experienced in the eucharist is not to be excluded" (Wanke, "κλαω," 2.296). "The symbolism is eucharistic. Had the narrator not wished to evoke the sacrament, he could simply have said, 'Paul ate'" (Pervo, *Acts*, 664).

101. "Even though the others do not share Paul's food, celebrating the Eucharist 'before all' so that all will eat shows a remarkable concern to benefit non-Christians through a central Christian practice" (Tannehill, *Narrative Unity*, 2.336). "Acts 27:33–38, like the 'sea stories' in Luke 5:1–11 and John 21:1–14, has a universal, missionary thrust. 'All persons' appears four times in vv. 33–37 (33, 35, 36, 37), redundancy underscoring its universalistic intent" (Pervo, *Acts*, 664).

Summary

The first meal scene in Luke, in which Jesus and his disciples eat with the tax collector Levi (Luke 5:27–32), indicates to the audience that their eucharistic banquets celebrate their past repentance in being baptized (cf. 3:3, 8) and becoming followers of Jesus like Levi. It also reminds them that at the Eucharist they share meal fellowship with the Jesus who calls them to recognize their moral or spiritual "sickness" and need to further repent and be forgiven (cf. 5:17–26). Finally, it encourages them not to shun but to call their fellow sinful followers to likewise repent and be forgiven in anticipation of the eschatological banquet.

Jesus' first meal with a Pharisee (7:36–50) presents the audience with a paradigm for their eucharistic meals. At the Eucharist they, like the sinful woman, have the opportunity to encounter Jesus and his divine authority to forgive sins. They may not only demonstrate their repentance and pray for the forgiveness of their sins, no matter how great or how many, but also express their loving gratitude for the divine forgiveness and salvific peace they can expect to receive as believers. The figure of Simon the Pharisee calls for all in the audience to ask themselves whether they have a sinfulness of which they are unaware or refuse to acknowledge (7:40–47). The meal ended without any indication of whether Simon recognized his need for repentance and without any narration of the actual eating of the meal. This invites the audience to complete the open ending of the meal scene with the eating of their eucharistic meals as repentant sinners with faith in Jesus to forgive and dismiss them in salvific peace.

Jesus' miraculously overabundant feeding of a large crowd (9:10–17) instructs the audience about their own eucharistic meals. Welcoming the crowds, Jesus, before he provided the meal, spoke to them about the kingdom of God, and cured those who had need of healing (9:11). This sets a pattern for the audience, who likewise before the Eucharist are to welcome and instruct participants about the kingdom of God. And those in need of the healing of the "sickness" of their sinfulness (cf. 5:17–32) are to be given the opportunity to repent and be forgiven. Jesus' overabundant feeding of the people to satisfaction indicates how the Eucharist can similarly satisfy the audience's spiritual hunger in anticipation of the eschatological banquet in the kingdom of God. But most of all, Jesus' enabling of his apostles, who did not think they could feed the crowds (9:12–13), to satisfy them with an overabundance so that there were twelve baskets of leftovers (9:17) indicates to the audience how their eucharistic meals likewise empower them to materially and spiritually feed hungry people to an overabundant satisfaction.

The meal with Martha and her sister Mary (10:38–42) presents the audience with complementary models for a proper understanding of and participation in the Eucharist. Mary indicates that the one thing necessary and the best portion (10:42) offered at the eucharistic meal is to hear and understand that the eschatological banquet in the kingdom of God, anticipated by the Eucharist (cf. 9:10–17), is made possible through the divine necessity of the suffering, death, and resurrection of Jesus. Rather than being distracted in trying to serve many things (10:40–41), Martha and the members of the audience are, like Mary, to listen to the word of Jesus indicating the one thing necessary for their proper participation and service not only in the eucharistic meal but as Jesus' disciples. Such service includes following Jesus by denying oneself and taking up one's cross daily in order to save one's life (9:23–25) and inherit the eternal life (10:25) of heavenly glory anticipated by the transfiguration of Jesus (9:29–31) and by the eucharistic meal, the goal of the best portion or part chosen by Mary and to be chosen by the audience.

Jesus' second meal with Pharisees (11:37–54) serves as a counter example for the eucharistic meals of the audience. By giving alms to the poor, the audience may cleanse themselves externally and internally, ritually and morally, for proper participation in the Eucharist by transforming their greed and wickedness into a selfless and compassionate concern for the needy. Jesus left the meal with the Pharisees, who failed to repent (11:53). By repenting and practicing almsgiving, the audience can properly and completely cleanse themselves so that Jesus will remain in union with them at their eucharistic meals. Jesus' woes to the Pharisees implicitly call the audience to repent by adding to their monetary donations their working for social justice and the love of God, and by seeking not adulation from others but authentic leadership of and service to others, in order to properly share a eucharistic meal with Jesus.

In his third meal with Pharisees (14:1–24) Jesus models for the audience how they are to have a compassionate care and concern for those who, like the man with dropsy, are in physical need, in order to celebrate appropriately their eucharistic meals. Jesus calls those invited to the Sabbath meal (14:7) and the audience to humble themselves in dependence upon God in their social interaction to be cured of their dropsical self-seeking (14:11). God will exalt them in places of honor at the eschatological banquet prefigured by their eucharistic meals. Similarly, Jesus invites the host of the Sabbath meal (14:12) and the audience to cure a dropsical, selfish craving for social honor by demonstrating a care and concern for the socially and economically unfortunate (14:13). God will repay them in the eschatological resurrection of the righteous (14:14) anticipated by their eucharistic meals.

The great dinner in Jesus' final parable during his third meal with Pharisees (14:16–24) characterizes the eschatological banquet in the kingdom of God (14:15) to which Jesus is inviting many to participate in by repenting. But in the parable a dropsical craving to acquire property and increase their wealth prevents those invited from attending. The parable reinforces for the audience their need to humble themselves (14:11) by rejecting a dropsical craving for wealth, in order to be exalted and blessed by God to dine at the eschatological banquet in the kingdom of God (14:15) foreshadowed by their eucharistic meals.

Jesus disclosed to his disciples his deep desire to eat "this" particular Passover meal "with you" before he "suffers" (22:15). This recalls that it is divinely "necessary" that he "suffer" much on his way to death and resurrection (9:22; 17:25) according to God's scriptural plan (18:31). His deep desire to share the special meal fellowship of this Passover with his disciples indicates its great importance for closely uniting the disciples with Jesus before he suffers a necessary sacrificial death like that of the Passover lamb. This impresses upon the audience how their eucharistic meals unite them with Jesus as the new sacrificial Passover lamb, who effects salvation not just for the people of Israel but for all peoples (2:30–32; 3:6).

The bread of his last Passover meal that Jesus gave thanks to God for and broke he gave to his disciples with a new symbolic interpretation: "This is my body which is being given for you" (22:19). In identifying the bread as his "body," that is, his whole person, his entire self, Jesus further associated his death with the sacrificial death of the Passover lamb, whose entire body was to be eaten roasted whole and without a bone broken, together with the unleavened bread and bitter herbs (Exod 12:8–9, 46; Num 9:11–12; Deut 16:2–3). The eating of the unleavened bread and the roasted body of the Passover lamb enabled the participants of the meal to experience in the communion of table fellowship the salvation God effected by the sacrificial death of the Passover lamb. So now in the same way the eating of the bread identified as the very body of Jesus in the Eucharist, their new Passover meal, enables the audience to experience in the communion of table fellowship the eschatological salvation God effected by the sacrificial death of Jesus.

As he did with the bread, Jesus gave the after-dinner cup to his disciples with a new symbolic interpretation: "This cup is the new covenant in my blood which is being poured out for you" (22:20). In identifying this cup of wine as the new covenant "in my blood," Jesus exploited the ability of wine, often described as the "blood" of grapes (LXX Gen 49:11; Deut 32:14; Sir 39:26; 50:15), to symbolize his own blood, that is, his actual life. He thus further interpreted his imminent death as a sacrificial offering to God of his total person, symbolized both by the bread that is his own body (self) and the wine that is his own blood (life). Both the body and blood of the sacrificed Passover lamb were instrumental in effecting God's salvation of the Israelites in the exodus event (Exod 12:7, 13, 22–23). Similarly, both the sacrificial body and blood of Jesus were instrumental in making his death a new event of God's salvation for his people, a salvation made present for the audience in their eating the bread/body and drinking the wine/blood of Jesus at their eucharistic meals.

The cup of wine Jesus designated as "the new covenant" in his blood (22:20) recalls the hope for a new covenant, after the establishment of the old Sinai covenant through the sacrificial "blood of the covenant" (Exod 24:6–8), by which God promises his new, definitive, eschatological forgiveness of sins (Jer 31:31–34). That the cup of wine, designated as the covenantal blood of Jesus, "is being poured out for you" (22:20) not only expresses Jesus' death by violent murder (cf. 18:32–33), but also underscores the sacrificial character of his death as an atonement for sins. As the Levitical priest "pours out" the blood of sacrificed animals on the altar as a sin offering to atone for the sins of the people (LXX Lev 4:7, 18, 25, 30, 34), so the sacrificial blood of Jesus "is being poured out" in death to establish the new covenant that definitively unites God to his people through his forgiveness of their sins. This indicates to the audience that in their eucharistic meals they are drinking the wine/blood of Jesus that effects and makes available for them God's forgiveness of their sins.

Jesus' pronouncement that "the hand of the one betraying me is with me at the table" (22:21) triggered in the disciples a questioning among themselves as to which one of them it could be who was going to do this (22:23). Their uncertainty serves as a poignant warning to the audience that their participation in the Eucharist does not guarantee that any one of them will not betray Jesus.

After inducing his disciples to agree that the one who reclines at a meal is surely greater than the one who serves it, Jesus continued his paradoxical reversal and transformation of what constitutes the greatness of leadership, as he shockingly stated that he is among them as the one who serves (24:27). Jesus thus indicated to his disciples and the audience that the new Passover meal of the Eucharist he has given them should issue in a leadership that imitates his humble life and sacrificial death, a leadership concerned not with the greatness of public acclaim but with the paradoxical greatness of lowly, selfless service of others.

Invited to be the guest of the Emmaus disciples, Jesus took on the role of the host of the meal as he performed the familiar eucharistic gestures (24:30). As soon as they recognized the risen Jesus, he disappeared from them (24:31). Before the disciples' eyes could be "opened" by God for them to recognize the risen Jesus, he had to "open" for them the scriptures concerning himself (24:27, 32). The Emmaus disciples' experience of the risen Jesus in both his scriptural teaching and breaking of the bread is paradigmatic for the audience's experience of the invisible risen Jesus in both their scriptural teaching and breaking of the bread whenever they celebrate the Lord's supper at the Eucharist.

By asking his disciples to give him something to eat (24:41), the risen Jesus continued to demonstrate that he is capable of resuming the eucharistic meal fellowship he enjoyed with his disciples before his death (cf. 24:30). That they gave over to him a piece of baked fish (24:42) recalls and complements how Jesus kept giving them broken bread and fish at the overabundant meal with eucharistic overtones (9:16). At his last Passover supper before his death Jesus solemnly declared: "How eagerly I have desired to eat this Passover meal with you before I suffer! For I say to you that I will never eat it again until it is fulfilled in the kingdom of God" (22:15-16). That Jesus actually "ate" with his disciples after his death (24:43) greatly bolsters the audience's hope of sharing meal fellowship with him at the final banquet in the future kingdom of God (14:15; 22:16-18, 29-30). This hope is nourished for the audience whenever they celebrate Jesus' last Passover supper in remembrance of him at the Eucharist.

The Jerusalem believers had all things in common (Acts 2:44) and were sharing their property and possessions with one another, "as any had need" (2:45). They were "breaking bread in their houses" and "sharing food with gladness and generosity of heart" (2:46). This serves as a model for the eucharistic celebrations of the audience. Now that the risen Jesus has ascended to heavenly exaltation and is no longer visibly present, their eucharistic breaking of the bread is a way of uniting them to the salvific benefits of his sacrificial death and invisible presence as the risen and ascended Lord (Luke 24:30-35, 41-43; Acts 1:4). Their eucharistic meal fellowship should result in a glad and generous sharing of their food and possessions with one another, especially those who are most needy among them.

The ideal meal fellowship of the Jerusalem believers (2:42-47) demonstrated one of the ways in which they were witnesses for the mission of proclaiming repentance for the forgiveness of sins to all nations beginning from Jerusalem (Luke 24:47-48; Acts 1:8). Likewise, through the eucharistic meal fellowship by which they celebrate their being saved by their own repentance and the forgiveness of sins, the members of the audience can be witnesses who attract others to be saved by repenting and being forgiven, and so share in the joy and generosity of their communal meal fellowship.

Saul, converted after persecuting the believers at Damascus and informed by Ananias that he is to be filled with the Holy Spirit (9:17), was baptized (9:18) and taking food was strengthened (9:19). Recalling how an angel appeared in answer to the prayer of Jesus, spiritually "strengthening" him (Luke 22:43), Saul was not only physically but spiritually "strengthened" after taking food suggestive of a Eucharist (Acts 9:19). That Saul was spiritually strengthened was confirmed when he began to proclaim in the synagogues that Jesus was the Son of God (9:20), and he was all the more "strengthened" (9:22). This suggests to the audience that eucharistic meal fellowship is a source of spiritual strength for their apostolic mission.

Saul's meal fellowship with the Damascus disciples for "some days" (9:19) and Peter's meal fellowship with the gentile household of Cornelius for "some days" (10:48) implied their sharing of eucharistic meals. So also the staying of Paul and his companions for meal fellowship with the newly baptized gentile household of Lydia (16:15), a worshiper of God (16:14), at Philippi for "some days" (16:12) implies their sharing of the Eucharist. This reinforces for the audience how their own eucharistic meals can be celebrations of God's salvation for newly baptized believers regardless of their ethnic origin or gender.

Paul's eucharistic meal at Troas (20:7–12) develops for the audience the life-giving and salvific benefits of their communal celebrations of the Eucharist. The miraculous revival of Eutychus from death, as a consequence of Jesus' resurrection from the dead commemorated and made present at the Eucharist, invites the audience to celebrate the Eucharist as a hopeful anticipation of their own ultimate participation in the eternal life of the risen Jesus at the eschatological banquet. That Eutychus was restored to life at the Eucharist "immeasurably encourages" (20:12) the audience that their fellow members who have died will ultimately share in the life of the risen Jesus at the eschatological banquet. The missionary Paul's revival of Eutychus's physical life and his spiritual encouragement of the community at his farewell eucharistic breaking of the bread serve as a model for the audience's eucharistic celebrations. The Eucharist empowers the audience, like Paul, to apply the life-giving effects of the death and resurrection of Jesus to both the physical and spiritual needs of the members of the community.

Paul's eating of a eucharistic meal before and on behalf of all on the ship (27:33–38) indicates that the eating of the Eucharist can empower the audience, like it did Paul, to extend the life-giving, salvific effects of the death and resurrection of Jesus to both believers and nonbelievers. The celebration of the Eucharist not only anticipates future eschatological salvation at the eschatological banquet, but can have salvific and life-giving effects in present situations of distress and despair. Their eating of the Eucharist can strengthen the individual members of the audience, like it did Paul, to encourage, help, and rescue all who are in need. And finally, the celebration of the Eucharist can unite the audience, like all of those on the ship with Paul, not only with their fellow believers but with nonbelievers to work together for the present and future salvation of all peoples to be completed at the eschatological banquet.

8

Conclusion

Detailed summaries can be found at the conclusions of the preceding chapters, which have provided a comprehensive presentation of all the various dimensions and different types of worship in Luke-Acts. There are chapters on the locations, leadership, and times for worship (ch. 2), true and false worship (ch. 3), laudatory worship (ch. 4), supplicatory worship (ch. 5), baptismal worship (ch. 6), and meals and eucharistic worship (ch. 7). These chapters demonstrate that Luke-Acts provides its audience with a basic foundation for, as well as key insights into, all of the various dimensions of Christian worship. This final chapter provides a more general concluding summary representative of the main points and themes. It serves as a summary of all of the preceding chapter summaries.

Locations, Leadership, and Times for Worship

Throughout Luke-Acts the focus of true worship for all peoples moves away from the Jerusalem temple and its Jewish leaders (chief priests, elders, synagogue officials, etc.) to the risen Lord Jesus and the leaders of the Christian community. Luke-Acts presents its audience with a concerted theme of the transition from inadequate worship, disbelief, and rejection of the gospel in Jewish synagogues, often on the Sabbath, to true worship, belief, and fellowship in Christian communities and houses, especially on the first day of the week, Sunday, the day of the revelation of the resurrection of the Lord Jesus (Luke 24:1; Acts 20:7). The Christian eucharistic meal is based upon but supersedes the Jewish Passover meal (Luke 22:15–20). And the exuberant outpouring of the Holy Spirit upon the believers in Jerusalem (Acts 2:1–11) marks the transition from the Jewish to the Christian feast of Pentecost, which celebrates the origin of the church's empowerment for its missionary activity.

True and False Worship

Luke-Acts provides its audience with a foundation for recognizing, appreciating, and practicing the true worship of the Lord God and the divine Lord Jesus rather than the false worship of earthly status, wealth, idols, the devil, or human beings. With the risen Lord Jesus as its foundational "cornerstone" (Luke 20:17), the Christian community is to become a new household of true worship to replace the Jerusalem temple whose leaders failed to make it God's "house of prayer" (19:46), a communal place for true worship. True worshipers are to "give to God what belongs to God" (20:25), that is, the total human person made in the "image" and likeness of God (Gen 1:26). Rather than giving to God dead animals in sacrificial worship in the temple, they are to give themselves as living human beings to God, since "he is not the God of the dead, but of the living, for all live to him" (Luke 20:38). In imitation of the poor widow who offered to God her whole livelihood (21:1–4), prefiguring the Lord Jesus himself, true worshipers are to give their whole lives to God in acts of self-sacrificial worship.

Supplicatory Worship

Jesus taught his disciples to submit to God by praying for the advancement of God's salvific plan (kingdom) for the world, before presenting God with petitions for their daily needs, forgiveness of their sins, and divine assistance in avoiding and overcoming temptations (Luke 11:1–4). One should not hesitate to pray to God, even with shameless audacity, because God will certainly give to one who prays to him whatever that person needs (11:5–10). Although those engaged in supplicatory worship may not receive precisely what they pray for, God will never give them anything detrimental but only what is beneficial for them. Even if petitioners do not explicitly ask for the gift of the Holy Spirit, but only for what they think they need, God will give those praying to him the Holy Spirit, as the greatest good that everyone needs (11:11–13).

The dramatic and decisive prayer of Jesus on the Mount of Olives, through which he was divinely strengthened to undergo his suffering and death (22:39–46), provides the audience not only the model but the

Conclusion

empowerment to be likewise strengthened to submit to God's will for them through prayer. In praying for the forgiveness of those who crucified him (23:33–34), Jesus provided a model for the audience to be generous in forgiving those who sin against them in accord with how he taught his disciples to pray (11:4; 6:28). The prayer of the dying Jesus, in which he entrusted his spirit into the hands of his Father (23:46), provides both the model and the empowerment for the audience to submit themselves completely to the will of God by praying, not only throughout life but at the time of death with confidence of ultimately being raised by God like Jesus to heavenly life.

Jesus' healing of the mother-in-law of Simon Peter after a petition was made to him on her behalf (4:38–39), the petitionary prayer of Peter for forgiveness (5:8), the prayer of a leper for healing (5:12), and Jesus' healing of the slave of a gentile centurion after intercession was made for him (7:1–10) provide models for the audience to pray with faith in the divine power of the Lord Jesus to forgive them and to heal the sick. The forgiveness of a sinful woman by Jesus serves as a model for the audience to repent of their sins, no matter how numerous or great, to receive forgiveness by demonstrating their faith and love through their supplicatory worship of Jesus (7:36–50). The criminal who prayed to Jesus on the cross (23:42) serves as a model for the audience to acknowledge their sinfulness and pray to join Jesus in the heavenly kingdom he has opened for them by his salvific death. And Jesus' raising of the daughter of Jairus (8:41–55) gives the audience a foundation for praying to Jesus on behalf of those who have fallen "asleep" in death, with faith that he can raise them to everlasting life in the kingdom of God.

The answered prayer of the church for the freeing of the imprisoned Peter (Acts 12:1–17), the prayers of the church at Antioch for Barnabas and Paul (13:1–3), the prayers of Barnabas and Paul for the elders in local churches (14:23), and the praying by the imprisoned Paul and Silas (16:25–34) provide foundational models encouraging the audience to pray not only for themselves when in need but for the needs of church leaders, so that they may fulfill their roles in advancing the evangelizing and pastoral missions of the church.

The examples of Paul praying while kneeling, like Jesus (Luke 22:41), Stephen (Acts 7:60), and Peter (9:40), before his fateful journey to Jerusalem (20:36; 21:3–6) serve as models for the audience to pray alone as well as with others at critical times of need for divine strength and guidance. And Paul's praying before healing the pagan father of Publius, the chief of the island of Malta (28:8–9), provides a model for the audience to pray for the health and salvation even of nonbelievers.

Laudatory Worship

Zechariah's joyful hymn of laudatory worship addressed to God (Luke 1:68–79) speaks not only for himself but for and to the audience of believers as the people of God. It abounds with references to "people," "we," "us," and "our." It invites the audience to join Zechariah in joyfully praising God not only for the birth of his son John but for the salvation God has brought to us in raising up Jesus to be born as the Davidic messiah and in raising Jesus from the dead for our salvation from the shadow of death (1:79).

Before the angel Gabriel informed Mary that she is to give birth to a son whom she will name Jesus (1:31), he greeted her with an exhortation: "Rejoice, favored one, the Lord is with you!" (1:28). After Elizabeth declared Mary "blessed" for believing that what the Lord spoke to her would be fulfilled (1:45), Mary responded to her and to Gabriel's exhortation to rejoice with a hymnic act of laudatory worship: "My soul magnifies the Lord, and my spirit rejoices in God my savior" (1:46–47). She praised God for looking upon her "lowliness" (1:48a) as an instance of how God has exalted the "lowly" (1:52). From now on not only Elizabeth but all generations "will call blessed" Mary (1:48b). In Mary God has helped the people of Israel, remembering his "mercy" (1:54), the "mercy" that is from generation to generation for those who revere him (1:50). Mary's hymn invites the audience to revere God by joining her in joyfully praising God by calling her blessed to be the mother of Jesus, the holy Son of God (1:35).

Simeon's exuberant laudatory worship (2:28–34) invites the audience to join him in blessing and praising God not only for the birth but for the resurrection of Jesus from the dead. Like Simeon, each member of the audience can face his or her inevitable death in peace, consoled by the hope of being raised from death because of the resurrection of Jesus from the dead. They can join Simeon in blessing and praising God for the birth and resurrection of Jesus, as the embodiment of salvation for all peoples (2:30–31), who sit in the darkness and shadow of death (1:79). As salvation personified, Jesus represents the light that reveals resurrection from death to the gentiles and the glory that fulfills the hope of the people of Israel for resurrection from the dead (2:32; cf. Acts 22:11; 26:23).

After the young Jesus was found in the temple, he told Mary that it was divinely "necessary" that he be "in the things of his Father" (2:49). This foreshadows that according to his Father's will it is "necessary" for him to undergo suffering and death before being raised from the dead (9:22; 17:25; 24:7, 26, 44). Mary again kept all these things in her heart (2:51; cf. 2:19). Mary thus indicates to the audience how their joyful laudatory worship is to include the praise of God not only for the birth but for the resurrection of Jesus, as they keep in their hearts the divine necessity for Jesus' suffering, death, and resurrection.

After Jesus raised from death the only son of a widow at Nain (7:11–15), those who witnessed it performed an act of laudatory worship as they "glorified" God, saying, "A great prophet was been raised among us!" and "God has visited his people!" (7:16). This recalls Zechariah's hymnic laudatory worship when he blessed the Lord the God of Israel "for he has visited and brought redemption to his people; he has raised up a horn of salvation for us in the house of David his servant" (1:68–69). The audience can again appreciate the double meaning. The great prophet Jesus "has been raised" among us by being born and by being raised from the dead. The Jesus who told the dead young man to "be raised" will himself be raised by God to eternal life. This scene invites the audience likewise to glorify God for "raising up" Jesus for our eschatological salvation.

Jesus performed an act of laudatory worship when he "rejoiced" in the Holy Spirit and said, "I praise you, Father, Lord of heaven and earth, because you have hidden these things from the wise and intelligent and revealed them to the childlike. Yes, Father, for thus has been your good pleasure" (10:21). He then proclaimed that all things have been handed over to him by his Father (cf. 4:6; 10:18), and no one knows who the Son is except the Father, and who the Father is except the Son and anyone to whom the Son wishes to reveal him (10:22). The members of the audience are to identify with the childlike disciples to whom Jesus has revealed the Father and the knowledge of the mysteries of the Kingdom of God (10:23; cf. 8:10). They are invited to join Jesus in praising his Father for revealing him as the Son, an agent of divine revelation, and thus worthy to be an object of laudatory worship as the divine Son of his divine Father.

When Jesus, mounted on a colt (19:35), was approaching the slope of the Mount of Olives, the whole multitude of the disciples, "rejoicing," began to "praise" God with a loud voice for all the "mighty deeds" they had seen (19:37). The whole multitude of disciples thus performed an act of joyful laudatory worship, as they climactically praised God for all the mighty deeds of Jesus' ministry. This leads the audience to likewise praise God joyfully for all of the mighty acts God has enabled Jesus to perform for their salvation.

Before his death Jesus called out in prayer, quoting LXX Ps 30:6, "Father, into your hands I entrust my spirit" (23:46). The centurion who saw this performed an act of laudatory worship, as he "glorified" God, saying, "Certainly this man was righteous!" (23:47). The centurion thus acknowledged that Jesus died as the suffering "righteous one" (cf. LXX Ps 30:19; Acts 3:14; 7:52; 22:14), with full confidence in God. That Jesus was "righteous" means that he died not only innocently but in accord with what God's will commanded for him. The centurion's laudatory worship invites the audience to join him in glorifying God for Jesus' accomplishment of God's salvific will in and through his death as God's "righteous one."

The risen Jesus led his disciples out as far as Bethany, and lifting up his hands, he performed an act of laudatory worship, as he "blessed" them (Luke 24:50), implicitly praising God for what he had done for them in raising Jesus from the dead and in anticipation of their being given the Holy Spirit (24:49; Acts 1:4–5, 8). While he was "blessing" them he parted from them and was taken up into heaven (Luke 24:51) by God. After "worshiping" him, the disciples complemented his praise, as they returned to Jerusalem with great joy (24:52), and they were continually in the temple "blessing" God (24:53). This final, climactic scene of laudatory worship in Luke invites the audience likewise to bless God for exalting Jesus to heaven to be an object of worship and source for the gift of the Holy Spirit to all believers, as promised by John the Baptist (3:16; Acts 2:33).

"All the people" who saw the lame man, whom Peter had "raised" up (Acts 3:7), "praising" God (3:9), complemented his laudatory worship, as they appropriately "glorified" God (4:21), who "glorified" Jesus (3:13) by raising him from the dead (3:15). The healing of the lame man was considered a "sign" (4:22; cf. 4:16), which indicated to "all the people" that it was in the name of the risen Jesus Christ that the man was healed (4:10). It also pointed to and established a hope for an eschatological salvation that goes beyond this healing, as to "the people" the apostles were proclaiming in Jesus the resurrection of the dead (4:2). The laudatory worship of the "raised" lame man as well as that of all the people invite the audience to join them in praising and glorifying God not only for the continuing healing activity of the risen Jesus, but for the hope of a future resurrection from the dead for all people, based on the resurrection of Jesus.

Paul reported to James and the elders of the Jerusalem church what God had done among the gentiles through his ministry (21:17–19). When they heard this, they performed an act of laudatory worship, as they "glorified" God (21:20), bringing to a climax all of the previous instances in Luke-Acts of "glorifying" God. This laudatory worship invites the audience to likewise glorify God for giving Jews as well as gentiles the faith that brings believers salvation to eternal life.

When Paul was met by fellow Christian believers from Rome, he performed the final, climactic act of laudatory worship in Luke-Acts, as he "gave thanks" to God and took courage (28:15). After Paul met with the leaders of the Jews (28:17), some were persuaded, but others did not believe (28:24), and so Paul declared that this salvation of God has been sent to the gentiles, and they will listen (28:28). Paul's climactic act of laudatory worship invites

Conclusion

the audience to likewise give thanks to God not only for those among Jews as well as gentiles who have already become believers but for all those who are yet to listen and believe.

Baptismal Worship

Christian baptism, prefigured by and built upon the foundation of John's baptism of repentance, is a form of ritual worship that includes an ethical dimension. All baptized Christians should complete and live out their ritual reception of the sacrament of baptism with their corresponding ethical behavior, demonstrating their repentance and transformed life with an active care and concern for the poor and less fortunate among them (Luke 3:7–11). Baptized Christians, whatever their profession or way of life, are to be honest in their dealings with others and not use others to advance and satisfy their own greediness (3:12–14).

After Jesus' ascension, as the disciples were gathered together on the day of Pentecost (Acts 2:1), suddenly there came from heaven a noise like a strong driving wind, and it filled the entire house where they were sitting (2:2). And tongues spreading out like fire appeared to them and came to rest on each one of them (2:3). All were filled with the Holy Spirit and began to speak in different tongues as the Spirit enabled them to speak out (2:4). Each of the Jewish pilgrims who had come to Jerusalem for the feast (2:5, 9–10) heard them speaking in his own language (2:6) of the mighty acts of God (2:11). This baptism with the Holy Spirit by the risen Jesus (2:33) established the sacrament of Christian baptism, which brings with it the ability to communicate to others what God has done in raising Jesus from the dead (2:22–24).

Paul testified to the Jews in the synagogue in Corinth (18:4) that Jesus was the Christ (18:5). When they opposed and reviled him, he told them that he is now going to the gentiles (18:6). Paul then left the synagogue and entered the house of a man named Titius Justus, a gentile who worshiped God (cf. 16:14), whose house was next to the synagogue (18:7). Crispus, the synagogue official, believed in the Lord together with his entire household, and many of the Corinthians who heard believed and were baptized (18:8; cf. 1 Cor 1:14). This continues to develop the trend of entire households of various sociological types believing and being baptized. Baptism has now brought into the church believers of entire households headed by a gentile God-fearing man (Cornelius), a gentile God-fearing woman (Lydia), a gentile pagan jailer, and a Jewish synagogue official. Christian baptism includes and embraces a wide variety of different kinds of people, uniting them within a community of those who believe in the Lord Jesus Christ.

Paul found some disciples in Ephesus (19:1) who had not yet received the Holy Spirit (19:2), as they had been baptized only with the baptism of John (19:3; cf. 18:25). He informed them that John baptized with a baptism of repentance, telling the people to believe in the one who was to come after him, that is, in Jesus (19:4), who will baptize them with the Holy Spirit (Luke 3:16; Acts 1:5; 2:33). When they heard this, they were baptized in the name of the Lord Jesus (19:5). And when Paul laid his hands on them, the Holy Spirit came upon them, and they spoke in tongues and prophesied (19:6), just like those who received the Holy Spirit in Jerusalem at Pentecost (2:4, 11, 17–18). This reinforces for the audience how John's baptism of repentance for the forgiveness of sins prepared for and was complemented by Christian baptism with the Holy Spirit (2:38). The Holy Spirit that believers receive at Christian baptism inspires and empowers them to communicate and bear witness to the risen Lord Jesus to all the peoples of the world (Luke 24:46–49; Acts 1:4–5, 8; 13:47).

Meals and Eucharistic Worship

The first meal scene in Luke, in which Jesus and his disciples eat with the tax collector Levi (Luke 5:27–32), indicates to the audience that their eucharistic banquets celebrate their past repentance in being baptized (cf. 3:3, 8) and becoming followers of Jesus like Levi. It also reminds them that at the Eucharist they share meal fellowship with the Jesus who calls them to recognize their moral or spiritual "sickness" and need to further repent and be forgiven (cf. 5:17–26). Finally, it encourages them not to shun but to call their fellow sinful followers to likewise repent and be forgiven in anticipation of the eschatological banquet.

Jesus' miraculously overabundant feeding of a large crowd (9:10–17) instructs the audience about their own eucharistic meals. Welcoming the crowds, Jesus, before he provided the meal, spoke to them about the kingdom of God, and cured those who had need of healing (9:11). This sets a pattern for the audience, who likewise before the Eucharist are to welcome and instruct participants about the kingdom of God. And those in need of the healing of the "sickness" of their sinfulness (cf. 5:17–32) are to be given the opportunity to repent and be forgiven. Jesus' overabundant feeding of the people to satisfaction indicates how the Eucharist can similarly satisfy the audience's spiritual hunger in anticipation of the eschatological banquet in the kingdom of God. But most of all, Jesus' enabling of his apostles, who

Conclusion

did not think they could feed the crowds (9:12–13), to satisfy them with an overabundance so that there were twelve baskets of leftovers (9:17), indicates to the audience how their eucharistic meals likewise empower them to materially and spiritually feed hungry people to an overabundant satisfaction.

The bread of his last Passover meal that Jesus gave thanks to God for and broke he gave to his disciples with a new symbolic interpretation: "This is my body which is being given for you" (22:19). In identifying the bread as his "body," that is, his whole person, his entire self, Jesus further associated his death with the sacrificial death of the Passover lamb, whose entire body was to be eaten roasted whole and without a bone broken, together with the unleavened bread and bitter herbs (Exod 12:8–9, 46; Num 9:11–12; Deut 16:2–3). The eating of the unleavened bread and the roasted body of the Passover lamb enabled the participants of the meal to experience in the communion of table fellowship the salvation God effected by the sacrificial death of the Passover lamb. So now in the same way the eating of the bread identified as the very body of Jesus in the Eucharist, their new Passover meal, enables the audience to experience in the communion of table fellowship the eschatological salvation God effected by the sacrificial death of Jesus.

As he did with the bread, Jesus gave the after-dinner cup to his disciples with a new symbolic interpretation: "This cup is the new covenant in my blood which is being poured out for you" (22:20). In identifying this cup of wine as the new covenant "in my blood," Jesus exploited the ability of wine, often described as the "blood" of grapes (LXX Gen 49:11; Deut 32:14; Sir 39:26; 50:15), to symbolize his own blood, that is, his actual life. He thus further interpreted his imminent death as a sacrificial offering to God of his total person, symbolized both by the bread that is his own body (self) and the wine that is his own blood (life). Both the body and blood of the sacrificed Passover lamb were instrumental in effecting God's salvation of the Israelites in the exodus event (Exod 12:7, 13, 22–23). Similarly, both the sacrificial body and blood of Jesus were instrumental in making his death a new event of God's salvation for his people, a salvation made present for the audience in their eating the bread/body and drinking the wine/blood of Jesus at their eucharistic meals.

Invited to be the guest of the Emmaus disciples, Jesus took on the role of the host of the meal as he performed the familiar eucharistic gestures (24:30). As soon as they recognized the risen Jesus, he disappeared from them (24:31). Before the disciples' eyes could be "opened" by God for them to recognize the risen Jesus, he had to "open" for them the scriptures concerning himself (24:27, 32). The Emmaus disciples' experience of the risen

Jesus in both his scriptural teaching and breaking of the bread is paradigmatic for the audience's experience of the invisible risen Jesus in both their scriptural teaching and breaking of the bread whenever they celebrate the Lord's supper at the Eucharist.

By asking his disciples to give him something to eat (24:41), the risen Jesus continued to demonstrate that he is capable of resuming the eucharistic meal fellowship he enjoyed with his disciples before his death (cf. 24:30). That they gave over to him a piece of baked fish (24:42) recalls and complements how Jesus kept giving them broken bread and fish at the overabundant meal with eucharistic overtones (9:16). At his last Passover supper before his death Jesus solemnly declared: "How eagerly I have desired to eat this Passover meal with you before I suffer! For I say to you that I will never eat it again until it is fulfilled in the kingdom of God" (22:15–16). That Jesus actually "ate" with his disciples after his death (24:43) greatly bolsters the audience's hope of sharing meal fellowship with him at the final banquet in the future kingdom of God (14:15; 22:16–18, 29–30). This hope is nourished for the audience whenever they celebrate Jesus' last Passover supper in remembrance of him at the Eucharist.

The Jerusalem believers had all things in common (Acts 2:44) and were sharing their property and possessions with one another, "as any had need" (2:45). They were "breaking bread in their houses" and "sharing food with gladness and generosity of heart" (2:46). This serves as a model for the eucharistic celebrations of the audience. Now that the risen Jesus has ascended to heavenly exaltation and is no longer visibly present, their eucharistic breaking of the bread is a way of uniting them to the salvific benefits of his sacrificial death and invisible presence as the risen and ascended Lord (Luke 24:30–35, 41–43; Acts 1:4). Their eucharistic meal fellowship should result in a glad and generous sharing of their food and possessions with one another, especially those who are most needy among them.

Saul's meal fellowship with the Damascus disciples for "some days" (9:19) and Peter's meal fellowship with the gentile household of Cornelius for "some days" (10:48) implied their sharing of eucharistic meals. So also the staying of Paul and his companions for meal fellowship with the newly baptized gentile household of Lydia (16:15), a worshiper of God (16:14), at Philippi for "some days" (16:12) implies their sharing of the Eucharist. This reinforces for the audience how their own eucharistic meals can be celebrations of God's salvation for newly baptized believers regardless of their ethnic origin or gender.

Paul's eucharistic meal at Troas (20:7–12) develops for the audience the life-giving and salvific benefits of their communal celebrations of the Eucharist. The miraculous revival of Eutychus from death, as a consequence

Conclusion

of Jesus' resurrection from the dead commemorated and made present at the Eucharist, invites the audience to celebrate the Eucharist as a hopeful anticipation of their own ultimate participation in the eternal life of the risen Jesus at the eschatological banquet. That Eutychus was restored to life at the Eucharist "immeasurably encourages" (20:12) the audience that their fellow members who have died will ultimately share in the life of the risen Jesus at the eschatological banquet. The missionary Paul's revival of Eutychus's physical life and his spiritual encouragement of the community at his farewell eucharistic breaking of the bread serve as a model for the audience's eucharistic celebrations. The Eucharist empowers the audience, like Paul, to apply the life-giving effects of the death and resurrection of Jesus to both the physical and spiritual needs of the members of the community.

Paul's eating of a eucharistic meal before and on behalf of all on the ship (27:33–38) indicates that the eating of the Eucharist can empower the audience, like it did Paul, to extend the life-giving, salvific effects of the death and resurrection of Jesus to both believers and nonbelievers. The celebration of the Eucharist not only anticipates future eschatological salvation at the eschatological banquet, but can have salvific and life-giving effects in present situations of distress and despair. Their eating of the Eucharist can strengthen the individual members of the audience, like it did Paul, to encourage, help, and rescue all who are in need. And finally, the celebration of the Eucharist can unite the audience, like all of those on the ship with Paul, not only with their fellow believers but with nonbelievers to work together for the present and future salvation of all peoples to be completed at the eschatological banquet.

Bibliography

Avemarie, Friedrich. *Die Tauferzählungen Der Apostelgeschichte: Theologie und Geschichte*. WUNT 139. Tübingen: Mohr Siebeck, 2002.
Balentine, Samuel E. "Prayer." In *EDB* 1077–79.
Balz, Horst. "μαμωνᾶς." In *EDNT* 2.382–83.
———. "οὐαί." In *EDNT* 2.540.
Bauckham, Richard. *Jesus and the Eyewitnesses: The Gospels as Eyewitness Testimony*. Grand Rapids: Eerdmans, 2006.
Bergmeier, Roland. "πούς." In *EDNT* 3.143–44.
Bieder, Werner. "βαπτίζω." In *EDNT* 1.192–96.
Böcher, Otto. "αἷμα." In *EDNT* 1.37–39.
Bock, Darrell L. *Acts*. BECNT. Grand Rapids: Baker Academic, 2007.
———. *Luke 1:1—9:50*. BECNT. Grand Rapids: Baker Academic, 1994.
———. *Luke 9:51—24:53*. BECNT. Grand Rapids: Baker Academic, 1996.
Borchert, Gerald L. *Worship in the New Testament: Divine Mystery and Human Response*. St. Louis: Chalice, 2008.
Boring, M. Eugene. "Messianic Banquet." In *NIDB* 4.66–67.
Braun, Willi. *Feasting and Social Rhetoric in Luke 14*. SNTSMS 85. Cambridge: Cambridge University Press, 1995.
Bubbers, Susan I. *A Scriptural Theology of Eucharistic Blessings: Profiles from the History of Interpretation*. LNTS 495. London: Bloomsbury T&T Clark, 2013.
Bucur, Bogdan G. "Blinded by Invisible Light: Revisiting the Emmaus Story (Luke 24:13–35)." *ETL* 90 (2014) 685–707.
Burer, Michael H. *Divine Sabbath Work*. BBRSup 5. Winona Lake, IN: Eisenbrauns, 2012.
Burke, Trevor J. "The Parable of the Prodigal Father: An Interpretative Key to the Third Gospel (Luke 15:11–32)." *TynBul* 64 (2013) 217–38.
Butticaz, Simon. "'Le récit des événements accomplish parmi nous' (Lc 1,1): Euvre de Dieu ou actes d'apôtres?" *RTP* 148 (2016) 607–25.
Byrne, Brendan. *The Hospitality of God: A Reading of Luke's Gospel*. Collegeville, MN: Liturgical, 2000.
Campbell, William Sanger. *The "We" Passages in the Acts of the Apostles: The Narrator as Narrative Character*. SBLStBL 14. Atlanta: SBL, 2007.
Carpinelli, Francis Giordano. "'Do This as *My* Memorial' (Luke 22:19): Lucan Soteriology of Atonement." *CBQ* 61 (1999) 74–91.
Carroll, John T. *Luke: A Commentary*. NTL. Louisville: Westminster John Knox, 2012.

Coleridge, Mark. *The Birth of the Lukan Narrative: Narrative as Christology in Luke 1–2*. JSNTSup 88. Sheffield: JSOT, 1993.

Cosgrove, Charles H. "A Woman's Unbound Hair in the Greco-Roman World, with Special Reference to the Story of the 'Sinful Woman' in Luke 7:36–50," *JBL* 124 (2005) 675–92.

Crump, David Michael. *Jesus the Intercessor: Prayer and Christology in Luke-Acts*. WUNT 49. Tübingen: Mohr, 1992.

———. *Knocking on Heaven's Door: A New Testament Theology of Petitionary Prayer*. Grand Rapids: Baker Academic, 2006.

De Long, Kindalee Pfremmer. *Surprised by God: Praise Responses in the Narrative of Luke-Acts*. BZNW 166. Berlin: de Gruyter, 2009.

De Santis, Massimo. "La visita di Dio alla vedova di Nain (Lc 7,11–17) e la risurrezione di Gesù (Lc 24)." *RivB* 62 (2014) 49–74.

Dillon, Richard J. "The Benedictus in Micro- and Macrocontext." *CBQ* 68 (2006) 457–80.

———. "A Narrative Analysis of the Baptist's Nativity in Luke 1." *CBQ* 79 (2017) 240–60.

Dinkler, Michal Beth. *Silent Statements: Narrative Representations of Speech and Silence in the Gospel of Luke*. BZNW 191. Berlin: de Gruyter, 2013.

Downing, Francis Gerald. "Theophilus's First Reading of Luke-Acts." In *Luke's Literary Achievement: Collected Essays*, edited by C. M. Tuckett, 91–109. JSNTSup 116. Sheffield: Sheffield Academic, 1995.

Edwards, James R. *The Gospel According to Luke*. The Pillar New Testament Commentary. Grand Rapids: Eerdmans, 2015.

Endres, John C. "Praise." In *NIDB* 4.578–79.

Esposito, Thomas. *Jesus' Meals with Pharisees and Their Liturgical Roots*. AnBib 209. Rome: Gregorian & Biblical Press, 2015.

Eve, Eric. *Writing the Gospels: Composition and Memory*. London: SPCK, 2016.

Farkasfalvy, Denis. "The Eucharistic Provenance of New Testament Texts." In *Rediscovering the Eucharist: Ecumenical Conversations*, edited by Roack A. Kereszty, 27–51. Mahwah, NJ: Paulist, 2003.

Feldkämper, Ludger. *Der betende Jesus als Heilsmittler nach Lukas*. Veröffentlichungen des Missionspriesterseminars St. Augustin bei Bonn 29. Bonn: Steyler, 1978.

Fitzmyer, Joseph A. *The Acts of the Apostles: A New Translation with Introduction and Commentary*. AB 31. New York: Doubleday, 1998.

———. *The Gospel According to Luke I–IX*. AB 28. Garden City, NY: Doubleday, 1981.

———. *The Gospel According to Luke X–XXIV*. AB 28A. Garden City, NY: Doubleday, 1985.

García Serrano, Andrés. "Anna's Characterization in Luke 2:36–38: A Case of Conceptual Allusion?" *CBQ* 76 (2014) 464–80.

Garland, David E. *Luke*. Zondervan Exegetical Commentary on the New Testament. Grand Rapids: Zondervan, 2011.

Gathercole, Simon. "The Heavenly ἀνατολή (Luke 1:78–9)." *JTS* 56 (2005) 471–88.

Gaventa, Beverly Roberts. *Acts*. ANTC. Nashville: Abingdon, 2003.

Glavic, J. A. "Eutychus in Acts and in the Church: The Narrative Significance of Acts 20:6–12." *BBR* 24 (2014) 179–206.

Gorman, Frank H. "Passover, Feast Of." In *EDB* 1013–14.

———. "Pentecost." In *EDB* 1027.

Green, Joel B. *Conversion in Luke-Acts: Divine Action, Human Cognition, and the People of God.* Grand Rapids: Baker Academic, 2015.

———. *The Gospel of Luke.* NICNT. Grand Rapids: Eerdmans, 1997.

Guinan, Michael D. "Praise." In *EDB* 1076–77.

Hamm, Dennis. "Acts 3:1–10: The Healing of the Temple Beggar in Lucan Theology." *Bib* 67 (1986) 305–19.

———. "Acts 4:23–31—A Neglected Biblical Paradigm of Christian Worship (Especially in Troubled Times)." *Worship* 77 (2003) 225–37.

———. "The Freeing of the Bent Woman and the Restoration of Israel: Luke 13:10–17 as Narrative Theology." *JSNT* 31 (1987) 23–44.

———. "Praying 'Regularly' (not 'Constantly'): A Note on the Cultic Background of *dia pantos* at Luke 24:53, Acts 10:2, and Hebrews 9:6, 13:15." *ExpTim* 116 (2004) 50–52.

———. "The Tamid Service in Luke-Acts: The Cultic Background Behind Luke's Theology of Worship (Luke 1:5–25; 18:9–14; 24:50–53; Acts 3:1; 10:3, 30)." *CBQ* 65 (2003) 215–31.

———. "What the Samaritan Leper Sees: The Narrative Christology of Luke 17:11–19." *CBQ* 56 (1994) 273–87.

Harris, Sarah. *The Davidic Shepherd King in the Lukan Narrative.* LNTS 558. London: Bloomsbury T&T Clark, 2016.

Hays, Richard B. *Echoes of Scripture in the Gospels.* Waco, TX: Baylor University Press, 2016.

Head, Peter. "The Temple in Luke's Gospel." In *Heaven on Earth: The Temple in Biblical Theology,* edited by T. Desmond Alexander and Simon Gathercole, 101–19. Waynesboro, GA: Paternoster, 2004.

Hegermann, Harald. "διαθήκη." In *EDNT* 1.299–301.

Heil, John Paul. *The Book of Revelation: Worship for Life in the Spirit of Prophecy.* Eugene, OR: Cascade, 2014.

———. *The Gospel of John: Worship for Divine Life Eternal.* Eugene, OR: Cascade, 2015.

———. *1–3 John: Worship by Loving God and One Another to Live Eternally.* Eugene, OR: Cascade, 2015.

———. *The Letter of James: Worship to Live By.* Eugene, OR: Cascade, 2012.

———. *The Letters of Paul as Rituals of Worship.* Eugene, OR: Cascade, 2011.

———. *The Meal Scenes in Luke-Acts: An Audience-Oriented Approach.* SBLMS 52. Atlanta: Society of Biblical Literature, 1999.

———. *1 Peter, 2 Peter, and Jude: Worship Matters.* Eugene, OR: Cascade, 2013.

———. "Reader-Response and the Irony of Jesus Before the Sanhedrin in Luke 22:66–71." *CBQ* 51 (1989) 271–84.

———. "Reader-Response and the Irony of the Trial of Jesus in Luke 23:1–25." *ScEs* 43 (1991) 175–86.

———. *The Transfiguration of Jesus: Narrative Meaning and Function of Mark 9:2–8, Matt 17:1–8 and Luke 9:28–36.* AnBib 144. Rome: Editrice Pontificio Istituto Biblico, 2000.

———. *Worship in the Letter to the Hebrews.* Eugene, OR: Cascade, 2011.

Henrichs-Tarasenkova, Nina. *Luke's Christology of Divine Identity.* LNTS 542. London: Bloomsbury T&T Clark, 2015.

Holladay, Carl R. *Acts: A Commentary.* NTL. Louisville: Westminster John Knox, 2016.

Holmås, Geir Otto. "'My House Shall Be a House of Prayer': Regarding the Temple as a Place of Prayer in Acts within the Context of Luke's Apologetic Objective." *JSNT* 27 (2005) 393–416.

———. *Prayer and Vindication in Luke-Acts: The Theme of Prayer within the Context of the Legitimating and Edifying Objective of the Lukan Narrative*. LNTS 433. London: Bloomsbury T&T Clark, 2011.

Jipp, Joshua W. "Paul's Areopagus Speech of Acts 17:16–34 as *Both* Critique *and* Propaganda." *JBL* 131 (2012) 567–88.

Johnson, Luke Timothy. *The Gospel of Luke*. SP 3. Collegeville, MN: Liturgical, 1991.

———. *The Acts of the Apostles*. SP 5. Collegeville, MN: Liturgical, 1992.

Just, Arthur A. *Luke 1:1—9:50*. Concordia Commentary. St. Louis: Concordia, 1996.

———. *Luke 9:51—24:53*. Concordia Commentary. St. Louis, Concordia, 1997.

———. "Luke's Canonical Criterion." *CTQ* 79 (2015) 245–60.

Keener, Craig S. *Acts: An Exegetical Commentary*. Vol. 1, *Introduction and 1:1—2:47*. Grand Rapids: Baker Academic, 2012.

———. *Acts: An Exegetical Commentary*. Vol. 2, *3:1—14:28*. Grand Rapids: Baker Academic, 2013.

———. *Acts: An Exegetical Commentary*. Vol. 3, *15:1—23:35*. Grand Rapids: Baker Academic, 2014.

———. *Acts: An Exegetical Commentary*. Vol. 4, *24:1—28:31*. Grand Rapids: Baker Academic, 2015.

Koenig, John. *The Feast of the World's Redemption: Eucharistic Origins and Christian Mission*. Harrisburg, PA: Trinity International, 2000.

Kuhn, Karl Allen. "Beginning the Witness: The αὐτόπται καὶ ὑπηρέται of Luke's Infancy Narrative." *NTS* 49 (2003) 237–55.

———. "Deaf or Defiant? The Literary, Cultural, and Affective-Rhetorical Keys to the Naming of John (Luke 1:57–80)." *CBQ* 75 (2013) 486–503.

———. *The Heart of Biblical Narrative: Rediscovering Biblical Appeal to the Emotions*. Minneapolis: Fortress, 2009.

———. *The Kingdom according to Luke and Acts: A Social, Literary, and Theological Introduction*. Grand Rapids: Baker Academic, 2015.

Kurz, William S. *Acts of the Apostles*. Catholic Commentary on Sacred Scripture. Grand Rapids: Baker Academic, 2013.

———. "Narrative Models for Imitation in Luke-Acts." In *Greeks, Romans and Christians: Essays in Honor of Abraham J. Malherbe*, edited by D. L. Balch, E. Ferguson, and W. A. Meeks, 171–89. Minneapolis: Fortress, 1990.

Lanier, Gregory R. "'From God' or 'from Heaven'? Ἐξ ὕψους in Luke 1,78." *Bib* 97 (2016) 121–27.

Lincoln, Andrew T. "From Sabbath to Lord's Day: A Biblical and Theological Perspective." In *From Sabbath to Lord's Day: A Biblical, Historical, and Theological Investigation*, edited by D. A. Carson, 343–412. Eugene, OR: Wipf & Stock, 1999.

———. "Sabbath, Rest, and Eschatology in the New Testament." In *From Sabbath to Lord's Day: A Biblical, Historical, and Theological Investigation*, edited by D. A. Carson, 197–220. Eugene, OR: Wipf & Stock, 1999.

Magdalene, F. Rachel. "Bless, Blessing." In *EDB* 192.

Matera, Frank J. *Passion Narratives and Gospel Theologies: Interpreting the Synoptics Through Their Passion Stories*. Mahwah, NJ: Paulist, 1986.

Matson, David L. *Household Conversion Narratives in Acts.* JSNTSup 123. Sheffield: Sheffield Academic, 1996.
Maxwell, Kathy Reiko. *Hearing Between the Lines: The Audience as Fellow-Worker in Luke-Acts and Its Literary Milieu.* LNTS 425: London: T&T Clark International, 2010.
May, David M. "The Straightened Woman (Luke 13:10–17): Paradise Lost and Regained." *PRSt* 24 (1997) 245–58.
McBride, S. Dean. "Bless." In *NIDB* 1.476–77.
McGowan, Andrew B. *Ancient Christian Worship: Early Church Practices in Social, Historical, and Theological Perspective.* Grand Rapids: Baker Academic, 2014.
McHugh, John. *The Mother of Jesus in the New Testament.* Garden City, NY: Doubleday, 1975.
Mekkattukunnel, Andrews George. *The Priestly Blessing of the Risen Christ: An Exegetico-Theological Analysis of Luke 24, 50–53.* European University Studies 714. Bern: Lang, 2000.
Metzger, Bruce Manning. *A Textual Commentary on the Greek New Testament.* 2nd ed. Stuttgart: Deutsche Bibelgesellschaft, 1994.
Millar, J. Gary. *Calling on the Name of the Lord: A Biblical Theology of Prayer.* New Studies in Biblical Theology 38. Downers Grove, IL: InterVarsity, 2016.
Moles, John. "Luke's Preface: The Greek Decree, Classical Historiography and Christian Redefinitions." *NTS* 57 (2011) 461–82.
Nolland, John. *Luke 18:35—24:53.* WBC 35C. Dallas: Word, 1993.
O'Toole, Robert F. "Paul at Athens and Luke's Notion of Worship." *RB* 89 (1982) 185–97.
———. "Some Exegetical Reflections on Luke 13:10–17." *Bib* 73 (1992) 84–107.
Padilla, Osvaldo. *The Acts of the Apostles: Interpretation, History and Theology.* Downers Grove, IL: IVP Academic, 2016.
———. *The Speeches of Outsiders in Acts: Poetics, Theology and Historiography.* SNTSMS 144. Cambridge: Cambridge University Press, 2008.
Papademetriou, Kyriakoula. "Illustrating the Meaning of the w. ἀνατάξασθαι and Its Sense in the Preface of Luke (Lk 1:1)." *EstBib* 74 (2016) 365–87.
Patsch, Herrman. "πάσχα." In *EDNT* 3.49–51.
Paulsen, Henning. "ἐνεδυναμόω." In *EDNT* 1.451.
Perrin, Nicholas. *Jesus the Temple.* Grand Rapids: Baker Academic, 2010.
Pervo, Richard I. *Acts: A Commentary.* Hermeneia. Minneapolis: Fortress, 2009.
———. *Luke's Story of Paul.* Minneapolis: Fortress, 1990.
Peterson, David G. *The Acts of the Apostles.* The Pillar New Testament Commentary. Grand Rapids: Eerdmans, 2009.
———. *Engaging with God: A Biblical Theology of Worship.* Downers Grove, IL: InterVarsity Press, 1992.
Phillips, Thomas E. "Why Did Mary Wrap the Newborn Jesus in 'Swaddling Clothes'? Luke 2.7 and 2.12 in the Context of Luke-Acts and First-Century Literature." In *Reading Acts Today: Essays in Honour of Loveday C. A. Alexander*, edited by Steve Walton et al., 29–42. LNTS 427. London: Bloomsbury T&T Clark, 2011.
Plymale, Stephen F. *The Prayer Texts of Luke-Acts.* AUSTR 118. New York: Lang, 1991.
Pope, Michael. "The Downward Motion of Jesus' Sweat and the Authenticity of Luke 22:43–44." *CBQ* 79 (2017) 261–81.
Reardon, Timothy W. "Cleansing through Almsgiving in Luke-Acts: Purity, Cornelius, and the Translation of Acts 15:9." *CBQ* 78 (2016) 463–82.

Rebell, Walter. "χιτών." In *EDNT* 3.468.

Resseguie, James L. *Narrative Criticism of the New Testament: An Introduction.* Grand Rapids: Baker Academic, 2005.

Rosner, Brian S. *Greed as Idolatry: The Origin and Meaning of a Pauline Metaphor.* Grand Rapids: Eerdmans, 2007.

Roth, Stephen J. *The Blind, the Lame, and the Poor: Character Types in Luke-Acts.* JSNTSup 144. Sheffield: Sheffield Academic, 1997.

Rowe, C. Kavin. *Early Narrative Christology: The Lord in the Gospel of Luke.* Grand Rapids: Baker Academic, 2006.

———. "The Grammar of Life: The Areopagus Speech and Pagan Tradition." *NTS* 57 (2010) 31–50.

———. *World Upside Down: Reading Acts in the Greco-Roman Age.* Oxford: Oxford University Press, 2009.

Ryan, Jordan J. "Jesus and Synagogue Disputes: Recovering the Institutional Context of Luke 13:10–17." *CBQ* 79 (2017) 41–59.

Schnabel, Eckhard J. *Acts.* Zondervan Exegetical Commentary on the New Testament. Grand Rapids: Zondervan, 2012.

Schottroff, Luise. "ζω." In *EDNT* 2.105–9.

Seo, Pyung Soo. *Luke's Jesus in the Roman Empire and the Emperor in the Gospel of Luke.* Eugene, OR: Pickwick, 2015.

Shellberg, Pamela. *Cleansed Lepers, Cleansed Hearts: Purity and Healing in Luke-Acts.* Minneapolis: Fortress, 2015.

Sick, David H. "Zacchaeus as the Rich Host of Classical Satire." *BibInt* 24 (2016) 229–44.

Smit, Peter-Ben. "Negotiating a New World View in Acts 1.8? A Note on the Expression ἕως ἐσχάτου τῆς γῆς." *NTS* 63 (2017) 1–22.

Smith, Dennis E. "Meals." In *EDB* 874–76.

Smith-Christopher, Daniel L. "Fasting." In *EDB* 456.

Snodgrass, Klyne. *Stories with Intent: A Comprehensive Guide to the Parables of Jesus.* Grand Rapids: Eerdmans, 2008.

Spencer, F. Scott. *Journeying through Acts: A Literary-Cultural Reading.* Grand Rapids: Baker Academic, 2004.

Staudinger, Ferdinand. "ἐλεημοσύνη." In *EDNT* 1.428–29.

Sylva, Dennis D. "The Cryptic Clause *en tois tou patrous mou dei einai me* in Lk 2:49b." *ZNW* 78 (1987) 132–40.

———. "The Temple Curtain and Jesus' Death in the Gospel of Luke." *JBL* 105 (1986) 239–50.

Szukalski, John A. *Tormented in Hades: The Rich Man and Lazarus (Luke 16:19–31) and Other Lucan Parables for Persuading the Rich to Repentance.* Eugene, OR: Pickwick, 2013.

Tannehill, Robert C. *The Narrative Unity of Luke-Acts.* Vol. 1, *The Gospel According to Luke.* FF. Philadelphia: Fortress, 1986.

———. *The Narrative Unity of Luke-Acts.* Vol. 2, *The Acts of the Apostles.* FF. Minneapolis: Fortress, 1990.

———. "Should We Love Simon the Pharisee? Hermeneutical Reflections on the Pharisees in Luke." *CurTM* 21 (1994) 424–33.

Taylor, Joan E. "Baptism." In *NIDB* 1.390–95.

Thompson, Alan J. *The Acts of the Risen Lord Jesus: Luke's Account of God's Unfolding Plan.* New Studies in Biblical Theology 27. Downers Grove, IL: InterVarsity, 2011.

Thompson, Michael B. "Paul in the Book of Acts: Differences and Distance." *ExpTim* 122 (2011) 425–36.
Tipei, John Fleter. *The Laying On of Hands in the New Testament: Its Significance, Techniques, and Effects.* Lanham, MD: University Press of America, 2009.
Turner, Max. *Power from on High: The Spirit in Israel's Restoration and Witness in Luke-Acts.* Journal of Pentecostal Theology Supplement Series 9. Sheffield: Sheffield Academic, 1996.
Untergassmair, Franz Georg. "ἐκχέω." In *EDNT* 1.424.
Von der Osten-Sacken, Peter. "δεξιός." In *EDNT* 1.285–86.
Walton, Steve. "A Spirituality of Acts?" In *Reading Acts Today: Essays in Honour of Loveday C. A. Alexander*, edited by Steve Walton et al., 186–201. LNTS 427. London: Bloomsbury T&T Clark, 2011.

———. "A Tale of Two Perspectives? The Place of the Temple in Acts." In *Heaven on Earth: The Temple in Biblical Theology*, edited by T. Desmond Alexander and Simon Gathercole, 135–49. Waynesboro, GA: Paternoster, 2004.
Wanke, Joachim. "κλαω." In *EDNT* 2.295–96.
Winter, Bruce W. *Divine Honours for the Caesars: The First Christians' Responses.* Grand Rapids: Eerdmans, 2015.
Witherington, Ben. *The Acts of the Apostles: A Socio-Rhetorical Commentary.* Grand Rapids: Eerdmans, 1998.
Witherup, Ronald D. "Cornelius Over and Over and Over Again: 'Functional Redundancy' in the Acts of the Apostles." *JSNT* 49 (1993) 45–66.
Wolter, Michael. *The Gospel According to Luke.* Vol. 1, *Luke 1—9:50.* Waco, TX: Baylor University Press, 2016.
Yamasaki, Gary. "Point of View in a Gospel Story: What Difference Does It Make? Luke 19:1–10 as a Test Case." *JBL* 125 (2006) 89–105.

Scripture Index

OLD TESTAMENT

Genesis

1:26 (LXX)	12, 34, 38, 142
2:1–3	108
49:11 (LXX)	123, 136, 149

Exodus

3:1	17
3:12	17
12:1–30	120n53
12:6	121
12:7	124, 137, 149
12:8–9	122, 136, 149
12:13	124, 137, 149
12:14 (LXX)	29, 123
12:17	123
12:21 (LXX)	121n58
12:22–23	124, 137, 149
12:24	123
12:27 (LXX)	121n58
12:46	122, 136
13:9 (LXX)	123
13:10	123
16:3 (LXX)	111
20:8–11	108
24:6–8	124, 137

Leviticus

4:7 (LXX)	124, 137
4:18 (LXX)	124, 137
4:25 (LXX)	124, 137
4:30 (LXX)	124, 137
4:34 (LXX)	124, 137
23:9–21	29
24:5–9	21, 108
25:10	19

Numbers

9:11–12	122, 136, 149

Deuteronomy

6:13	12, 32
6:16	12
16:1–8	120n53
16:2–3	122, 136, 149
16:2 (LXX)	121, 121n58
16:4–6 (LXX)	121n58
16:5–6	121
16:9–11	29
22:9 (LXX)	121n61
32:14 (LXX)	123, 136, 149

1 Samuel

21:1–6	21
21:2–7	108

2 Kings

4:41–44	111n18
5:7	32, 48

Psalms

15:5 (LXX)	113n26

Psalms (continued)

15:8–11 (LXX)	79, 81n68, 84
15:9–11 (LXX)	79
30:6 (LXX)	9, 46, 77, 89, 145
30:19 (LXX)	78, 89, 145
77:19–20 (LXX)	111
90:11–12 (LXX)	12
110:1	34
117:22 (LXX)	13, 16, 34

Sirach

39:26	124, 136, 149
50:15	124, 136, 149
50:20–21	78n60

Hosea

2:18	108n6
2:21	108n6

Amos

9:13–15	111

Joel

2:24–26	111

Zechariah

3:8 (LXX)	65
6:12 (LXX)	65

Isaiah

9:1 (LXX)	65
25:6–8	111
32:12 (LXX)	121n61
40:3–5 (LXX)	93
53:7–8 (LXX)	97
53:12 (LXX)	52
54:5—55:5	108n6
54:5–8	108n6
55:1–2 (LXX)	107n4, 108
55:7 (LXX)	107n4
56:7	13, 33
58:6	18
61:1–2	18
62:5	108n6
66:1	17

Jeremiah

2:2	108n6
7:11	13, 33
23:5 (LXX)	65
31:14	108
31:31–34	124, 137

Ezekiel

16:7–8	108n6

NEW TESTAMENT

Matthew

6:24	34n8
26:26	110

Mark

14:22	110

Luke

1–2	59
1:1–4	2, 4–7
1:1	4, 5, 6
1:2	4, 5, 6
1:3–4	4, 93, 106
1:3	4, 5, 6
1:4	5, 6, 6n20, 7, 64, 110
1:5–13	39
1:5–7	9
1:6	78n58
1:7–9	64
1:9	8, 9
1:10	9, 39, 64
1:11	9
1:13	40, 55, 64
1:14	64, 66, 80, 86
1:15–17	65
1:17	9, 40, 93
1:19	64
1:20	64

Scripture Index

1:21	8	2:10	68, 86
1:22	8	2:11	12, 21, 32, 40, 68, 69, 71, 86
1:24	66	2:13	68, 76, 80, 86
1:25	66	2:14	68, 69, 77, 86
1:27	21, 64	2:16–17	71
1:28	66, 86, 144	2:16	68, 86
1:31	66, 86, 144	2:17	68, 86
1:32	21, 31, 64	2:18	71
1:33	31	2:19	71, 72, 87
1:35	19, 20, 44, 67, 82, 86, 144	2:20	68, 72, 76, 80, 84, 86
1:38	68	2:25	68, 69, 71
1:41	66	2:26	11, 68, 69
1:42–43	86	2:27–28	69
1:42	66, 80	2:27	11, 68
1:43	12, 32, 40, 65, 66, 68, 86	2:28–34	70, 86, 144
1:44	66, 80	2:28	11, 68, 93
1:45	67, 86, 144	2:29–32	77
1:46–55	67	2:29	68, 69
1:46–47	67, 86, 144	2:30–32	93, 121, 136
1:46	11, 33, 38, 71, 82	2:30–31	71, 86, 144
1:47	73	2:30	11, 22, 40, 69, 93n6
1:48	67, 86, 144	2:31	11, 69
1:49	67	2:32	11, 69, 71, 87, 144
1:50	67, 86, 144	2:34	70
1:52	67, 86, 144	2:35	21, 71
1:54	67, 86, 144	2:36	11, 40, 71, 87
1:57	66, 85	2:37	11, 40, 71, 87, 107
1:58	66, 86	2:38	11, 40, 71, 87
1:62	64	2:46	11
1:63	64	2:47	11
1:64	64	2:49	11, 72, 87, 144
1:67	64	2:51	72, 87
1:68–79	65, 85, 144	3:2	93
1:68–69	73, 88, 145	3:3–6	107
1:68	64, 65, 71, 87	3:3	92, 93, 96, 98, 99, 103, 107, 113, 120, 134, 148
1:69	21, 22, 64, 65, 66, 69, 71, 87		
1:70	65	3:4	12, 65, 93, 120
1:71	22, 65, 66, 69	3:6	22, 77, 93, 93n6, 121, 136
1:72–73	65	3:7–14	120
1:74	65	3:7–11	102, 147
1:76	65, 93	3:7	93
1:77	22, 65, 66, 69, 73, 87, 93	3:8	93, 107, 113, 134, 148
1:78	65, 66, 68	3:9	93
1:79	65, 66, 68, 69, 71, 85, 86, 144	3:10	93, 96
		3:11	93, 113
2:4	21	3:12–14	102, 147
2:9–12	72	3:12–13	107
2:9	68, 86	3:12	94, 96, 120

Luke *(continued)*

3:13	94
3:14	94, 96
3:15	94
3:16	79, 90, 92, 95, 99, 101, 102, 104, 105, 146, 148
3:21–22	42, 44, 60, 92, 95, 102
3:21	43
3:22	19, 31, 43
3:31	21
4:1–13	31, 42
4:1	43
4:2–13	43
4:3	19
4:5–8	38, 44
4:5	31
4:6	31, 73, 88, 145
4:7	31
4:8	12, 14, 32, 34, 35
4:9	12, 19
4:10–11	12
4:12	12
4:13	45
4:14	42, 44, 60, 72, 87
4:15	18, 19, 72, 87, 120n57
4:16–21	72
4:16	18, 21
4:18–19	18
4:18	20, 23, 24, 42, 44
4:19	20, 21, 22, 23, 24, 44
4:20	19
4:21	4, 19, 20, 23, 24, 44
4:22	19, 20, 72
4:24	19, 72, 87
4:25–27	19
4:28	19
4:29–30	19
4:29	72, 87
4:30	72, 87
4:31–37	47
4:31	19, 120n57
4:32	19
4:33	20
4:34	20
4:35	20, 47
4:36	20
4:38–39	61, 143
4:38	20, 47
4:39	20, 47
4:40	59
4:43	32, 48
5:1–7	47
5:3	120n57
5:5	32
5:6–7	32
5:8	32, 32n3, 47, 49, 50, 61, 143
5:9	47
5:10	32, 48
5:12	32, 32n5, 48, 49, 51, 61, 75, 143
5:13	32, 48
5:15	44
5:16	44, 60
5:17–32	111, 134
5:17–26	107, 111n19, 134, 148
5:17	44, 120n57
5:19	72
5:20	59, 72, 87
5:21–24	109
5:21	72
5:22–23	72
5:22	21
5:24	72, 87, 108, 109
5:25–26	84
5:25	73, 87
5:26	73, 87, 134, 148
5:27–32	134, 148
5:27	76, 107
5:28	51, 76, 107
5:29	107
5:30–35	60
5:30	40, 107, 117
5:31–32	111n19
5:31	107
5:32	107, 109
5:33	40, 107
5:34	40, 107
5:35	40, 108
6:1–4	108
6:1	21
6:2	21
6:3	21
6:4	21
6:5	21, 22, 23, 24, 74, 88, 108
6:6	21, 120n57
6:7	21, 23

Scripture Index

6:8	21	8:13–15	122
6:9	21, 24, 115	8:13	45
6:10	22	8:27	49
6:12	44, 60	8:28	49
6:13–16	44, 60	8:29	49
6:13	33, 45	8:30	49
6:17–18	44, 60	8:31	49
6:19	44, 60	8:32	49
6:21	49n27, 111n18	8:33	49
6:25	49n27	8:35	111
6:28	43, 46, 60, 143	8:38	49
7:1–10	61, 143	8:39	49
7:1–2	48	8:41–55	61, 143
7:1	22	8:41	22, 36, 50, 51, 75
7:3	48	8:42	22, 50
7:4	48, 49	8:43	50
7:5	22, 48	8:44	50
7:6	22, 48	8:47	50
7:7	22, 48	8:48	50, 51, 59, 75
7:9	22, 48, 59	8:49	22, 50, 120n57
7:10	22, 48	8:50	22
7:11–17	73n38	8:51–55	50, 55
7:11–15	88, 145	8:51	22
7:11–13	73	8:54–55	22
7:12	50	8:54	55
7:13	49n27	9:10–17	110, 112, 122, 134, 135, 148
7:14	73	9:11	111, 134, 148
7:15	50, 73	9:12–13	111, 134, 149
7:16	73, 84, 88, 145	9:12	110
7:29–30	113	9:14–17	111n18
7:32	49n27	9:14	110
7:36–50	49n28, 61, 108, 110, 134, 143	9:16	110, 122, 126, 127, 133, 138, 150
7:36–37	48	9:17	111, 111n18, 122, 134, 149
7:36	109	9:18	44, 60
7:37	109	9:20	44, 60
7:38	49, 109	9:22	45, 64, 72, 87, 95, 102, 112, 121, 136, 144
7:40–47	110, 134	9:23–25	112, 135
7:40–43	109	9:23–24	95, 102
7:40	120n57	9:23	51, 61, 76, 89
7:44–47	109	9:24	51, 61
7:44–46	49	9:26	45
7:47	49, 109	9:28–37	50
7:48–50	109	9:28	44, 60
7:48	49, 109	9:29–31	112, 135
7:49	109	9:29	44, 60
7:50	49, 50, 51, 59, 75, 109	9:30–31	45
8:10	74, 88, 145		

Luke (continued)

9:31	50, 111
9:35	45, 112
9:38	50, 120n57
9:39	50
9:40	50
9:41	50
9:42	50
9:44	112
9:46	125
9:47–48	125
9:51	13, 111
10:1–9	40
10:2	40
10:13	76
10:18	73, 88, 145
10:21	42, 73, 80, 84, 88, 145
10:22	74, 88, 145
10:23	74, 88, 145
10:25	112, 112n26, 120n57, 135
10:38–42	112, 119n50, 135
10:38	111, 119n50
10:39	111
10:40–41	112, 135
10:40	112
10:41–42	112n24
10:41	112
10:42	112, 135
11:1–4	60, 142
11:1	40, 120n57
11:2–4	40
11:2	46
11:4	42, 45, 46, 46n17, 60, 143
11:5–10	60, 142
11:5	41
11:6	41
11:7	41
11:8	41
11:9–10	41
11:11–13	60, 142
11:11–12	41
11:13	41
11:29–36	113
11:37–54	115n34, 135
11:37	113
11:38	113
11:39–44	113
11:39	113, 116
11:40–41	113
11:42–44	114
11:42	114, 114n32
11:43	22, 114, 116
11:44	114
11:45–52	113
11:45	120n57
11:46	114
11:47–48	114
11:49–51	114
11:52	114
11:53–54	113, 114
11:53	113, 114, 135
12:11	22
12:13	120n57
12:50	95, 95n13, 102
13:10–12	74, 88
13:10	23, 120n57
13:11	23
13:12	23, 24
13:13	23, 59, 74, 84, 88
13:14	23, 74, 88
13:15–16	115
13:15	23, 24
13:16	23, 74, 88
13:17	74, 76, 88
13:22	120n57
13:26	120n57
13:29	121
13:33	72, 87
13:35	77
14:1–24	115, 117n42, 135
14:1	23, 115
14:2	24, 115
14:3–6	115
14:3	24
14:4	24
14:5	24
14:7–14	128
14:7	116, 135
14:8–11	116
14:11	67, 116, 117, 135, 136
14:12	116, 135
14:13	116, 135
14:14	116, 135
14:15–24	128
14:15	116, 117, 121, 127, 136, 138, 150

Scripture Index

14:16–24	116, 136	18:11	13, 42
14:18	116	18:12	13, 42
14:19	116	18:13	13, 43
14:20	116	18:14	13, 43, 67
14:21	117	18:18	120n57
14:22–24	117	18:31–34	76, 77, 89
15:2	117	18:31–33	51
15:3–6	117	18:31	119, 121, 136
15:7	117, 118	18:32–33	124, 137
15:8–10	117	18:35–43	51
15:11–23	117	18:35–41	75, 89
15:24	117	18:35	51, 76
15:28	117	18:38	51
15:29	117	18:39	51
15:30	117	18:41	51
15:31	117	18:42	51, 59, 75, 89
15:32	117	18:43	51, 76, 84, 89
16:13	34, 34n8	19:1	119
16:19–31	118, 119n48	19:2–3	119
16:21	118	19:5	119
16:22	118	19:6	119
16:23	118	19:7	119
16:24–26	118	19:8	119
16:27–30	118	19:9	119
16:31	118	19:11–27	77
17:3	46	19:35	76, 89, 145
17:12–19	61	19:37	76, 80, 89, 145
17:12	50	19:38	77
17:13	50, 51	19:39	120n57
17:14	50	19:45	13, 33
17:15	51, 75, 84, 88	19:46	13, 14, 33, 34, 38, 142
17:16	36, 51, 75, 88	19:47	13, 34, 120n57
17:17	51, 75, 89	20:1	12, 13, 34, 120n57
17:18	36, 51, 75, 76, 89	20:9–19	34
17:19	51, 59, 75, 89	20:9	13
17:20–37	42	20:13	13
17:25	72, 87, 121, 136, 144	20:14–15	13
18:1–8	60	20:15	34
18:1	42, 43	20:16	34
18:2	42	20:17	13, 16, 34, 38, 142
18:4	42	20:19	11, 13, 14
18:5	42	20:20	78n58
18:6	42	20:21	11, 120n57
18:7	42	20:22	12
18:8	42, 43	20:24	12, 34
18:9–14	60	20:25	12, 34, 37, 38, 142
18:9	12, 42, 43, 78n58	20:27	70
18:10	13, 42	20:28	120n57

Scripture Index

Luke (continued)

20:33	70
20:35	70
20:36	70
20:38	34, 37, 38, 142
20:39	120n57
20:41–44	34, 34n10
20:46	22, 43
20:47	42
21:1–4	35, 38, 142
21:5	11, 14
21:6	14, 17
21:7	120n57
21:12	22
21:36	43
21:37	14, 34, 120n57
21:38	14
22:1–15	28
22:1	28, 120
22:3	45
22:7	28, 120
22:8	29, 120
22:9	120
22:11	29, 120, 120n57
22:12	120
22:13	29, 120
22:14–20	45
22:14	29
22:15–20	30, 141
22:15–16	127, 138, 150
22:15	29, 121, 136
22:16–18	127, 138, 150
22:16	121
22:17–20	29
22:17	85n83
22:18	121
22:19–20	120, 132
22:19	29, 85n83, 110, 122, 123, 126, 127, 133, 136, 149
22:20	45, 123, 124, 136, 137, 149
22:21	125, 130, 130n92, 137
22:22	125
22:23	125, 137
22:24–27	128
22:24	125
22:25	125
22:26–27	112n23
22:26	125
22:28	121
22:29–30	52, 127, 138, 150
22:30	122, 130, 130n92
22:31	45
22:32	45
22:34	45
22:39–46	60, 142
22:39	45
22:40	45, 46n17
22:41	45, 53, 55, 58, 62, 143
22:42–46	58
22:42	45, 47, 53, 78
22:43	45, 55, 129, 139, 150
22:44	45
22:45	46
22:46	46, 46n17
22:47	125
22:52	14
22:53	14
23:5	120n57
23:33–34	60, 142
23:33	46, 51
23:34	33, 46, 53
23:39	52
23:41	52
23:42	52, 61, 143
23:24	77
23:45	9, 77
23:46	9, 33, 47, 53, 60, 78, 89, 143, 145
23:47	47, 78, 84, 89, 145
23:54	24
23:55	24
23:56	24
24:1	24, 28, 30, 141
24:2–8	24
24:5	37, 131
24:6	64
24:7	72, 87, 144
24:13	6
24:19–21	126
24:25–27	6
24:26	72, 87, 126, 144
24:27	126, 137, 138, 149
24:28–35	130
24:29	130
24:30–35	128, 131, 138, 150

Scripture Index

24:30	126, 127, 133, 137, 138, 149, 150	2:1–11	30, 80, 98, 104, 142
24:31	6, 6n20, 126, 138, 149	2:1–4	82, 90
24:32	126, 138, 149	2:1	29, 95, 102, 147
24:34	12, 14, 64	2:2	95, 102, 147
24:35	6, 127	2:3	95, 102, 147
24:36	69, 126	2:4	30, 95, 101, 102, 105, 147, 148
24:41–43	128, 138, 150	2:5–11	30
24:41	126, 138, 150	2:5	95, 102, 147
24:42	126, 138	2:6	96, 102, 147
24:43	127, 138	2:9–10	95, 102, 147
24:44–46	4	2:11	96, 101, 102, 105, 147, 148
24:44	72, 87, 144	2:14	96
24:46–49	101, 105, 148	2:17–18	101, 105, 148
24:46–48	92	2:21	81
24:47–48	128, 138	2:22–24	96, 102, 147
24:48	4n18	2:23	79
24:49	29, 78, 90, 95, 146	2:24	65, 79
24:50–53	78n60	2:25	81n68
24:50	14, 78, 90, 146	2:26–30	81n68
24:51–52	14	2:26–28	79, 84
24:51	14, 79, 90, 146	2:26–27	70
24:52	12, 36, 79, 90, 146	2:27–28	83
24:53	8, 12, 14, 79, 79n62, 90, 146	2:29–31	79
		2:31	70
		2:32	5n18, 96, 103

Acts

		2:33	67, 79, 80, 82, 90, 92, 96, 101, 102, 105, 146, 147, 148
1:1–2	2, 4–7	2:36	6, 96
1:1	4, 5, 6, 106	2:37–38	127, 129
1:2	33, 45, 95	2:37	96
1:3	37, 131	2:38	80, 96, 97, 101, 102, 103, 105, 128, 148
1:4–5	78, 90, 101, 105, 146, 148	2:40	5n18, 81, 128
1:4	95, 128, 138, 150	2:41	96, 103, 106, 127, 129
1:5	92, 95, 99, 101, 104, 105, 148	2:42–47	138
1:8	5n18, 78, 82, 90, 92, 96, 97, 101, 103, 105, 128, 138, 146, 148	2:42	52, 80, 106, 127, 129, 131
		2:44	128, 138, 150
1:14	52	2:45	128, 138, 150
1:15–20	32	2:46	15, 16, 28, 80, 106, 108, 128, 129, 129n83, 131, 138, 150
1:15	45	2:47	15, 80, 81, 128
1:16–22	45	3:1	15
1:16	45	3:2	15, 80
1:21	32	3:3	15
1:22	5n18, 32, 70, 96, 103	3:6–8	81
1:23	32, 45	3:6	15, 54, 80
1:24	33, 45, 52	3:7	80, 80n68, 90, 146
1:25	45		
1:26	33, 45		

Acts (continued)

Reference	Pages
3:8–9	15
3:8	15, 81
3:9	81, 90, 146
3:10	15
3:11	16
3:12	46
3:13	81, 90, 146
3:14	47, 78, 89, 145
3:15	5n18, 46, 64, 81, 90, 146
3:16	54
3:17	46
3:19	46
4:1	16
4:2	70, 81, 82, 90, 146
4:3	16
4:5	16
4:6	16
4:7	16, 80
4:9	81
4:10	16, 54, 64, 80, 81, 90, 146
4:11	16
4:12	16, 81
4:16	81, 90, 146
4:18	52
4:21	81, 83, 84, 90, 146
4:22	81, 90, 146
4:23	52
4:24	52
4:25–28	52
4:29–31	61
4:29	52
4:30	52
4:31	53, 57
4:33	70
5:12	16
5:17–18	16
5:19	16
5:20	16
5:21	16
5:24	16
5:25	16
5:30	64, 67
5:31	67, 83, 99
5:32	5n18
5:40	16
5:42	16
6:1–4	53
6:3	53
6:4	5n18, 52
6:5–6	53
6:6–7	61
6:6	53
6:7	17, 53
6:8	17
6:9	25
6:12	35
6:13	17
6:14	17
6:15	35
7:1	35
7:7	17
7:33	17
7:40–48	38
7:40	35
7:41	35
7:42	35
7:43	35
7:47	10, 17, 35
7:48	10, 17, 35
7:49	10, 17
7:52	78, 89, 145
7:55–56	33, 53
7:58	25
7:59–60	15, 61
7:59	33, 53
7:60	33, 53, 54, 58, 62, 143
8:1	25
8:3	25
8:5	96
8:9	33, 97, 103
8:12	96, 103
8:14	54, 96, 103
8:15–17	61
8:15	54, 97, 103
8:16	33, 54, 97, 103
8:17	54, 97, 103
8:18–19	33
8:18	97, 103
8:19	97, 103
8:20	97, 103
8:22	33
8:24	33
8:25	5n18
8:27	97
8:28	97

8:29–31	97	10:10	55, 58
8:32–33	97	10:11–12	55
8:32	97	10:13–14	55
8:35	97, 103	10:15	55
8:36	97, 103	10:24	82
8:37	97n21	10:25–26	36, 37, 38
8:38	97, 103	10:25	35
8:39	97, 103	10:26	35
9:1–9	98	10:27	82
9:1	25	10:28	55, 100, 104
9:2	25	10:30	55
9:3–19	25	10:31	55
9:3–9	54	10:32	55
9:3	69	10:37	98, 99
9:10–12	98	10:38	98
9:10	54	10:39	5n18
9:11–20	61	10:40–42	82
9:11	54	10:40	64
9:12	54, 59	10:41	5n18
9:15–16	98	10:42	5n18
9:15	54	10:43	98, 99, 103
9:16	54	10:44	82, 98, 99, 103
9:17–18	98, 103	10:44–48	55
9:17	54, 129, 139	10:45	82, 129
9:18	54, 129, 139	10:46	11, 33, 38, 82, 83, 98, 104
9:19	129, 129n83, 129n87, 130, 150	10:47–48	98, 99, 104
		10:48	100, 104, 129, 129n87, 130, 139, 150
9:20	25, 98, 103, 129, 139	11:2–3	82, 90
9:22–25	98, 103	11:5	56, 58
9:22	25, 129, 139	11:6	58
9:23	25	11:9	58
9:24–26	25	11:15–18	58
9:26–30	98, 103	11:15	82, 90
9:34	54	11:16	99, 104
9:36–41	62	11:17	82, 99, 104
9:36–37	54	11:18	82, 83, 84, 90, 99
9:38–39	54	12:1–17	62, 143
9:40	54, 55, 58, 62, 143	12:1–2	36
9:41	55	12:1	56
10:1—11:18	62	12:3–4	36, 56
10:1–48	82, 90	12:5	36, 56
10:1–2	82, 98, 103	12:6–10	56
10:1	35, 55	12:11	36, 56
10:2	35, 55	12:12	56
10:3	35, 55	12:13–16	56
10:4	35, 55	12:17	33, 56
10:5	55	12:19	36
10:9	55, 58		

Acts (continued)

12:21	36
12:22–23	37, 38
12:22	36
12:23	33, 36
13:1–3	62, 143
13:1	33, 40, 56
13:2–3	60
13:2	33, 40, 56
13:3	40, 56
13:5	25
13:6	25
13:7	25
13:8–11	25
13:9	25
13:12	25
13:14	25, 83, 90
13:15–41	25
13:24	99, 104
13:27	46
13:30	64, 83, 90
13:31	5n18
13:33	83, 90
13:34	65, 83, 90
13:37–38	99, 104
13:37	64, 83, 90
13:42	25
13:43	25
13:44–45	83, 90
13:44	25
13:45	25, 99, 104
13:46–48	85
13:46–47	84
13:46	25, 83, 90, 99, 104
13:47	69, 101, 105, 148
13:48	25, 83, 84, 90, 99, 104
13:50	25
14:1	26
14:2	26
14:5	26
14:6	26
14:7	26
14:8–10	36
14:9	59
14:11–15	38
14:11	36
14:12	36
14:13	36
14:14	36
14:15	36
14:23	57, 60, 62, 143
14:26	57
15:7	5
15:21	28
16:10–17	5
16:12	26, 130, 139, 150
16:13	26
16:14	26, 100, 104, 130, 139, 147, 150
16:15	26, 100, 104, 130, 139, 150
16:23–24	57
16:25–34	62, 143
16:25	57
16:26	57
16:29–30	57
16:30–32	84
16:30–31	131
16:31	57, 100, 104
16:33	57, 100, 104, 131
16:34	57, 84, 100, 104, 130, 130n92, 131
17:1	26
17:2	26
17:3	26
17:4	26
17:8	26
17:10	26
17:11	26
17:12	26
17:13	26
17:14	26
17:15–16	26
17:16–33	38
17:16	37
17:17	26
17:18	10, 37, 70
17:23	10, 37
17:24–30	37
17:24	10
17:31	37
17:32	10, 37, 70
17:33	37
18:1	27
18:2–3	27
18:4	27, 100, 104, 147
18:5	5n18, 27, 100, 104, 147

Scripture Index

18:6	27, 100, 104, 147	21:17	84
18:7	27, 100, 104, 147	21:18	84
18:8	27, 100, 104, 147	21:19	84
18:19	27	21:20	84, 91, 146
18:20–21	27	21:21	17
18:24	27	21:23	17
18:25	6, 27, 101, 105, 148	21:26	17
18:26	6, 27	21:27	17
18:27	27	21:28	17
18:28	27	21:29	17
19:1	101, 105, 148	21:30	17
19:2	101, 105, 148	21:39	58
19:3	101, 105, 148	22:1	18
19:4	101, 105, 148	22:3	111
19:5	101, 105, 148	22:6	69
19:6	101, 105, 148	22:9	69
19:8	27	22:11	69, 87, 144
19:9	27	22:13	69
19:10	27	22:14	47, 78, 89, 145
19:13	38	22:15	5n18
19:14–27	38	22:16	98, 193
19:14–16	38	22:17	18, 58
19:17	11, 33, 38	22:18	18, 59
19:21	85	22:19	28
19:24–25	37	22:20	5n18
19:24	10	22:21	18, 59
19:26	10, 37	23:6	70, 71, 81, 85, 87
19:27	11, 38	23:8	70
20:5–15	5	23:11	5n18, 85
20:6	28	24:1	18
20:7–12	132, 139, 150	24:3	18, 70
20:7	28, 30, 131, 141	24:6	18
20:8	28	24:11	18
20:9–10	131	24:12	18, 28
20:10	132	24:14	28
20:11	131	24:15	70, 71, 81, 85, 87
20:12	131, 132, 133, 139, 150	24:18	18
20:17–35	58	24:21	70
20:21	5n18	25:8	18
20:24	5, 5n18	26:2	70
20:36	58, 62, 143	26:6–8	81
21:1–18	5	26:6–7	85
21:3–6	62, 143	26:6	70
21:3–4	58	26:7	70, 71, 87
21:5	58	26:8	70
21:6	58	26:11	28
21:14	58	26:16	5, 5n18
21:17–19	91, 146	26:17–18	69

Acts (continued)

26:19	69
26:21	18
26:22	18
26:23	11n10, 18, 69, 70, 71, 87, 144
26:28–29	59
27:1—28:16	5
27:22	133
27:33–38	133, 139, 150
27:33–34	133
27:35–36	133
27:35	85n83, 133
27:36–38	133
27:44	133
28:1	59
28:3–5	59
28:6	59
28:7	59
28:8–9	62, 143
28:8	59
28:9	59
28:14	85
28:15	85, 91, 146
28:17	69, 85, 91, 146
28:20	70, 71, 81, 85, 87
28:23	5n18, 85
28:24	85, 91, 146
28:28	85, 91, 146

1 Corinthians

1:14	100, 104, 147
11:23–24	110

Philippians

2:8–9	67n18

Author Index

Avemarie, Friedrich., 96n17

Balentine, Samuel E., 39n1
Balz, Horst., 34n8, 114n30
Bauckham, Richard., 5n17
Bergmeier, Roland., 111n21
Bieder, Werner., 92n3
Böcher, Otto., 124n67
Bock, Darrell L., 4n16, 9n5, 10n6,
   15n25, 20n37, 24n47, 34n9,
   36n16, 37n19, 48n24, 50n30,
   53n39, 55n45, 58n53, 65n10,
   67n19, 68n23, 71n31, 73n37,
   74n39, 76n51, 79n63, 80n67,
   81n71, 92n4, 94n11, 96n17,
   98n23, 108n7, 114n31, 118n47,
   127n77
Borchert, Gerald L., 1n5
Boring, M. Eugene., 107n4
Braun, Willi., 115n36, 116n38,
   116n41
Bubbers, Susan, I., 120n53
Bucur, Bogdan G., 126n75
Burer, Michael H., 19n34, 108n9
Burke, Trevor J., 118n45
Butticaz, Simon., 4n15
Byrne, Brendan, 19n35, 67n19, 68n21

Campbell, William Sanger., 5n19
Carpinelli, Francis Giordano., 124n70
Carroll, John T., 3n9, 9n4, 34n9,
   42n8, 64n6, 65n8, 68n21, 69n24,
   75n47, 78n60, 127n77, 130n89
Coleridge, Mark., 9n4

Cosgrove, Charles H., 49n27, 109n14
Crump, David Michael., 1n3, 41n6,
   41n7, 42n8, 42n9, 43n11, 45n15,
   45n16, 46n18, 47n21

De Long, Kindalee Pfremmer., 1n2,
   63n3, 64n4, 65n10, 66n12,
   67n16, 73n37, 74n39, 74n43,
   77n53, 77n55, 78n56, 79n64,
   80n67, 81n69, 82n73, 83n75,
   83n79, 85n82, 85n84
De Santis, Massimo., 73n38
Dillon, Richard J., 64n6, 66n11
Dinkler, Michal Beth., 2n7, 115n37
Downing, Francis Gerald., 3n12
Edwards, James R., 3n9, 18n32,
   20n36, 21n40, 23n44, 32n4,
   32n6, 34n9, 41n5, 43n10, 49n27,
   50n31, 52n37, 52n38, 64n5,
   66n14, 68n22, 69n26, 71n32,
   73n38, 74n40, 74n41, 76n49,
   77n54, 79n62, 93n6, 94n10,
   95n13, 110n16, 111n20, 115n34,
   115n37, 117n43, 118n44,
   123n66, 126n75, 126n76

Endres, John C., 63n1
Esposito, Thomas., 1n4, 3n11, 24n47,
   49n28, 106n2, 109n11, 109n12,
   109n13, 115n34, 115n35, 117n42
Eve, Eric., 3n10

Farkasfalvy, Denis., 3n11
Feldkämper, Ludger., 1n3

Author Index

Fitzmyer, Joseph A., 4n14, 9n3, 29n55, 29n57, 40n4, 65n9, 76n49, 81n69, 82n74, 95n15, 110n17, 111n21, 112n26, 118n47, 121n61, 123n63, 125n73, 125n74, 127n80, 129n82, 131n94, 131n95

García Serrano, Andrés., 71n31
Garland, David E., 2n6, 3n9, 13n16, 13n17, 14n18, 14n20, 19n34, 20n37, 23n46, 32n6, 35n11, 44n12, 46n19, 50n31, 51n35, 52n36, 54n44, 65n9, 66n14, 69n25, 72n36, 74n42, 77n54, 78n56, 78n57, 79n63, 94n10, 110n15, 118n44, 119n50, 119n51, 120n55, 121n59, 123n66, 125n74, 126n75
Gathercole, Simon., 65n9
Gaventa, Beverly Roberts., 3n9, 27n50, 53n39, 99n26, 100n31, 101n32, 132n97
Glavic, J. A., 132n98
Gorman, Frank H., 29n54, 30n58
Green, Joel B., 2n6, 3n9, 4n15, 5n17, 9n1, 14n19, 15n22, 20n38, 21n41, 22n43, 23n45, 24n47, 31n1, 39n2, 48n23, 52n37, 65n7, 68n19, 69n25, 76n50, 77n52, 78n59, 79n62, 93n7, 107n5, 110n15, 116n40, 120n54
Guinan, Michael D., 63n1

Hamm, Dennis., 9n2, 13n16, 14n22, 51n33, 53n39, 75n43, 75n44, 75n46, 78n60, 79n62, 79n63, 81n69
Harris, Sarah., 11n11
Hays, Richard B., 3n8
Head, Peter., 1n1, 13n18
Hegermann, Harald., 124n68
Heil, John Paul., 1n4, 20n39, 45n14, 46n17, 49n28, 112n22, 113n26
Henrichs-Tarasenkova, Nina., 32n2
Holladay, Carl R., 3n9, 80n66, 99n25, 131n94

Holmås, Geir Otto., 1n1, 1n3, 44n13, 45n14, 45n15, 46n20, 47n22, 50n32, 53n41, 54n43, 54n44, 55n45, 56n47, 56n48, 57n49, 57n51, 58n52, 58n54, 59n55, 59n56

Jipp, Joshua W., 10n7, 37n18
Johnson, Luke Timothy., 18n30, 83n79, 84n80, 100n30, 114n31, 118n47, 121n61
Just, Arthur A., 3n9, 3n13, 6n21, 7n22, 15n23, 21n41, 22n43, 29n56, 32n4, 35n11, 41n5, 49n29, 51n33, 51n34, 66n13, 71n33, 71n34, 74n39, 75n45, 76n48, 77n55, 79n61, 93n5, 95n12, 95n14, 106n1, 107n3, 108n10, 109n12, 110n17, 112n25, 113n28, 114n30, 115n33, 117n43, 119n49, 120n56, 121n60, 122n62, 123n64, 124n71, 126n75, 127n78

Keener, Craig S., 36n13, 36n15, 56n46, 58n53, 59n55, 71n31, 80n65, 81n71, 83n76, 83n78, 84n80, 85n83, 95n15, 97n19, 97n20, 98n24, 99n28, 101n34, 128n81
Koenig, John., 1n4
Kurz, William S., 3n9, 53n42

Lanier, Gregory R., 65n9
Lincoln, Andrew T., 19n34, 24n48

Magdalen, F. Rachel., 63n2
Matera, Frank J., 125n73
Matson, David L., 129n84, 129n85, 130n88, 130n89, 130n90, 131n92
Maxwell, Kathy Reiko., 2n7
May, David M., 75n43
McBride, S. Dean., 63n2
McGowan, Andrew B., 24n48
McHugh, John., 72n35
Mekkattukunnel, Andrews George., 14n21

Author Index

Metzger, Bruce Manning., 68n20, 70n30, 97n21, 112n24
Millar, J. Gary., 1n3
Moles, John., 6n21

Nolland, John., 123n65

O'Toole, Robert F., 37n18, 74n43

Padilla, Osvaldo., 2n6, 3n9, 10n7, 10n8
Papademetriou, Kyriakoula., 4n15
Patsch, Herman., 120n53
Paulsen, Henning., 129n85
Perrin, Nicholas., 1n1
Pervo, Richard I., 3n9, 10n7, 36n14, 59n56, 69n27, 107n2, 130n91, 132n96, 133n100, 133n101
Peterson, David G., 1n1, 27n50, 29n57, 56n48, 57n51, 57n52, 59n55, 70n28, 80n66, 82n72, 83n77, 84n81, 96n17, 97n20, 99n27, 100n29, 101n32, 101n35
Plymale, Stephen F., 1n3
Pope, Michael., 46n16

Reardon, Timothy W., 114n29
Rebell, Walter., 93n8
Resseguie, James L., 2n7
Roth, Stephen J., 116n39
Rowe, C. Kavin., 10n7, 19n33, 21n40, 32n2, 32n4, 32n6, 34n10, 37n17, 37n18, 38n20, 48n26, 66n15, 108n8
Ryan, Jordan J., 75n43

Schnabel, Eckhard J., 3n9, 27n51, 37n18, 58n53, 58n54, 67n18, 69n27, 81n70, 81n71, 82n74, 84n81, 96n17, 97n18, 97n22, 98n24, 99n26, 127n79, 129n86

Schotroff, Luise., 131n95
Seo, Pyung Soo., 94n9
Shellburg, Pamela., 56n47
Sick, David H., 119n52
Smit, Peter-Ben., 98n22
Smith, Dennis E., 113n27
Smith-Christopher, Daniel L., 40n3
Snodgrass, Klyne., 41n6, 41n7, 42n9, 43n10, 118n44, 118n46
Spencer, F. Scott., 3n9, 15n25, 16n26, 17n29, 53n39, 57n50, 97n20, 98n22, 100n32, 101n35
Staudinger, Ferdinand., 114n29
Sylva, Dennis D., 10n6, 11n12
Szukalski, John A., 119n48

Tannehill, Robert C., 2n6, 67n17, 110n15, 131n93, 133n99, 133n101
Taylor, Joan E., 92n3
Thompson, Alan J., 1n1, 4n16, 15n24, 15n25, 16n27, 16n28, 17n29, 33n7, 35n12, 96n16
Thompson, Michael B., 5n19
Tipei, John Fleter., 53n40, 57n49, 57n50
Turner, Max., 29n57, 101n33

Untergassmair, Franz Georg., 124n69

Von der Osten-Sacken, Peter., 21n42

Walton, Steve., 1n1, 18n31, 128n81
Wanke, Joachim., 133n100
Witherington, Ben., 18n30
Witherup, Ronald D., 56n47
Wolter, Michael., 3n9, 48n25, 68n20, 70n29, 93n8

Yamasaki, Gary., 119n52

www.ingramcontent.com/pod-product-compliance
Lightning Source LLC
Chambersburg PA
CBHW020851160426
43192CB00007B/884